A New Australia

A New Australia

Discarding delusions and organising for the wellbeing of all

Geoff Davies

A BetterNature Book

Book 8 in the **Seventh Generation** series.

First published 2023 by BetterNature Books

Braidwood NSW, Australia

http://betternaturebooks.net

Davies, Geoffrey Frederick, 1944-

Design and layout: BetterNature Books

Text version 24 April 2023. File, clean version 24 April 2023

ISBN: 978-0-6482968-5-0

Praise

"The stories we live by - that human nature is fundamentally selfish, and that the planet has infinite space to absorb abuse – have turned deadly. ... *A New Australia* is an urgent and necessary contribution to the big ideas our age demands." – **Scott Ludlam**, writer, former senator.

"... a bold philippic that calls for the rekindling of our national spirit, a rebirthing of the dream of decency and fairness that we held in earlier days, a re-energising of the will to make this a better, fairer, kinder land." – **Julian Cribb AM**, science journalist and author

" Geoff Davies' book *A New Australia* should be required reading for anyone who cares about the future of Australia, or indeed humanity at large. ... Geoff draws on his wide scientific and life experience to chart the way to overcome this existential challenge, creating a genuinely sustainable and prosperous society where the common good is respected and individual freedoms are balanced with corresponding responsibilities. **A tour de force. Thoroughly recommended." – Ian Dunlop, Member, The Club of Rome**, Formerly: Chair Australian Coal Association, CEO Australian Institute of Company Directors. "

"In his latest book *A New Australia,* Davies boldly argues the need for a new direction in the structure and operation of Australian society. I have followed the author's journey for several years, and I consider that what he is proposing in this book is stimulating and constructive, and that the arguments he presents, need to be seriously considered by politicians, decision-makers and leading thinkers across Australia." – **Em Prof Bob Douglas AO**; Founder of *Australia 21,* formerly the Founding Director of the National Centre for Epidemiology and Population Health at The Australian National University.

Contents

	Acknowledgement	vi
	Uluru Statement from the Heart	vii
1.	To fail or succeed	1
2.	We are clan	11
3.	Belonging	43
4.	Birth of the treadmill	53
5.	Housekeeping	71
6.	Working together	87
7.	Pulling apart	105
8.	Too many promises	123
9.	Growing Up	147
10.	Peace making	163
11.	Good growth	181
12.	Cycling	201
13.	Our place	211
	Appendix I: A field bereft of intellectual integrity	227
	Appendix II: Anthem words	233
	Bibliography	235
	About the author	249

Acknowledgement

I write these words on Yuin Country. I pay my respects to Yuin elders past and present. I acknowledge that this Country and this whole land were brutally stolen, and that the surviving descendants of the First Australians suffer still. I look forward to the day when we take up the invitation of the *Uluru Statement from the Heart* and walk together, in mutual respect, to create 'a fuller expression of Australia's nationhood'.

Uluru Statement from the Heart

Our Aboriginal and Torres Strait Islander tribes were the first sovereign Nations of the Australian continent and its adjacent islands, and possessed it under our own laws and customs. This our ancestors did, according to the reckoning of our culture, from the Creation, according to the common law from 'time immemorial', and according to science more than 60,000 years ago.

This sovereignty is a spiritual notion: the ancestral tie between the land, or 'mother nature', and the Aboriginal and Torres Strait Islander peoples who were born therefrom, remain attached thereto, and must one day return thither to be united with our ancestors. This link is the basis of the ownership of the soil, or better, of sovereignty. It has never been ceded or extinguished, and co-exists with the sovereignty of the Crown.

How could it be otherwise? That peoples possessed a land for sixty millennia and this sacred link disappears from world history in merely the last two hundred years?

With substantive constitutional change and structural reform, we believe this ancient sovereignty can shine through as a fuller expression of Australia's nationhood.

Proportionally, we are the most incarcerated people on the planet. We are not an innately criminal people. Our children are aliened from their families at unprecedented rates. This cannot be because we have no love for them. And our youth languish in detention in obscene numbers. They should be our hope for the future.

These dimensions of our crisis tell plainly the structural nature of our problem. *This is the torment of our powerlessness.*

We seek constitutional reforms to empower our people and take a *rightful place* in our own country. When we have power over our destiny our children will flourish. They will walk in two worlds and their culture will be a gift to their country.

We call for the establishment of a First Nations Voice enshrined in the Constitution.

Makarrata is the culmination of our agenda: *the coming together after a struggle*. It captures our aspirations for a fair and truthful relationship with the people of Australia and a better future for our children based on justice and self-determination.

We seek a Makarrata Commission to supervise a process of agreement-making between governments and First Nations and truth-telling about our history.

In 1967 we were counted, in 2017 we seek to be heard. We leave base camp and start our trek across this vast country. We invite you to walk with us in a movement of the Australian people for a better future.

– *The Uluru Statement, 2017*[1]

1

To fail or succeed

... today we are subjected in every conceivable sphere to the signs of a seriously fractured social order. - Sara Dowse[2]

The subtitle of Jared Diamond's book *Collapse*[3] is "*How societies choose to fail or succeed*". The book recounts the stories of ten or so societies that encountered existential crises. Some societies recognised their imminent crisis, chose a different strategy and survived. Other societies failed to perceive their peril, or failed to make suitable changes, and collapsed.

To some, Australia in 2023 will seem far removed from the Mayan jungles or Norse Greenland, and the possibility of our society collapsing fanciful. It is true there are challenges at present, they will say, but we are dealing with them. There have always been challenges, and there are always some people crying doom.

To others the prospect of drastic, unpleasant change is real, even terrifying. The science of global warming gives us a very clear warning that we are dangerously close to triggering runaway warming leading to a hellish climate. Nuclear confrontation is looming again as politicians fall into the same old mistakes of power plays and, in Australia's case, cringing dependence. A serious nuclear exchange would quickly collapse global civilisation and endanger many of the Earth's species, including us. Short of that, crises in biodiversity, fresh water supply, soil fertility and general environmental degradation beset Australia and the world as a whole.

Australian society is also degrading. Having peaked in social wellbeing around the nineteen eighties, we now have much higher wealth inequality, increasing poverty, absurdly expensive housing, increasing homelessness, pervasive insecurity of livelihoods and increasing divisiveness and extremism. Our First People, despite many individual successes and their obvious abilities and talents, still battle discrimination and vilification and many still live in very deprived communities. We imprison children as young as ten.

It is true we have implemented some more tolerant policies and attitudes towards some minorities, yet scapegoating is still all-to-easy for those so inclined. We can look to the United States to see how such social tensions can lead to a society that seems increasingly to be on the brink of violent disintegration, yet there are those who continue to push us towards emulating that unhappy place.

There are vigorous debates on how to deal with these challenges. The political mainstream, meaning the old political parties and most of the mainstream media, is still firmly pursuing business as usual, with a few tweaks they hope or imagine will be sufficient. Many others are loudly advocating more substantial changes, some of them fairly radical.

This book argues that we are indeed in a perilous state, but that even the more fundamental changes commonly mentioned will still not be enough to get us through the dangers. The reasons are that some erroneous beliefs and destructive attitudes are still not widely recognised, and a more integrated vision is required.

One can find in the analysis that follows some twenty or more beliefs basic to our governance that are erroneous or quite misguided. Some are to do with economic management, which is in a deplorable state. Some are broader, to do with what human nature is really like and how we can cultivate our better angels, so we work better together and work better with the natural world, as our ancestors mostly did. To have the best chance of avoiding collapse we need to address all the erroneous beliefs.

The required changes range so broadly they are not commonly brought together. For example they range from the banking system to connecting more deeply with each other. Those who understand the banking system are less likely to have focussed on our intimate connections, and *vice versa*. The more we can get right the more all the positive changes will synergise.

The sum of the changes advocated here may seem radical. From the point of view of the narrow and extremist ideology that has prevailed for four decades they are indeed radical, but from a broader and more humane perspective they are not so radical. Some are a return to things we used to do routinely, before our leaders were seduced by neoliberal snake oil salesmen. Some are a recreation of how most people used to live, and how many outside the global consumerist machine still do. Some are things many of us wish for but don't know how to get, like having less pressure in our lives and more time for family, friends and community. Some are fairly novel, but their benefit ought to be fairly easy to see or demonstrate.

This is not to minimise the challenge of adopting the proposed changes. Much of that challenge will be persuading people to recognise and step away from the mistaken or destructive beliefs that saturate our public conversation, things that have become quite deeply entrenched in our culture. There will of course be strident resistance from those who benefit from present arrangements, who will assure us the sky will fall if we go anywhere near these subversive thoughts. That resistance is not to be minimised: people regularly die who get in the way of the powerful.

Yet many people are highly dissatisfied and looking for something better. A few key changes made early on could bring a lot of those people along. For example, raising the minimum wage can not only help the battlers directly and promptly, but it would benefit our anaemic economy as well, because more people would have more money to spend. Such thinking is decried by the short-sighted big-business lobby and denied by the deluded economics establishment, but a recent Nobel prize was awarded for showing how it happened in the real world.

Around sixty years ago Donald Horne made a scathing assessment of Australian governance in his book *The Lucky Country*[4]. He portrayed our leadership class, in and out of government, as complacent and smug, uninterested in the wider world or the big social and political changes already discernible in 1964, though even Horne could not foresee the power of the changes that washed through the world in the following decade. The famous summary line from the book is

> 'Australia is a lucky country run mainly by second rate people who share its luck.'

He meant the book title, *The Lucky Country*, to be taken ironically. He meant we were living on our luck, and it was unlikely to last. He went on to say

> '[Australia] lives on other people's ideas, and, although its ordinary people are adaptable, most of its leaders (in all fields) so lack curiosity about the events that surround them that they are often taken by surprise.'

Perhaps our second-rate leaders lifted their game a little over the following decade or two, but by now they have regressed and are much worse. Having immersed themselves in the cults of materialism and selfishness, having scuttled back to the shelter of the the colonial mentality, and having opened themselves to more corruption and to outright capture, they have set us up for failure.

There have recently been some encouraging signs in Australia of change for the better, even though the political mainstream has hardly shifted.

Australia fended off the disease afflicting many of the world's democracies. That disease has featured demagoguery, misinformation, cultivation of division, and disregard for norms, conventions, protocols and even the law, along with excessive secrecy, corruption and incompetence. In the 2022 federal election we removed an anarchic government and installed one that has returned to actually governing and (mostly) to abiding by conventions and laws. But the change is a remission, not a cure. The new government still hews to old beliefs that we need to move beyond, and it is still heavily corrupted.

The election of a clutch of community independents to federal parliament has the potential to get nearer the source of disease. Together with the Greens, they can help to reduce the toxicity and corruption of parliamentary culture, and of our broader political culture, and bring more focus onto what the country needs.

Yet there is a deeper malaise whose source we need to find. We are a materialist society, compared with many past and traditional societies, and the materialism has been raised to new heights by the deliberate cultivation of selfishness and greed. The greed promotes political corruption and is obviously helping to drive the endless growth that our economic managers strive for so relentlessly. The greed leads some people to take more than their share of stuff, leaving other people with not enough, so driving wealth inequality. They have also taken more than the planet can provide, without itself suffering decline.

Why are these people so greedy? There have been many societies in which such greed was constrained, if it existed at all, so we need not resort to the dead-end explanation that greed is just part of human nature. Something provokes or facilitates the greed.

Our materialist focus gets in the way of social connection and love, which are essential to our sense of belonging and being valued, and to our emotional health. Consumerist marketing exploits this by persuading us that buying stuff will satisfy our craving for connection, but of course it does not. Behind the marketing is a deliberate fostering of selfishness. We are exhorted to be rugged individuals and to compete with each other. Cooperation is seen either as weakness or collusion. One consequence is that livelihoods have become very insecure, by design. In our insecurity we are prone to turning on each other. We have become fractious and divided. Those divisions in turn are exploited by the holders and seekers of power. The conflict consumes our 'social capital', the fund of trust required to keep our society functioning.

Yet selfishness and greed still do not fully explain the perilous situation we are in. The feudal lords were selfish and greedy too, and the lower orders suffered, but feudal society did not grow inexorably, to consume itself and the world.

A feature of our modern governance is to ensure there is never quite enough of something essential. A prime example at present is employment. For a time, postwar, employment was maintained close to a sufficient level, and our society prospered. However for decades now employment has been deliberately kept insufficient, under the bogus guise of combating inflation. So we compete for livelihoods and accept less than we might deserve out of desperation. This keeps us on a treadmill that serves the greedy. The treadmill has been operating for centuries, probably since the land enclosures of late Mediaeval times.

Our modern greed is thus fostered and implemented in way that requires ever more 'economic growth', and that growth requires ever more of everything: materials, people, land, water, crops, poisons, products, devices and so on. We have built a machine with unlimited demands. There is ever less room for anything else on the planet. Nor is there time to stop and enjoy the sunset, to have surprise and poetry in our lives. Uncontrolled and unlimited growth of this kind is correctly called a cancer.

The workings of this lurking machine are obscured by a fog of misconceptions and delusions. We do things that keep the machine grinding along, but tell ourselves we are doing something else. Some of the things not properly understood include banks, money, markets and how we count success. There are also things not acknowledged, in the corridors and forums of power, like being kept subservient, even infantile, in a hierarchy. There are factors not recognised as being significant, like our being physically unable to know everyone personally in a large society, let alone in another society. There are things neglected or forgotten, like our connection with the rest of the natural world, so we fail to understand how it works and how we fit within it.

To address the deep dysfunction in Australian society we require a wider-ranging, deeper and more forensic analysis to support the diagnosis, and to point to potential remedies. There *are* remedies. We can stop harming ourselves, our land and the planet, and we will live more fulfilling lives as we do so.

Two deep streams of belief underlie much of what we are experiencing. Each has brought benefits, but each has been pursued too narrowly and too far. First, the European Enlightenment gave rise to the scientific and industrial revolutions, but also to an increasing focus on materialism at the expense of relationship. Second, though Christ preached love, Christianity has a history of viewing people as separate from and above the rest of the natural world. It inherited this attitude from the earliest cities, which limited most 'civilised' people's connection with the natural world. We have become too attached to our power over the natural world, power enhanced by our industrial system. So there are deep cultural forces propelling our materialism and our exploitation of the world.

Yet in the late 1990s in the United States, a country borne of the Enlightenment and where Christianity plays a prominent role, fully two thirds of adults agreed that humans are *part* of nature. Two thirds were concerned their children will inherit a degraded world, and four fifths agreed we should change the way we live now so future generations can enjoy a good quality of life.

Nine tenths of Americans thought a prosperous economy and protecting the environment should be compatible[5].

Currently, more than four-fifths of respondents from G20 (developed) nations want to do more to protect and restore nature, and more than two-thirds believe the benefits of action to protect 'the global commons' outweigh the costs[6]. Overall, most people agree we should move beyond focussing on gross domestic product and instead focus more on the health and wellbeing of people and nature.

There is good reason to believe these views are shared by Australians. For example, many Australians have downshifted: they have changed their employment in order to spend more time with their families, to find personal fulfilment, to lead a more balanced life or to look after their health[7].

These are startling numbers. However, according to surveyors, the discontented often don't realise how many others are discontented. Often people feel embarrassed to say what they really feel, afraid they will be ridiculed for disagreeing with what 'everybody knows'. So they feel isolated. Perhaps also it is discomforting to speak openly about, because we carry on with a lifestyle that we believe, deep down, is harming the world. People's real views only come out when they are allowed to feel comfortable and safe from judgement within focus groups and in-depth interviews[5].

These surveys reveal something profound about our society. We don't like it. *We think it will degrade the world and harm our children.*

These feelings are so widespread they must cross the usual political divides. Yet most of us continue to live the way our society demands. Mostly we still vote for those who will continue it. We evidently feel trapped. To deal with materialism and destructive consumerism we need a big change of direction but we don't know how to do that. Perhaps we don't believe it is even possible.

Yet this materialist, competitive, unsatisfying, destructive society we find ourselves in is the creation of human beings. It must therefore be possible for us to uncreate it. Societies in other times and places have functioned differently, so the present form of society is not inevitable.

If the world is to survive for our grandchildren, clearly it is not enough just to *want* it to survive. We must figure out how to *stop* the machine we have created, the machine that is chewing up all the trees, and everything else. To do so, we must understand some basic things about ourselves and our society. Why does our society seem like an unstoppable machine? What drives it? Where is the off switch?

Not everyone feels trapped. There are many who have a vision of a better way to live and are working to bring it about: houses that require no energy input, cities that don't require you to migrate long distances every day, farming without poisons that draws carbon back into the soil, community organisations that re-connect people, companies with a positive social role, money that supports rather than exploits, and much more.

Yet these alternatives don't get enough traction, and the old system rolls on. The old habits of thought, the old power networks, the old social institutions like media and parliament have continued in their old ways. There is now the prospect of some change of political culture, and perhaps that change might gather pace if we cultivate it.

How do we tilt the balance? How do we promote the big shifts, so the positive alternatives can replace the old? There are many sources we can draw on. Psychology tells us we are better than we often think. Archaeology and anthropology show us we have more options than we have tended to believe. Resources can be used much more efficiently. There are better ways to run a democracy. Banking and money can be made much simpler and more constructive.

The economy can be harnessed to power the good things we want, instead of subverting them. That may seem to be a radical claim, but consider this: the economy has been erroneously placed above society, and it is currently the locus of power. However 'the economy' is not a separate thing, it is the means by which our society provides for its material needs. Coming from this viewpoint it is evident that a lot of the concepts and practices underpinning the present economic system are misguided or just wrong. It is not hard to understand the problems, if we can shut out the noise of apologists trying to keep the old system staggering along.

Rebecca Huntley[8] researches people's attitudes to climate, energy and related matters, using surveys and focus groups. One of her methods is to put statements of well-documented fact in front of people and ask if they believe them. One of her subjects asserted that fossil fuels are good for Australia not only because of the jobs they provide but also because of the taxes and royalties they pay. He also asserted that renewable energy is heavily subsidised by government whereas fossil fuels get no subsidies.

Huntley: You don't think coal and gas get subsidies from the government?

Subject: They don't.

Huntley: Would it surprise you to know they get billions of dollars a year in subsidies and some of these companies that are foreign-owned don't pay tax or royalties?

Subject: I don't believe that.

Huntley notes that the *Australia Institute* found fossil fuels received $10.3 billion in subsidies over the previous financial year (2020-21), just within Australia.[9] Renewable energy receives a small fraction of that. It is becoming well-known that many large companies, including foreign-owned companies, pay little or no tax.

Huntley finds that people are often reluctant to accept well-documented facts as true. Either they say they can't be right, as in the above example, or they assume the government or the country must be getting something in return for subsidies. They don't want to believe the government is being dudded or is just giving our wealth away. In one group the subjects reluctantly supposed it must be true that there are more jobs in health and education than in mining, after Huntley showed them the numbers. However when she asked them did it *feel* right, they said no. Huntley's point is that the mining industry has invested in a lot of public relations aiming to get people to *feel good* about mining. Feelings trump facts.

2

We are clan

We are clan, not an individual; a lone human is not a functioning unit. – Steve Biddulph[10]

On the 22nd of April 2020 Richard Pusey of Melbourne outraged public decency.[11] He filmed a video on his phone of the aftermath of a freeway crash in which four police were dead or dying. He offered the victims no help at all, but kept filming for several minutes, at times making such remarks as 'Look at that ... Look at that ... Absolutely amazing ... Oh he's smashed.' He ignored pleas, from others who had stopped at the crash site, to help them tend to the injured, and kept filming.

Pusey was charged and convicted for the archaic common law offence of outraging public decency. The intricacies of the unusual legal situation are not the concern here. Rather, it is that Pusey's behaviour did cause widespread outrage. People were outraged that he offered no help and showed no concern or remorse, even though his actions had initiated the sequence of events that resulted in the tragic crash.

Pusey had been travelling well over the speed limit in his black Porsche on Melbourne's Eastern Freeway, not for the first time. He was pulled over by two police in an unmarked car. Because of his record they summoned two other police in a patrol car. As the police conferred by the roadside a truck veered into the emergency lane and crashed into the three stationary vehicles, fatally injuring the four police. Pusey was uninjured because he had gone into the roadside bushes to urinate, not having been arrested at that point. The truck driver was severely sleep-deprived and affected by drugs. He immediately wailed his remorse at the scene. He was given a heavy jail sentence, but he did not attract as much public outrage as Pusey even though he was more directly responsible for the police deaths.

Pusey, it seemed, showed no empathy at all for the victims of the crash. He was assessed by a psychiatrist as having prominent features of personality-based psychopathology. The media portrayed his behaviour as outrageous. He was, in other words, recognised by many people as being highly abnormal and his actions as being highly offensive. Some called him the most hated man in Australia.

Outrage is nothing unusual these days, either in our traditional media or in modern social media. Outrage is a staple of tabloid media, though all media cultivate it. Yet the outrage directed at Pusey is notable because, even though he was not as culpable as the truck driver, he was perceived as uncaring, as disconnected from normal human feelings, as repulsively negligent in not attempting to help the injured police.

The outrage is notable also because Pusey was behaving as we are all urged to behave by the imposed norms of the materialist consumer society we inhabit.

Empathy is social glue. It is the foundation of social cohesion. Large societies inevitably have many conflicting currents. People separate into neighbourhoods and groups according to occupational or cultural background, wealth and many other factors, and the different groups come to have different needs, wants and perceptions. The wealthy want to live in a quiet, leafy neighbourhood with people like themselves, and they want the government to keep out of their way. The working class, those who depend on relatively low wages, want an active government providing many services. Immigrant ethnic groups understandably like to live with their fellows, they tend to value initiative and education and they may regard government as helpful or threatening depending on their background. Family farmers, those that are left, tend to value independence but are usually willing to pitch in together in times of need; they tend to have mixed attitudes to government, resenting regulation and wishing for more help getting a fair go.

Out of such varied interests the cross-currents of a society emerge. Some societies manage their internal differences better than others. Older, more established societies tend to have well-established norms for managing differences, but societies with long-established religious or deep ethnic differences can sometimes explode into lethal conflict.

On the scale of societies around the world Australian society is relatively peaceful. This is especially so given that since 1945 we have absorbed people from almost every part of the world bringing a bewildering array of cultures and languages. By, say, 1990, it was possible to say that Australia's 'multiculturalism' was a resounding success, even though dissenting voices had begun to argue we were too diverse. Over the past thirty years those dissenting voices have grown much louder and have penetrated governments and affected policies. Yet still Australia's level of internal conflict is relatively low.

Perhaps we do not properly appreciate our distinctiveness. We are claimed, for example, to share many values with the United States, but there are some major differences in internal conflicts and attitudes, differences that have been highlighted by recent events.

A couple of major differences are Americans' addiction to guns and their refusal of a government-sponsored health insurance scheme. Yet another school massacre unleashed lamentation, but also fierce debate, with plenty of prominent people defending gun ownership. We have many fewer guns, we mostly want to keep it that way, and we support Medicare by clear majority – much more than the recent government in fact. A visiting Canadian musician once explained the difference between Canadians and Americans: a Canadian, he said, is like an unarmed American with health insurance.

Another difference was strikingly evident in the earlier stages of the Covid-19 pandemic in 2020. The virus swept through the US and only later was there some prospect of it declining, thanks to a major vaccination program instituted by a more competent and concerned President than he who presided through 2020. Australia had far fewer cases, despite hesitations, bungles and lack of preparedness by various governments. Until mid-2021, when the delta variant arrived, the virus had been confined to specific outbreaks and much of the country was able to proceed relatively normally without catching the virus. Later the omicron variant did spread more, facilitated by continuing bungles and the wish of Prime Minister Morrison and the NSW Premier to re-open the economy against the advice of health experts.

I think a major difference that worked in our favour is Australians' greater social cohesion, our greater willingness to restrain ourselves for the sake of everyone. Compliance with 'lockdowns' was high, notwithstanding a fair bit of grumbling and a slowly growing protest movement taking its lead from libertarians in the US. Some people claimed we are sheep who just do what we are told, but I think the bigger factor is simply that most of us appreciate that we will all be better off if we limit ourselves until the danger is passed. We do it for the greater good, which includes our own good. Australian (white) society early on developed a fairly strong ethic of helping each other through hard times. It is called mateship or egalitarianism, and it is less obvious now than it was a century ago, but it comes out during disasters, of which we have had plenty lately. (There is also a dark side to mateship, let it be acknowledged, that allows misbehaviour to be covered up, particularly misbehaviour towards women and minorities.)

The US, on the other hand, has a stronger tradition of rugged individualism. Rhetoric about 'freedom' permeates both society and politics. Given the social, governmental and corporate limitations on Americans' lives it is not really clear what they mean, but it seems to refer back to a semi-mythical frontier in which the lone settler battled the world, did as he saw fit and sought no help, except perhaps from John Wayne. This tradition of individualism has fuelled increasing division, as first the tea-party Republicans promoted anti-government libertarianism or anarchy and then President Trump compounded it with his chaotic personality, proclamations and exhortations. This is the background to the widespread refusal of many Americans to restrict themselves so as to limit the spread of the virus.

The 2022 federal election may come to be seen as a remarkable re-emergence of the ideas of decency and a fair go, after decades of having individuality thrust upon us. A significant section of the electorate turned its back on Trump-esque divisiveness, and elected community independents supporting climate action, anti-corruption and a fair and non-abusive go for women. The result vindicated my own feeling that an underlying streak of decency and generosity survived among Australians and just needed an avenue for its expression. At this writing there seems to be no equivalent shift towards moderation among comparable societies overseas.

In every society there is some balance between individuality and social restraint, but the balance is different in each place. Most Americans still stop at red traffic lights, even if they won't wear face masks in the pandemic. Australians mostly wear face masks when advised or required to and we mostly like government health insurance. Thus the balance is more towards the side of individuality in the US than in Australia.

Other countries have different balances again. The English are perhaps more compliant as a result of their historical class structure, the French and Italians perhaps more rebellious (in some ways), and traditional Japanese culture had very strong social norms and tolerated less individuality.

There is an intrinsic tension between individuality and social cohesion. Whether it is in our family, our social circles and workplaces or the whole society, we all make some concessions for the sake of the larger group. It cannot be otherwise. If we make no concession to our group, then our group ceases to exist as a functional entity. If group rules were enforced too rigidly then individuality would cease and we would become like Brave New World or like ants.

This tension between individual and group is quite fundamental to human societies, and even to life itself. We live in groups of various kinds, and we concede some freedom of action so the group can continue to function. We expect the benefits of being in the group outweigh the concessions it requires from us. All organisms and many groups of organisms involve this kind of compromise.

This was recognised by Taoists, who characterised the two 'polarities' as *yang* and *yin* and advised of the wisdom of balancing between them. However there is no simple formula for where a healthy balance lies at any given moment. That is what gives our lives much of their novelty and richness, along with their challenges.

Western culture has paid less attention to how to reconcile individuality and social cohesion. We tend to see things in more absolute terms and don't like unresolved tensions between opposing tendencies. We tend to see them as opposites between which we must choose, rather than as the extremes of a spectrum with a healthy middle. We also tend to lean more towards individuality than Eastern cultures, though compliance with social norms was very strongly enforced during the Middle Ages. We then swung the other way as the industrial revolution got going. It was convenient to the new industrialists to emphasise the benefits of (their) individuality. This shift was taken to an extreme about forty years ago, when the dominance of individuality was raised to a moral imperative and relentlessly expounded by our media, politicians and some intellectuals who should have known better. This shift was especially convenient to financial capitalists.

The tension between individuals and the group is perhaps the deepest of the conflicting currents in our society. We are exhorted to compete with each other as independent economic agents, because that is what free-market capitalism demands, and it is claimed this will yielded the greatest (material) good for the greatest number. On the other hand we know perfectly well that we often work together, we cooperate, because we get better results that way. Ask any football coach. Ask any (functional) family. Ask any golf club committee or Rotary service club or industry advocacy body.

Much of our present travail arises from a conflict between an economic ideology expounding competition and our natural impulses to work together. The tendency to cooperate is in fact deeply embedded in our nature: we are *hard wired to cooperate within our group*. The nature of human nature has been contentious through the ages, but it is rather better known by now than it was in the past. We will go into it more later, but the strength of our innate tendency to care and to cooperate is attested by the *revulsion* evoked by Richard Pusey's flagrantly uncaring behaviour.

Cooperation is intrinsic to human beings – but not all the time. Competition is also part of our makeup – but not all the time. We are not one thing or the other, but a more potent mix of two polarities. The attempt to override our innate human nature by insisting on only cooperation led to trauma and ultimate failure in the communist states. The attempt to insist on only competition is behind many of the ills afflicting our own society, and many of the ills we are inflicting on the world.

The claim that competition should take precedence over cooperation got a boost in the nineteenth century. The unlikely source of this boost was a mathematical theory, and the neglect of cooperation was, in significant part, for mathematical convenience.

In the late nineteenth century the Swiss mathematician Leon Walras thought to emulate his hero Isaac Newton. In doing so he set off some ideas that some people found very seductive and that have become deeply entrenched in our society, despite being rather obviously wrong.

Like many intellectuals at the time Walras was in awe of Newton for discovering the 'laws' by which the universe operates. He set about finding the 'laws' by which human societies operate. In particular he thought of a way to investigate what happens, collectively, when a lot of us interact by exchanging goods and money. He did this by adapting a theory from physics, specifically the kinetic theory of gases. Don't worry, we won't go into technical details here and there won't be a test.

The kinetic theory of gases assumes a gas is made of a lot of little hard bouncing balls – atoms. If you have a great many of these tiny 'atoms' in a box, and they are moving very fast, they will bounce off the walls of the box and off each other. *Wikipedia* will show you a nice little animation of the idea. The tiny pummelings of atoms against the walls will generate a pressure pushing outwards against the walls. If you can squeeze the lid of the box down so the box has only half the volume, the pressure will double. Physicists Maxwell and Boltzmann created mathematical descriptions of this picture and showed it accounted for observed relationships between pressure, volume and temperature of hot gases quite well. Temperature is a measure of the speed of the atoms, but don't ask, it's a bit complicated.

Anyway Walras, rather cleverly, adapted this theory to the context of an idealised human society. Instead of little hard balls he proposed little 'economic agents'. Instead of interacting by bouncing, he supposed his agents interacted by exchanging goods and money. He was able to adapt the physicists' mathematics to solve his problem and he came up with a result that was rather remarkable and quite misleading. Unfortunately quite a few influential people, for a hundred and fifty years or so, have been in awe of the 'remarkable' and oblivious to the 'misleading'.

Walras' result was that his little idealised 'society' would come to an equilibrium, just like the ideal gases. In that equilibrium all supplies would balance all demands. Because there are no waste and no shortages in this 'general equilibrium', it can be shown to be the most efficient state, in the sense of achieving maximum output (of goods) for minimum input (work and money). Oooh! It meant that if you can just set up markets for everything, and let them run 'freely', your toy society would achieve a state of optimal efficiency. You can probably see the appeal.

There was however a bit of a problem with Walras' theory. The problem was that every agent had to know what every other agent was willing to pay, in order for the mathematics to work out. It was as though there was a grand auctioneer who got all the successful bids lined up before anyone actually exchanged anything. Walras recognised the unreality of this artificial process, but he and others set about finding ways to remove this restriction and, hopefully, show that the general equilibrium would still come about.

They are still looking. In effect Walras had to assume the flow of time ceased while the auctioneer assembled all the bids. In the real world time flows and the bids occur sequentially, so I have to make my bid without knowing what your bid in the future might be. The equilibrium can only happen if the future is predictable, at least in a certain statistical sense. Did anyone predict the Covid pandemic? People predicted the possibility of a pandemic, but of course no-one could predict the detailed timing and development of the Covid pandemic. The future is unknown. Mathematicians outside the field of economics know the general equilibrium is actually impossible if time flows and we can't predict the future. That's fairly basic isn't it? But within the dominant 'school' of neoclassical economics they maintain a faith that the equilibrium is possible and someday someone will prove it. Perhaps some day two plus two will equal five.

There was another problem with Walras' theory, less recognised at the time but more pertinent to our current theme. The little economic agents only interacted by exchanging goods and money. There were no other kinds of interaction allowed for, because that would make the mathematics too hard. In particular, no social interactions were included. What if people bought something just because a clever salesman convinced them it would bring them happiness, or because it's the latest fashion? If people bought the latest model car before the old one was worn out would the little theoretical world still be operating at optimal efficiency? Possibly not.

Walras' theory had a seductive appeal. It gave a simple answer to a very big question: what is the best way to organise a society? Walras' answer is free markets. Set up markets for everything, keep the meddling government out of the way and your society will get the maximum benefit from inputs of resources, work and money.

The many people who set about exploring Walras' approach became known as economists. Before that the question of how exchanges of goods and money affect society had been known as political economy. Specifically the new, mathematical economists are known as *neoclassical* economists, we don't have to worry about why. There are other kinds of economist, like Austrian or Keynesian or ecological economists, but the neoclassical economists have been very influential for a long time and since the 1980s they have been the dominant school.

My career was in science, specifically in geophysics, the physics of how the Earth works. One of my scientific colleagues had a definition of *an influential scientist*. An influential scientist, he said, is one who can mislead an entire field of research for a decade. By this measure neoclassical economists are in a class of their own. They have been misleading themselves and most of the world for over a century.

You may have noticed I have sometimes been saying society but only really talking about the economy, the exchange of goods and money. The implication, built into the way these things are usually discussed, is that the broader aspects of society must be kept subordinate to markets. Inequality, poverty, democracy, minority rights, arts and culture, the environment, those are all very well but we can only attend to them after we get the economy working properly so we can afford all those optional extras. This is basically what we have been told for the past forty years, in only slightly different language: we will attend to the environment etc once we have ensured a decent rate of 'growth'.

Just a little more about this strange theory of an abstract little economy before we return to broader topics. When the physicists had constructed the kinetic theory of gases they compared its results with observations of actual gases. It had already been observed that if you halve the volume of a gas you double the pressure, approximately, and if you increase its temperature you increase its pressure by a certain amount. The theory said similar things, so this was encouraging. On the other hand careful accurate measurements showed that if the gas was cool enough to be near its condensation temperature, like steam just above the boiling point of water for example, then the real gas deviated from the theoretical result. If the steam actually condenses, or freezes, you observe quite different behaviour of course: you have water or ice rather than steam. To account for the latter behaviours you need to take account of the complicated interactions of atoms described by quantum mechanics, rather than just treating them like little hard balls.

Economists did not bother to compare their theoretical results with observations of real markets. Walras, William Stanley Jevons and others simply claimed they knew their founding 'axioms' were true, therefore their results would also be true. They were following the example of Euclid's geometry, which is mathematics not science: it is an internally consistent logical construction that may or may not resemble the observable world. For many centuries Euclid's geometry was presumed to be an obviously true description of the world, used successfully by surveyors and architects and designers of widgets. However in the nineteenth century other internally consistent geometries were conceived. Then Einstein showed that our three-dimensional space is not Euclidean in the presence of a gravitational field. If you want to apply Euclid's geometry you have to test to make sure it is an accurate description of what you are concerned with. If you want to describe events near a black hole it will be completely inadequate.

If you want to describe the effects of exchanging goods and money you need to take account of social interactions, and the flow of time, and a few other rather basic features of life. Otherwise the behaviour of your toy economy may bear little resemblance to real economies. In fact the differences are not hard to see.

Neoclassical economics is not science. It is a belief system dressed up in mathematics to look like science. It is, in other words, pseudo-science. I am far from the first person to point this out, but any economist who spells it out is banished to the fringes of the field by what economist James Galbraith calls 'a politburo for correct economic thinking'.[12]

The central result of the neoclassical approach is the general equilibrium. If you look at real modern economies you might wonder if you are looking at a system in equilibrium, in balance. New firms boil up all the time and dominate their sector for a time: Ford, Microsoft, Amazon, Google. House prices climb steadily, much faster than the incomes of those trying to buy them. Financial markets gyrate crazily and every now and then crash. In 1987 stock prices dropped by nearly half within one day.

There were other crashes, then an even bigger one in 2008. A collapsing financial market is not a system in balance.

The neoclassical theory has nothing useful to tell us about real modern markets. It is highly misleading. In particular, if the economy is not close to equilibrium there is nothing you can say about the *efficiency* of free markets because the central neoclassical result does not apply. Oops, we just demolished the whole neoliberal ideology.

I have walked you through this digression into economic theory to emphasise how deeply the cult of the individual has been entrenched into our society. This is not an accident. British Prime Minister Margaret Thatcher said in an interview in 1981 'Economics are the method; the object is to change the heart and soul'[13]. Apparently by 'change' Thatcher meant *desiccate*, reduce to a dry husk.

Neoclassical theory is built around 'economic agents' who are presumed to be rational calculators of their optimal path through life. They have been called 'rational economic man' or '*homo economicus*'. I call them calculating reptiles. They are devoid of social behaviour. All mammals have social behaviour to some degree. You have to go back to the reptiles of the Triassic age, pre-dinosaur, to find animals with little social behaviour. They hatch out of their eggs and go their own way. There is no such thing as lizard society.

Margaret Thatcher, under the influence of the deviant neoclassical world view, proclaimed in 1987 that 'there is no such thing as society'.[14] She was referring to human society. We are just individuals going our own way.

Richard Pusey, he who filmed the dying police, behaved a little like *homo economicus*. He observed his fellow creatures but seemed to experience no identification with their suffering. He showed no empathy, which is the foundation of social behaviour. So deeply embedded in human makeup is the urge to empathy that many of us experienced visceral outrage at his uncaring behaviour.

Psychologists have been exploring our tendency to empathy and cooperation and finding that it does indeed seem to be an innate part of human nature. An experimental psychologist might sound like your idea of a horror movie, but actually they're pretty harmless. They like to set up little situations and see how people respond to them. Sometimes they even give away money.

One experiment is to take people in pairs and to offer one of them some money, on condition they share some of it with the other person. If they don't offer to share or if the other person refuses their offer then neither gets any money[15]. For example one person might be offered \$20 on condition that some is shared with the other person. The 'rational' behaviour is for the person given the money to offer only a very small share to the other person, say \$1, and for the other person to accept anything that is offered. That way they would both be better off. However people very consistently reject offers of very small shares, and they do so with indignation, considering the offerer to be selfish and the offer to be unfair. They would rather go without anything than go along with such selfish behaviour. By refusing, they ensure the offeror also gets nothing, so in effect the offeror is punished.

This experiment has been called the Ultimatum Game, because there's only one offer that is either accepted or rejected. It has been repeated many times in different contexts and cultures. Offers to share anything less than about 30% of the money tend to be considered unfair, though the threshold of perceived fairness does vary among cultures.

In another experiment, called the Public Goods Game, four people in a group are each given some money[16]. They are invited to pool some of the money, and the experimenter will then double the pool and divide the resulting total equally among them. Commonly, people begin by sharing, but then someone decides they can do better by freeloading. Suppose each person is given \$10 to start. If they all pool their money to make \$40 total and the experimenter doubles this to \$80, then each will double their money to \$20. But if one person contributes nothing then the pool is only \$30, which is doubled to \$60, and then each person receives \$15 back. But the freeloader still has the \$10 that he started with, so he has finished the round with \$25. However once somebody starts freeloading the others usually reduce their sharing in subsequent rounds and soon nothing maybe shared. In this way one freeloader can make everyone worse off in the long run.

However things unfold differently if people can punish the freeloader, even if it makes the punisher worse off. For example, a player may be able to pay \$1 to have the freeloader's money reduced by \$4. Thus if you pay \$2 to punish the freeloader in the above game, their take will be reduced by

$8, so they will only receive $17 and be worse off than if they had cooperated. Once this option is introduced sharing usually returns to high levels, sometimes even if no one has actually been punished. Potential freeloaders understand their selfishness may hurt them, and they stop being selfish.

The role of the punisher in this game is interesting because they will be worse off than everyone else, receiving only $13. However they will be better off in the long run than if they had not punished, even though the others gain a little bit more than they do. Quite literally, they sacrificed some of their own interest for the sake of the group.

Furthermore, punishers in both games are usually motivated by indignation, not by doing a careful calculation of costs and benefits. In some experiments with the Ultimatum Game great care was taken to ensure the participants knew there was no possibility they would deal with the same person again. In that case the rational behaviour is to be selfish, because punishing someone will have no effect on the next round of the game. The results were unchanged: people reacted with the same indignation and punished selfish behaviour[15]. Another confirmation was made by requiring people in the Public Goods Game to respond quickly, before they have a chance to work out a rational strategy[16]. In fact the quicker our responses, the more we tend to reinforce sharing.

There *is* a rational strategy behind the punishers' behaviour, even if they do not realise it. The rationale is that they are better off being part of a functioning group than they are acting just as an individual. Our intuitive responses in both games reinforce sharing, and sharing is what binds a group together. Thus both of these games show we have *innate* behaviour that tends to strengthen a social group.

Such behaviour makes good sense in the context of small communities, including hunter-gatherer groups struggling to survive. If everyone cooperates and shares then more food is likely to be gained, and if anyone doesn't succeed in gathering food for a day or two they can survive with the help of the others until they have more success. This is also the logic behind the pervasiveness of social groups among mammals. Hunting is much more productive if hunters form cooperative groups, as lions and wolves demonstrate, as well as humans. Obviously the group strategy only works if everyone pulls their weight and if everyone is willing to share. If selfishness becomes too common within the group then others are likely to stop cooperating and the group will fall apart. Everyone's survival would then be at greater risk.

The fact that we often respond immediately and intuitively with cooperative behaviour indicates we are 'hard-wired' for working together in groups. Apparently this imperative has been working on us for so long it has become part of our innate emotional make up.

Daniel Kahneman, in his book *Thinking, Fast and Slow*[17], cites a long series of experiments that demonstrate our brains work in two distinct modes. What he calls *slow thinking* is what we usually call rational thinking. In fact by 'thinking' we usually mean conscious thought, which is generally slow. What Kahneman calls fast thinking we more usually call intuition. This kind of intuition always involves feelings. He argues that feelings are the drivers of our intuitive thoughts and responses. For example, it is people's feeling of indignation that leads them to reject an unfair offer or to punish a cheater. Feelings are quick. They pop up unbidden in an instant. They are not the product of conscious thought, although conscious thought is one way to trigger them.

Our brains do other things quickly and without conscious thought. If we're startled our reaction is immediate, and we may jump or shout in surprise. Thus our brains work in two distinct modes: quick reactions and feelings, and slow, deliberate, conscious thought.

Our fast responses in social situations tend to favour cooperation. In particular, we are *conditional cooperators*: we are generally willing to cooperate so long as others cooperate. The Public Goods Game in its first form demonstrated this: if one person stopped cooperating then the others did too. Both games show we're willing to punish, even at a cost to ourselves, to maintain group coherence. This has been called *altruistic punishing*. We can also be *forgiving* and *vengeful*. We can forgive selfishness because we know sometimes people make mistakes or can be induced to be more cooperative. On the other hand sometimes we punish extra to reinforce the message that selfishness isn't acceptable.

There is also a simpler argument that our sociability is innate. If we were not social, we would not need language. Language, by its essential nature, is about interacting with others. If we were not already highly social, language would not have developed, and language surely intensified our social nature because it offers a more intimate level of sharing, and empathy.

Without language neither would we have developed *culture,* the large body of shared ideas and values that comprise such a large part of any society's existence. Language and culture are shared, they can only exist in the context of social interaction. *We are intensely social beings.*

You can argue that our highly social behaviour even pre-dates language, because we have the most elaborate body language of any mammals. This is especially true of facial expressions. We display an astonishing range of feelings with our faces, many of them quite subtle. We can also read others' faces without even thinking. We instantly recognise an angry face, or a happy face, or a welcoming face. (At least most of us have this ability, but for example some people on the autistic spectrum may not.) Facial expressions are clearly deeply wired into our systems. They would not be if our ancestors had not been highly social for a long time, from even before language developed. Facial expressions and language intensify our social bonds.

There is one big qualification to this conclusion, emphasised by Joshua Greene[16]: we only *impulsively* cooperate with those who we perceive to be part of our group. To anyone we perceive as being an outsider we may be indifferent or even hostile. As Greene puts it there is a big gap between our responses to *us* and our responses to *them*. Our cooperation-inducing responses help to reconcile the tensions between an individual and a group; between *me* and *us*. We do not have a comparable suite of behaviours to reconcile the tensions between *our* group and *other* groups; between *us* and *them*.

It seems to be true, though, that the boundary of *us* is very flexible: in some contexts we stick with a small group, whereas for example in a big disaster we will often jump in and help complete strangers. We can adopt a group, like a sporting team, as *us* and reject other teams as *them*. We can adopt a political party as *us* and reject another party as *them*. Later we will look at conflict between groups, and what might be done about it.

Perhaps while reading about this evidence for our cooperative behaviour you have had a feeling that it must be wrong, or at least overstated. If you watch the evening news you see all sorts of examples of hostile behaviour, from politics to crime to vindictive court cases to terrorism and wars. Greed seems to be rampant, to the point of taking our society on a suicidal path. Toxic masculinity, domestic violence, racial vilification, on it goes. History seems to be an endless series of tyrannies and wars. Some people say we are irredeemably nasty and the planet would be better off without us.

Rutger Bregman has published a book titled, in its English edition, *Humankind*[18]. He argues that humans are kind. He dissects some of the well-known examples that are said to demonstrate human nastiness. A good example is the book *Lord of the Flies,* which tells of a group of English schoolboys marooned on an island who quickly descend into conflict and depravity. It is a work of fiction written by a man, William Golding, who turns out to have been very unhappy. On the other hand there was a real group of boys marooned near Fiji for a year. They cooperated without serious conflict and survived quite well, until found by a passing yachtsman.

Quite a few other examples supposedly proving our nastiness turn out to have been misreported, manipulated or faked. An experiment at Stanford University was manipulated. Another experiment, supposedly showing most people can be ordered to inflict pain on others, turns out to have been inaccurately reported and to be a not-so-simple interplay of bullying and most people's good sense and resistance.

The media commonly seize on the negative and sensational, so much so they can portray events as the opposite of what they really were: the aftermath of Hurricane Katrina or a murder in New York in which neighbours supposedly ignored screams for help. In fact there was no murder in the New Orleans stadium, people helped each other, and the neighbours in New York either did not realise what was happening or did help. Suppose there was a drug, Bregman says, that is highly addictive and that causes a misperception of risk, anxiety, lower mood levels, learned helplessness, contempt and hostility towards others, and desensitisation. There is such a drug. It is called the evening news.

The story of Easter Island is often taken as a metaphor for our modern situation. I have used it this way myself. The conventional story is that the people of the island became so caught up in a competition building their great stone statues that they depleted the island of trees, their ecosystem and population collapsed, and only a sad remnant of the population remained. Much of that story turns out to be based on misreporting and even fabrication. The people survived very well, even after the trees were depleted, probably by rats eating the seeds, and were eventually brought down by slave traders and smallpox. It is a story of resilience, cooperation and good sense, not of ambition and greed, except from outsiders.

There is a lot of bad behaviour in the world, that cannot be denied. According to Robin Grille, in his *Parenting for a Peaceful World*[19], we are remarkably traumatised by the misguided societies in which we live, and traumatised people can behave badly. If we can but raise our children from infancy immersed in love, as many traditional cultures have done, then much of the conflict of the world would not occur. Is that too idealistic? We will see.

Philosopher Jean Jacques Rousseau reflected on the first man who proclaimed his ownership over land, and found people simple enough to believe him. Instead, someone could have said 'Be sure not to listen to this imposter; you are lost, if you forget that the fruits of the earth belong equally to us all, and the earth itself to nobody!' The civilisation we have inherited, based on ownership of land, has been a mixed blessing.

By ignoring our empathy and social interactions economic theorists have overlooked a fundamental part of our humanity, and it matters. One of our human characteristics is that we tend to go along with what our group is doing: if everybody else is running this way, or buying this toy, or investing in this hedge fund, then it must be for a good reason. In other words we have herd behaviour. We identify with groups, or tribes. Financial market traders can be stampeded into a big sell-off and the result is a market crash.

The stock market crash of 1987 provides a clear illustration. Over the course of a single day stock prices around the world dropped by thirty to forty percent. This episode illustrates several things. First, it shows that traders do not have as accurate an assessment of the value of a stock as they might claim. Their collective evaluation of stocks changed by nearly a factor of two even though there was no change in the physical world of the productive economy. Thirty percent of the world's factories had not been bombed overnight. The change was entirely within the minds of the traders.

A second thing the crash illustrates is that markets do not always integrate individual actions into a positive collective result, as Adam Smith's *invisible hand* is claimed to do. When stock prices are falling everyone tries to sell quickly to minimise their losses, but that only accelerates the fall, so everyone ends up worse off. This has been called the effect of the *invisible foot*.

A third lesson of the crash is that financial traders do indeed move in herds. Their valuation, before the crash, depended on what other traders valuations were, not just on some allegedly objective assessment of the value of a stock. In other words financial traders exhibit social behaviour. Even they are not socially oblivious calculating reptiles.

Financial market crashes are among the biggest and most destructive economic events. They usually trigger recessions and depressions. They destroy livelihoods and often lives as well, and they inflict misery on millions through unemployment, poverty and lost dreams. By excluding social interactions economists completely miss the phenomenon of a market crash.

This was starkly in evidence through the Global Financial Crisis of 2008. Just two months before the crisis began, the Chief Economist of the Organisation for Economic Cooperation and Development (OECD) predicted that 'sustained growth in OECD economies would be underpinned by strong job creation and falling unemployment'. After the crisis hit mainstream economists claimed it was a completely unpredictable event, impossible for anyone to have foreseen. They called it a 'black swan' event, as inconceivable as black swans were to Europeans before they encountered black swans in Australia. Except quite a few people had pointed out the likelihood of a crash, and some of them were even (marginalised) economists.

Market crashes are not even possible within the theoretical models used by mainstream economists, because those models always predict equilibrium conditions, or conditions close to equilibrium. A crash can only happen if there are imbalances, and the crash is a clear departure from near-equilibrium. The theoretical models leave out several important factors: social interactions, debt and, unbelievably, money. Debt plays a key role in setting up the conditions for a crash, as we will look at later. Once the conditions are there, social interactions play a large role in magnifying small events into a large crash.

What is economic theory for, if not to help us to avoid the worst dysfunctions of a modern economy? Apparently the monumental failure to anticipate the 2009 crash is of no great concern to the neoclassical economists who have come to dominate the profession. As James Galbraith has said, when their theories fail, they don't change their theories, they change the subject, and carry on as before. No-one is disgraced. No-one gets fired[20].

The obsession with individuality has much wider repercussions through our society than just through the management (or mismanagement) of the economy, important as that is. It has given rise to a stream of political thought known as neoliberalism (I won't grace it with the label 'political philosophy'). Basically it says we should all aspire to be rugged individualists who advance ourselves through our own efforts and by being better and more selfish competitors than others. We should certainly not look to government for any help because, as Ronald Reagan said, 'government is not the solution to the problem, government *is* the problem'.

If you're a multi-millionaire aspiring to be a billionaire that probably all sounds pretty reasonable. On the other hand if you're a struggling single mum you might be aware that neighbourhoods are not as strong as they used to be, government services have declined, and those that remain are harder to access. Such government support as may exist comes with highly intrusive requirements to divulge personal information and to regularly jump through hoops in order to continue receiving benefits.

Those receiving unemployment support (variously known by insidious names like jobsearch, newstart or JobSeeker) must show they have applied for a ridiculous number of jobs every two weeks and attended some kind of training. The fact that there are usually at least three times as many unemployed as there are jobs advertised is ignored (and lately the ratio has gone as high as fifteen). If you are unemployed it is your fault, not the system's fault.

Modern Coalition politicians seem to actively despise disadvantaged people[21], if not literally hate them. Perhaps poor people spoil the vision of a soup of little atomic economic agents all selfishly promoting the greater material good. Perhaps the right-wing politicians picked up their attitudes at posh private schools, which necessarily claim to be better than the common ruck in public schools (though it is not true) and that still explicitly or implicitly propagate the English upper class attitude of being born to rule.

For whatever reason, the Coalition created the scheme that became known colloquially as *robodebt,* in which computers were used to check government records of you to see if there are any inconsistencies, and especially to see if you might possibly have received more money than you were due. They soon found tens of thousands of inconsistencies. Many of the inconsistencies were because *robodebt* was making rather crude and incomplete comparisons, in other words it was making a lot of errors or unfounded claims. Nevertheless the government required the accused victims either to prove they had not been paid more than they were due or to pay back the claimed amounts.

The accused were people who were already flat strap trying to live on measly allowances, cope with disabilities and conditions of poverty and little education and jump through the other hoops already prescribed. Proving their innocence often required producing many years' records of their lives. Many failed to satisfy the requirements, whether or not they were 'guilty'. There are many claims that some victims suicided, but the government simply denied they were responsible.

Robodebt was eventually found to be illegal. Not being too concerned about the rule of law, the Coalition government still took several months to actually terminate the program. They were reportedly planning to re-start it with some of the worst features modified.

The context of this sort of harassment of those who used to be known as *the undeserving poor* is a society in which unemployment is higher and employment has become far less secure than they used to be, wages have not been increasing and have decreased in many jobs, and wages have been stolen from employees who either don't know their rights (like immigrant workers) or are too intimidated to demand their rights. Industrial unions have become far less powerful than they used to be, so it is difficult for the abused to push back.

This situation is the product of what is called *labour market flexibility.* Prices in the labour market (i.e. your wages) should be determined by the market, with no interference from social groupings, like unions or a government. Apart from the fact that free markets are as likely to produce instability as optimality, according to our earlier discussion, there is the complicating factor that your labour comes with you attached – you, an actual human being with all your rich and wonderful physical, emotional, social, mental and spiritual complexities. Perhaps you want more from life than working two or three low-paid insecure jobs doing low-skilled drudgery and having no time for your family, friends and community. Even if the theory of free markets had some validity in the real world, it would still only be serving the brute physical needs for food and (some kind of) shelter (but not always). This system expects us all to be calculating reptiles.

The other part of the context of the elevation of the individual over social groups is that some people have been making out like bandits. The deck was already stacked in favour of the already-wealthy, but as government has been pruned back the scope for 'entrepreneurs' has expanded. It is a widely remarked feature of our society that it has become markedly more unequal, in income and wealth, over the past forty years.

This has come about not just because the Government does not monitor and regulate as it used to, but because it flagrantly favours the wealthy. When it emerged that large amounts of its JobKeeper payments, intended to enable businesses to retain employees through the interruptions of the pandemic, went to large companies whose profits increased during the pandemic, the Government was not willing even to ask those companies to repay the money, let alone make the effort to identify and require the return of many billions of dollars[22]. This is in stark contrast to the trouble and expense of *robodebt*, searching for alleged cases of overpayment of poor battlers.

It is claimed by apologists that the poor have become richer, even though the rich have become richer faster, so no-one has reason to complain. This is a narrow and simplistic view. Even in strictly material terms it fails to account for the lower level of government services provided, even if wages might have increased a little in real dollar terms. (In the United States even that is not true: median incomes have actually been *stagnant* since about 1980.[23]) Battlers can see that some people are creaming off a lot of the wealth produced in our society, and they can see a lot of cheating going on – wage theft, tax avoidance, political corruption, whatever. House prices have been rocketing up, for reasons we'll look at later, and prices are so high many people have been made homeless. Even though incomes might be slightly higher in dollar terms, a person made homeless is a poorer person. This society cannot even ensure the basics: food, shelter and safety.

Most of all this view ignores the corrosive effect of stress on people's wellbeing. Working long hours for a barely-sufficient income that might be cut off at any time is highly stressful. We can feel 'less than', especially when there are plenty of politicians who openly blame the disadvantaged for their situation. We can become demoralised. We become less tolerant of any irritation, less able to maintain relationships, more prone to physical illness and less able to maintain healthy balances in our lives.

Australia scores poorly on an international ranking of human rights performance produced by Rights Tracker[24]. Australia recorded some strikingly poor results, particularly in terms of who is most at risk of rights abuses. Across education, food, health and work the Rights Tracker assessment gave Australia a 'bad' score of 7.9 out of 10 given its status as a high-income country. Aboriginal and Torres Strait Islanders in Australia were highlighted as being particularly at risk of arrest, detention and torture (torture?), as well as being unlikely to enjoy their rights to education, health, housing and work.

It should not be surprising that our social fabric has become increasingly frayed and torn. We are more divided and less tolerant of different social groups. There is more domestic violence (though there has always been a distressing amount, even in better times). The ailments of both poverty and affluence abound – poor nutrition, lack of exercise, obesity, diabetes, heart disease, asthma, hypertension, cancer and addictive states like alcoholism and drug abuse. In many ways we are a fortunate and generally wealthy society. When asked, people tend to rate their lives as good. But this should not blind us to the high level of poor functioning and dysfunction in modern Australia. We are not very happy campers. We could be much happier campers with a few perverse practices rectified.

We seem to be paying quite a high price in personal and social health and wellbeing for this grand experiment to which we are being subjected, this business of being selfish competitors so we will all be better off, somehow. So how is the material side of things going? How fares the economy under the neoliberal regime of the past four decades?

A few numbers can give us the gist. An increasing Gross Domestic Product (GDP) is the holy grail of modern economic management. So although that is a profoundly misguided goal, let us use the conventional measure to see how we have been going. In the postwar decades, 1950s through the early 1970s, GDP increased by 5% or more per year – a very rapid rise. Unemployment averaged 1.3%, a very low rate. Inflation averaged around 3% per year, quite moderate. Even better, the increasing wealth, as measured by the GDP, was widely shared around, so that most people could see their 'standard of living' rising year by year.

Since the 1990 recession GDP growth has struggled to be much more than 3% per year and lately has been hardly greater than population growth at 1.5-2%. Unemployment has rarely been below 5% and has at times been much higher. Inflation was held to 2-3% for some time, then was less before the pandemic.

The pandemic, the war in Ukraine and disruptions to supply lines have pushed prices up significantly early in 2022 (whether this should be called inflation will be taken up later). Unemployment did drop during the pandemic, when immigration was reduced to near zero, though almost no-one admitted any connection between those facts. In any case, many people feel worse off than they did ten or twenty years ago.

Thus the two eras, postwar and neoliberal, have been fairly dramatically different. The neoliberal era, since around 1980, has never come close to the economy's performance in the postwar decades. This may be a little surprising, because we have been told, rather incessantly, that the old economy, pre-1980, was heavily protected (from overseas competition), was constricted by militant unions, suffered from too much government interference, was highly inefficient as a result and was a bit of a basket case and only going to get worse. We have also been told that the Hawke-Keating 'reforms' of the 1980s set the economy up for an unprecedented run of prosperity, which is not what the above numbers seem to say. What's going on here?

There are three deceptions behind these claims. One is to pretend the postwar decades were like the 1970s, never mentioning anything before about 1972. Another is to mis-diagnose the problems of the 1970s and to offer snake oil solutions. The third is to cherry-pick the measure of prosperity you use for the neoliberal era.

There were two big disruptions in the 1970s. The price of oil quadrupled because the oil-producing states got together and raised the price. At the same time the US tried to pay for its Vietnam war by printing money, and then by detaching the dollar from the gold standard, which resulted in inflation being exported to the world. The high oil price slowed most economies because most activities were more expensive. This registered in economic statistics as stagnation, a lack of GDP growth, or a recession, a decreasing GDP.

The combination of stagnation and inflation, called *stagflation*, was not supposed to happen: it could not happen in the economic models used at the time. Mainstream economists were flummoxed, although a bit of common sense might have revealed to them what I described in the previous paragraph.

This provided an opportunity for neoliberals to step in and claim to have the cure for the ailing economies. All the way back in 1947 the Austrian economist Friedrich Hayek had founded the Mont Pelerin Society dedicated to promoting free markets and minimal government.[25] He soon found plenty of sponsorship from rich people who liked the idea of minimal restraint on their money-making activities. Chicago economist Milton Friedman acknowledged that in the prosperous post-war era it would be hard to get traction for their ideas and advocated waiting until there was some kind of crisis. This they did, so they were ready to run when the crisis developed in the 1970s.

The neoliberals blamed the troubles on the so-called Keynesian policies of the postwar years, never mind that those policies had been an outstanding success for about 25 years. They paraded their snake-oil theory that free markets yield the best of all possible worlds. Presumably because most Keynesian economists did not properly understand what was going on and most politicians don't understand any kind of economics, the neoliberals won the argument and became the courtiers and high priests to the powerful.

It is strange though that the parties of the nominally democratic-socialist left also swallowed the snake oil, though it was obvious at the time that neoliberal policies would favour the rich over the working people. So it was that Lange's Labour in New Zealand, Hawke and Keating's Labor in Australia, then Blair's Labour in Britain and Clinton's Democrats in the US all set about deregulating, privatising, outsourcing and cutting government, sometimes with greater zeal than their more conservative predecessors.

A particular factor in Australia may have been that many in Labor had been spooked by the experience of the Whitlam Government. Whitlam pursued an economic expansionist agenda, though it was not strongly socialist, and he reformed many dated laws and practices that had accumulated through the somnolent Menzies era. This was upsetting to conservatives, on top of the fact that it was not them being the government, which evidently they had come to see as their natural right. However the real problem was that Whitlam was on the point of challenging the penetration of US power into Australian domestic and foreign affairs. It is clear enough that this was one of the main underlying reasons for his dismissal. The claimed reasons were unconvincing. It is also quite clear that the Queen was aware that her representative here, the Governor General, was contemplating dismissing Whitlam and she made no move to stop him[26].

So it appears the 'right' factions in Labor resolved never again to offend the real holders of power, though it severely limited the scope of their policies. Or perhaps they were simply right-wing anyway, imposters in a supposedly left-wing party. Historians might have to disentangle those questions.

It has emerged recently that Bob Hawke was regularly passing information to the US, both when he was a senior union leader and after he entered parliament[27]. This would have been extremely useful to the US in protecting its considerable interests within Australia, from monitoring union resistance and protest movements to, presumably, promoting the interests of those politicians who shared its views. Had Hawke been passing such information to the Russians or the Chinese he would undoubtedly be labelled a subversive and a traitor and have spent a long time in jail.

Whitlam was also vilified for supposedly being an incompetent economic manager, and for a scandal involving a non-conventional loan. That scandal was fairly small beer compared with what was going on under the recent Coalition Government. As to Whitlam's economic management, it is usually overlooked that the inflation blamed on him was first of all a world-wide phenomenon originating in the US. Large increases in award wages may have added a component to that, but against that Australia was the only country not to suffer a recession in the early 1970s. And one of Whitlam's early actions was to cut tariffs on overseas goods by 25%, something his conservative predecessor was unwilling to do. So the economic competence of the Whitlam Government requires a rather more nuanced examination to separate actuality from the hysterical right-wing propaganda of the time.

Returning to the account of recent economic history, neoliberal policies were progressively imposed around the world from 1979 onwards and we were supposed to be entering a period of unprecedented economic prosperity. Indeed it is still claimed that we did. The actual record tells a rather different story, as we have just seen.

Hawke and Keating deregulated Australia's financial sector. The result was that banks competed to throw money at fast-talking entrepreneurs like Alan Bond and Christopher Skase, among many. The result of that was a boom through the 1980s fed by borrowed money that had to be paid back. By 1990 the business debt was unsustainable, and a series of collapses triggered the worst Australian recession since the 1930s Great Depression. Paul Keating infamously called it 'the recession we had to have', but we did not have to have it and it deserves to be known as the Keating Recession. It caused great hardship and shifted Australian politics in an ugly direction.

This brings us to the neoliberal claim that the Hawke-Keating reforms set the conditions for our greatest ever run of prosperity. Well they didn't: they created the Keating Recession. What the neoliberal spin doctors mean is that there had not been a recession *since* 1990, until the pandemic recession of 2020. That was indeed an unusual run, but the claim neglects three important factors. First, the severe Keating Recession was caused by neoliberal policies. Second, the economy since has been increasingly anaemic under the continued weight of misguided neoliberal policies. Third, we avoided another recession in 2008 by temporarily abandoning neoliberal policies.

Following the Keating Recession the Treasury Department, unusually for economists, looked at what they could have done better and concluded that the government needed to spend money to replace private spending that was collapsing, as debt defaults proliferated and people withheld spending; such spending is a classic Keynesian approach. When the Global Financial Crisis was threatening in 2008 the newly-elected Labor Prime Minister Kevin Rudd asked what they could do. Treasury's answer was to spend, and to 'go early, go hard and go households'. In other words the Government should put money in householders' accounts and spend on useful projects that could be ramped up quickly. This they did and Australia, again uniquely among developed nations, avoided a recession.

The commercial media and the conservative Opposition ignored this success and falsely portrayed the spending as wasteful and financially irresponsible. They claimed it led to the deaths of four inexperienced workers who were electrocuted while installing 'pink batt' insulation, though the death rate due to such accidents was no larger than usual, unfortunate as they were. The 'big-spending Labor' mantra was relentlessly pushed for over a decade, but the tune suddenly changed when the pandemic started shutting down the economy in 2020. Even the Morrison Government realised that it had to spend some money to get us through, in defiance of neoliberal doctrine, and the severity of the pandemic recession was reduced as a result.

The more accurate version of recent economic history is thus rather different from the revisionist neoliberal version. The economy boomed in the postwar decades under Keynesian policies aimed at full employment and involving regulation of bank lending, protection from cheap foreign competition and substantial government spending, especially during recessions. This run of prosperity was interrupted in the 1970s by oil embargoes and inflation driven by the United States' excessive spending on the Vietnam war.

Neoliberals falsely blamed Keynesian policies for the difficulties of the 1970s and gained power with the elections of Margaret Thatcher in 1979 and Ronald Reagan in 1980. Subsequent neoliberal policies led to an excessive build-up of private debt that collapsed into the 1990 recession. Later recessions in Australia were only avoided by briefly reverting to Keynesian government spending. In any case the economy has never performed as well under neoliberal policies as it did in the postwar decades. Such life as the economy has shown has depended heavily on steadily accumulating private debt, this time mostly household debt used to pay for severely inflated house prices. There is a continuing danger of that debt mountain collapsing and triggering a severe recession.

One more thing about recent economic history. The prosperity of the postwar decades was widely shared: incomes at the lower end rose steadily and inequality was at historic lows. This was because unions were strong and they insisted on the pie being shared around. Big business interests routinely claim that raising wages will cause unemployment and slow the economy, but the experience of the postwar decades was the opposite: ordinary people got regular pay rises, unemployment was at historic lows (1.3%, even in spite of high immigration!) and the economy boomed. How could this be?

Here is a different interpretation. What is good for one boss is not necessarily good for all bosses. To see the point, imagine all bosses stopped paying their workers. No-one would have money to buy anything and the economy would collapse. The bosses would go broke too. More realistically, if all bosses reduce the wages they pay, people will have less to spend, the economy will slow and profits will fall. The economy flourishes when everyone gets busy and is rewarded for their efforts. The money has to *circulate* to do its job.

Now imagine that one boss, say a Mr. Harvey, was a bit smarter and demanded the right to pay lower wages but insisted that all the other bosses should pay higher wages. Then the other boss' employees would be able to afford Mr. Harvey's products, sales would be high, he would be paying low wages and his profits would boom. Do you think Mr. Harvey could persuade his Business Council colleagues to go along with this scheme? Unlikely. Paying lower wages is good for one boss to do, but it is self-defeating if all bosses do it.

This point seems to elude the Business Council of Australia, which keeps droning on about labour market flexibility and wage restraint. This is plausibly a major reason why the economy has been increasingly anaemic over the past decade or more: wage growth has slowed and almost stopped.

The point is reinforced by the 2021 'Nobel' prize in economics (it is from the Swedish central bank, not Alfred Nobel). The prize was awarded to people who actually looked at the real world instead of just theorising. They showed in 1993 that in the real world a rise in the minimum wage led to an increase in employment, because there was more money circulating. The response of the neoclassical establishment was hostile. Fellow Nobelist James Buchanan said

> 'Such a claim, if seriously advanced, becomes equivalent to a denial that there is even minimal scientific content in economics, and that, in consequence, economists can do nothing but write as advocates for ideological interests.
>
> 'Fortunately, only a handful of economists are willing to throw over the teaching of two centuries; we have not yet become a bevy of camp-following whores.'

Buchanan's first statement is accurate: there is no scientific content in neoclassical economics. His second statement is a statement of faith and a personal attack in lurid language.[28]

There will of course be a limit on how high wages can go. Too high and the wage bill will cut into re-investment in the business. Too high and inflation might be triggered. In the extreme the business would go broke. There will be an optimal level of wages. The experience of the postwar decades seems to indicate we are well below the optimum wage level.

Inflation will not be a concern while unemployment is high. Inflation occurs when too much money is chasing too few goods. If wages were increased slowly, the extra spending would stimulate businesses to take up slack and increase their production, so that more goods would be available (and unemployment would fall). Only when unemployment is almost eliminated would businesses be unable to expand production, a point stressed by US economist Stephanie Kelton, who we will meet later[29]. Inflation would then be a possibility. We know low unemployment is possible because it averaged 1.3% through the 1950s and 60s, and inflation was also low.

Bob Menzies almost lost the 1961 election because unemployment was approaching 3%. After he squeaked back in he stole Labor's supposedly wicked big-spending policies and the economy picked up again. If a handful of votes had gone the other way in a couple of electorates Menzies would be less of a demigod to Liberals. It is worth noting that Labor had to recover from a disastrous split in 1954, and that Menzies' opponent was Arthur Calwell, whose grating voice and soap-box rhetorical style was not very appealing to many voters compared with Menzies' smooth and witty barrister's delivery, yet Menzies still only scraped in.

Socialists used to be accused of wanting to indulge in *social engineering* (shudder). Well, for the past four decades we have been subjected to a giant experiment in social engineering. We have been exhorted to be selfish and competitive, the economy has been re-structured to encourage or enforce selfish competition, and government and the public service have been shrunk to the point of being unable to perform properly when they are needed, as the pandemic has made all too obvious.

The expectation that selfishness would lead to good results has never been an obvious proposition. By now we have established that humans are highly social and innately inclined to cooperate within their group, and to ensure others cooperate as well. Individual expression is encouraged up to a point, and is essential to maintaining our diversity of talents and perceptions, but it must be balanced against the need for the group to function healthily. To try to depend only on selfishness is as misguided as to try to depend only on cooperation, and both experiments in social engineering, the neoliberal and the communist, have been proven failures.

The more overt expression of the selfishness doctrine, the free-market fetish of economic management, is clearly inferior to what went before, and the evidence is readily available and straightforwardly interpreted. It is only ignorance, wilful or otherwise, that allows us to pretend this is not so.

The broader insistence on selfishness, or rugged individualism, across society is widely perceived to have diminished our social cohesion, as indeed was intended, but to the detriment of most people. The evidence is less obviously clear cut than for economic performance, but there is still a great deal of evidence that the advantaged have worked to rapidly increase their advantage, and the disadvantaged have fallen further behind, in both relative and absolute terms. The quality of life of many who are not rich has been declining, and the divisions within our society have become sharper and more destructive. Why would this be so if the neoliberal ideology was as beneficial as is claimed?

The political expression of neoliberalism has never been pure, here or abroad. It is more of a convenient cover for those who wish to twist the powers of the state to their own advantage. It is also a cover for reactionary conservatism, which found its expression in the so-called culture wars.

The culture warriors attack anything that is not consistent with their presumptions, prejudices or gut reactions. Thus they claim global warming is a hoax, non-binary gender must be hidden away or stamped out, history demonstrates the glories of their class and their ancestors, and so on. Their attacks necessarily fall on knowledge-holders and the institutions of knowledge because the reactionaries' presumptions are often inconsistent with what we know, as the earlier discussion of human nature illustrates. Thus universities, the ABC and the National institutions (Library, Museum, Art Gallery, Archives and so on) have been attacked and defunded. This used to be done (by both sides) under the mendacious guise of so-called 'efficiency dividends', through which funding was shaved every year with the injunction to be more efficient, but more recently it became flagrant cutting.

These people, the free-marketers and the reactionaries, claim to value Western civilisation yet they are systematically dismantling its presence in Australia by attacking our knowledge-holders. They are destroying everything of value that makes us a civilised society (in the cultural sense). They claim to be expert economic managers, but their doctrine of selfishness is most clearly demonstrated to be a failure in the domain where it was most explicitly applied, the economy.

Neoliberal economics is based on a theory that bears no useful resemblance to the observable economic world. Putting it more colloquially, it is based on a theory that is plainly wrong. The history of neoclassical economics since Walras has been a history of desperately excluding anything from the theory that threatens the general equilibrium. Thus they exclude social interactions and the unpredictability of the future, along with economies of scale, debt, money and more. Not only that, but according to economist Steve Keen even their mathematics is wrong in several key places so that, for example, the law of supply and demand has no valid basis in the calculus used to develop it[30].

The discipline of neoclassical economics is without intellectual integrity. That is a very serious charge, but it is attested by many, some of whom are mentioned for example by Keen[30] and James Galbraith[12,31]. The case is elaborated in Appendix I. Other academic disciplines ought to investigate neoclassical economics because it is an impostor in their midst, and also because its false doctrines have done much to fundamentally damage universities, reducing them towards being merely training and consulting enterprises.

We are social. We are clan. We crave connection, we crave being valued, we crave love, and we thrive when we have them. In Zulu and related African languages, *Ubuntu* can be translated as 'I am because we are'[32]. Our very identities depend on being in relationship with others.

We can lay a foundation for a better world when we reject being treated as calculating reptiles and express our social nature in the ways that come naturally to us.

Yet there are still other malevolent forces at work in this benighted society and age, and we need to understand them too.

3

Belonging

Richard Manning is a writer and journalist who lives in Montana, USA. He likes to hunt and fish, and he eats what he kills. He says it is one of the few ways he has of sustaining a life that is visibly coupled to the forces that created it. Even so, he says, he does it less for the killing than for the seeing.

> ... I am able to perceive more detail—literally. Hidden layers become visible. Every subtle shift of shape or sound in the forest may signal the advent of an important moment. Hunting enlivens the senses like no other experience, giving me a taste of what it must be like to truly see and hear.[33]

Manning tells of one experience fishing a favourite creek as dusk thickened into darkness. He had been catching fish, and so continued even though he could no longer see. The mind tends to fill in the blanks left by failing vision, though often mistakenly. On this occasion however his mind zoomed to a spot across the creek that he perceived in close-up and fully illuminated. A large trout arched from the water, in this vision. Automatically he tensed his rod to set the hook in the phantom fish, and felt it set in a real trout that he soon landed, and recognised as the one from his 'imagination'.

Manning's book, *Against the Grain: How Agriculture Has Hijacked Civilization*[33], argues that humans traded a large measure of our sensual lives for the bit of security that comes with agriculture. You can make what you will of his story of the fish seen in the dark. I don't really know what to do with it, except I find it among the more credible accounts of what we might be capable of perceiving if our senses were not dulled by living sensually deprived lives in square boxes with only a handful of other species within our purview. If we are fully in the natural world there are thousands of species around us, and hundreds that we might know as food if we were raised to it.

Some people claim our brains are measurably different if we are regularly immersed in the sensual complexity of the natural living world. The Japanese, heavily urbanised, call it 'tree therapy' to spend a bit of time in a proper forest. Sometimes I take a small road out of my small town. I turn onto a dirt road that winds through the bush. Then the road gets smaller, and smaller again, until it is not sensibly passable because it is heavily washed out as it turns down a slope. I park the car, turn off the motor, step out and stand. There are no sounds of traffic, nor any other noise from humanity. There are bird calls and insects buzzing. As my brain tunes down to where I am, I hear the breeze sighing through the tree tops. I am immersed in the gentle breathing of the woodland. It washes through me and my body sighs in response. It feels like home.

First Australians do not own their Country, it owns them. They belong to the place where they were born. Their role is to care for it, to see that it is healthy and can continue indefinitely to be healthy. They are custodians. They may be the apex beings, but their role is not to dominate. They may be like a keystone predator species, but keystone species cannot eat all their prey because then they will starve. A keystone species is still a part of their ecosystem.

Like indigenous cultures everywhere, First Australians knew their Country intimately. Some still do, to varying degrees. The role of caring for Country required that they knew thousands of species, and knew a great deal about each species: where it likes to grow, whether it needs moist or dry conditions, whether it is fire tolerant, what its seasons are, how it reproduces, whether it is edible, how it must be prepared and so on and on.

Being part of the ecosystem does not mean having no effect on it. First Australians extensively modified the landscape. Fire was a primary tool, used not just to remove old grassy growth and encourage new green shoots favoured by kangaroos, but to determine where woodland and grasslands occurred. Some observant early European settlers noticed that trees were limited to poorer grounds and rocky rises, with grass growing in the best soil. In Europe the natural distribution is the reverse of this. A few perceptive observers realised the Australian landscape was not natural, that First Australians were managing it[34].

Management went well beyond 'firestick farming'. Yams were harvested and replanted, and in some places the soil was deep and soft, evidently from the regular action of women's digging sticks. There are some early reports of terracing on hillsides. Weirs were common on water ways, with associated fish traps. Fish traps were also used along the coasts. One of the most substantial examples of water management was an extensive system of ponds, channels and traps at Budj Bim in western Victoria, used to farm and harvest eels on their annual breeding migration. Smaller systems existed along other southern Victorian waterways. A major system of fish traps existed on the Barwon River at Brewarrina, extending for kilometres along the river and estimated to be many thousands of years old. This was a place of gathering for many groups in the region, because of the abundance of food available in peak season.[35]

Belonging to Country is also manifest in songlines, which are routes along which ancestral stories are embedded within features in the landscape. Many of the stories involve ancestral beings whose various escapades caused them to be turned to stone or hills, where they are preserved to remind everyone of the lessons of their story.

It turns out our brains are very good at associating ideas with physical features, whether they be in the landscape, among the stars or within artificial 'memory spaces', according to Lynne Kelly[36]. She argues that monumental arrangements like Stonehenge are memory spaces, but small, hand-held decorated plates can also function in this way, and are used in many traditional cultures. So it is with the songlines, with stories embedded in features of the landscape. A great deal of practical, social and spiritual wisdom was preserved in this way.

The most abundant animal group on Earth is not human beings, it is the ants, which may well exceed other groups not only in numbers of individuals but also in total body weight[37] (though possibly excepting beetles). There are few environments where ants will not be found in large numbers. Yet rapacious hordes of ants are not destroying the world's forests, degrading the soil, poisoning the environment from pole to pole, fouling their living places and killing every species that gets in their way. Ants' presence is to us and to most species only a marginal intrusion and occasional annoyance. They certainly have a large effect on Earth's biosphere, which would be different in many ways without them, yet other life forms thrive around them and with them. This is possible because ants live within the imperatives of the biosphere.

I say imperatives not because the Green Police will arrest you if you don't follow the rules but because consequences will inevitably flow and those consequences will, in the long run, decrease your descendants' chances of survival. So if you want your descendants to persist within the Earth's biosphere there are some things you need to do, and some other things you need to avoid. Following are some of the main rules.

You should not emit ***persistent toxins*** into the environment. In the scramble for survival many organisms produce substances that are poisonous to other organisms. Plants especially rely on poisons as one of their main defences. There is an arms race between plants and the digestive systems of herbivores. As plants develop more potent poisons, those that feed on them shift their metabolisms to neutralise the poison. However there is one thing that distinguishes natural poisons from many human-made poisons, which is that the natural poisons degrade rapidly, within hours or days. Any organism that produced a persistent poison would soon pollute its environment. The ecosystem on which it depended would sicken, and eventually the survival of the organism itself would be threatened.

You also need to ensure your 'waste' is ***recyclable***, so it doesn't accumulate and foul your nest. Living systems recycle *all* materials. One organism's 'waste' becomes food for others so that all the atoms of your body come from other organisms and return to other organisms. The water that forms much of your bulk has been cleaned by other organisms.

Having to recycle may sound a bit inconvenient to our present way of life, not to say onerous. Does it mean we're supposed to learn how to recycle *everything*? Yes it does. We need always to remember our connections, because what we do affects others. Those connections are not just with other organisms but connections within ourselves and the connections that make us part of something larger. We may have to reduce our consumption of alcohol because it's bad for our liver. Those things we are part of, called society and civilisation, need our attention too, to assure their viability, because if they fail our lives will become harder, and perhaps impossible.

You need to carefully manage your ***boundaries***. All organic systems, be they single cells, multicellular organisms, or insect colonies, carefully regulate what passes through their boundaries. We know we must not ingest poisons nor lose our life blood. Cultural boundaries are important for people, and the principle holds for them too.

We need to be mindful of how we deal with our neighbours. That does not mean just shutting them out, because then we can't live. Nor does it mean letting them take anything they like from us. Rather, it means managing our boundaries, allowing some interactions that are of mutual benefit but being careful to avoid others that may harm us.

You need to recognise you are ***part of something larger*** whose health you must protect. Conversely there are parts of you that need your protection in turn. Arthur Koestler[38] defined a *holon* as something that is simultaneously a whole and a part of something larger. A holon has a degree of self-regulating autonomy, yet it is part of a greater whole. He called a hierarchy of holons a *holarchy*. Examples are cells that make up our organs, organs that make up our bodies, individuals who make up a social system, and so on.

The imperative for recycling leads to the imperative of ***connection***. The Earth's living systems must long ago have become globalised. This probably occurred when there were only 'primitive' bacteria, and possibly before any currently surviving kind of organism had even developed. The reason is that every organism requires a flow of nutrients and produces a flow of wastes. It would not have taken long, on the scale of Earth's ancient aeons, for a proliferating organism to use up all of the readily available naturally-occurring nutrients and to fill the Earth with its wastes, and thus to threaten its own survival. A way through the resulting impasse would have awaited the development of other organisms that could make use of those wastes and turn them back into something that were nutrients for the first organism. Every farmer and gardener understands this.

In nature, ***competition and cooperation*** *coexist*. There may be an underlying competition for resources, but cooperation is a pervasive survival strategy. Cooperation is manifest as creatures flock and school and form social groups. It is manifest within our own bodies as the coordination of trillions of cells that comprise our organs, and in the bodies of all the other multicellular organisms, animal, plant and fungus. It is even manifest in the individual nucleated cells that make up our bodies, for they are the product of an ancient symbiosis between formerly separately living bacteria. Each species has its own level of cooperation, from little or none to the multicellular organisms that are the most visible manifestation of life to our senses.

Humans are highly social and evolved living in small groups and clans. It is essential to our physical and emotional health that we have the acceptance and approval of a community. It is essential that we maintain a *balance* between our individuality and our need for social connection. This was expressed long ago in Taoism, which counsels a *balance* between the *yang* and the *yin*.

Life is unpredictable: we encounter it often in our personal lives and a look at history will show that critical episodes can shift the trajectory of events unfolding. This has been recognised in biology and in systems theory as well, that a complex system is prone to sudden shifts that punctuate relatively stable times. It means we should not make our plans too specific and we should always be ready to adapt to unexpected developments.

Thus there are indeed imperatives applying to our lives:

- produce no persistent toxins
- recycle all materials
- carefully manage our interactions and boundaries
- be aware of being part of something larger, and of having smaller parts
- be aware of our connections; each of us is intricately and intimately connected with every other living organism on the planet
- maintain an appropriate balance between competing and cooperating
- maintain resilience and adaptability, avoid becoming too rigid.

Violation of these imperatives will lead to certain and possibly swift extinction.

First Australians say they belong to Country, but in a very literal sense we all belong to country. We are intimately linked into our local ecosystem, and through that to every other ecosystem in the global biosphere. Even if we work at the top of a glass and concrete tower, and move about in air-conditioned capsules, and live in boxes that exclude most other living creatures, we are still connected.

- All of our food comes from other organisms.
- All of the water essential to our survival is purified by other organisms.
- All of the oxygen we breathe is produced by other organisms.

Our modern societies violate every one of the biosphere's imperatives. This is particularly true of the industrial economies we have developed over the past couple of centuries. The implication is simple: either our societies change or they will not survive. Many of us may perish with them.

However we should not lose heart. People have done this before. People have lived in accordance with the imperatives of the biosphere, so we know it can be done. We may need to make some major changes, but there are those among us who are well along with figuring out how we can transition to a more viable collective way of life.

By the way, this business of being part of a *holarchy* is another blow to a political philosophy that has been popular for the past couple of centuries. It means there is no such thing as abstract *freedom* in nature. Rather there is a natural, and healthy, tension between individual autonomy and supporting the needs of the larger and smaller entities containing and contained by us.

I am fortunate to be able to live in a small town with much less of the noise and frenetic activity of a big city, although big mining and quarry trucks do rumble and roar through the main street, reminding us of our continuing imposition on the land. I have lived in large cities but always with the awareness of its artificiality, and of my preference for getting out in 'nature' when I could. What would it be like to spend long periods in a more natural environment?

Robert Wolff has done that in various parts of the non-industrial world, and notably in the highlands of Malaysia[39]. There he got to know the Sng'oi, non-Malay indigenous people who lived in the rapidly-diminishing mountain forests. He wrote in 2001, so their way of life may no longer exist. Wolff's little book tells of experiences with a number of non-Western cultures who interact with each other and the world in a variety of ways, but generally with gentleness and regard for integrity. They remind us there are many ways to be human.

I do not know what to do with this particular anecdote, just as I'm not sure what to do with Richard Manning's encounter with his trout, recounted earlier. Wolff got to know the Sng'oi over many visits, often sleeping over in their small, raised huts. One day the shaman, the man who had special knowledge and authority, asked Wolff if he would like to walk together the next day. No purpose was stated. Next morning they set out, carrying nothing, and walked through the jungle for many hours. Eventually Wolff asked for water and the shaman punctured a vine that yielded a drink. They returned to camp in the evening and he was none the wiser. No reasons had been offered and it was clear he should not ask.

There is little point in trying to use my second-hand words to do more than crudely summarise Wolff's English words as he attempted to convey his experience. For two more days they walked. Then Wolff had to return to his other life for a time. There were more visits, during which they walked again. Wolff, in his Western-style life in Malaysia, developed a rash and other symptoms with no clear cause. After many weeks of ill-ease the symptoms subsided and he had a sense of having come through some kind of crisis. He returned to the Sng'oi, who were pleased to see him, as always, and who asked no questions about his longer-than-usual absence. The next day and the day after they walked. There are more details to the story that I won't include here. Wolff did have some sense of being on the brink of something.

Next day they walked. After a time Wolff realised his head was full of thoughts and puzzles and he was not paying attention to the jungle, which had become much more familiar from their many walks. He consciously focussed his senses on the jungle around him, and stopped abruptly. 'The jungle was suddenly dense with sounds, smells, little puffs of air here and there. ... It was as if all this time I had been walking with dirty eyeglasses.'

He was thirsty. He focussed inside himself, as the shaman had indicated to do in other conversations. He sensed, and found nearby, a leaf with some water cupped in it. After studying minute details in fascination, and drinking, he became aware not just of the water and the leaf, but the plant it was attached to, the soil, the myriad other plants around it, then beyond. 'All was one, the same thing: water-leaf-plant-trees-soil-animals-earth-air-sunlight and little wisps of wind. The all-ness was everywhere, and I was part of it.'

Wolff realised his guide was nowhere to be seen, and briefly panicked. But then he re-focussed, and knew which way to go. He became aware that his guide was a little way off. He also became aware that there was a tiger down the way, beyond sound and sight but he knew it was there. As he returned towards the camp the tiger was moving parallel to his path, and he did not fear it.

There are other accounts of people having this kind of peak experience, feeling one-ness with all the world. Often it is reached through meditation, something I do not much relate to. I have never had such an experience. Wolff's account of reaching that hyper-awareness is more plausible to me because he reached it by being immersed in the living world. We may each have our interpretation of his story, that it was made up, or imagined, or that he connected through a spirit world of some kind. My version, provisional, is that our amazing bodies and minds are capable of a greater integration of all that we sense than we in the jaded civilised world are usually aware of. Some people think we go into a state of synaesthesia, a merging of our several senses[40]. Psychologist Steve Biddulph says we have a *supersense,* an unconscious synthesis of all that we sense and experience, and that often manifests as an intuition, if we pause long enough to let it emerge[10].

Whatever it might be, I am with Richard Manning in wondering what we have traded away, in return for this civilised life that we were never built for.

4

Birth of the treadmill

In 1843 two young men drove 1000 cattle from the Melbourne district, where their families had prospered, to 'settle' on the Murray River near present-day Swan Hill. They saw many substantial weirs around the river system, and they were forced to conclude the weirs must have been built by the local 'blacks'. One day one of the whitefellas, James Kirby, observed a native catching fish. The native had set up a flexible pole, thick end planted in the ground and a line with a loop attached to the thin end. The loop was hooked over a peg in the water within a small channel that cut through the weir. If a fish tried to swim through the channel it dislodged the loop which caught the fish and the fish was sprung out of the water by the flexible pole. The native would 'in a most lazy manner' reach back, undo the fish and reset the loop in the water. Kirby recorded that

> I have often heard of the indolence of the blacks and soon came to the conclusion after watching a blackfellow catch fish in such a lazy way, that what I had heard was perfectly true.[35]

My first reaction to this anecdote was that it takes quite a level of contempt of blackfellas to see the incident as displaying indolence (laziness) rather than ingenuity. The contempt was undoubtedly there, as was common at the time, but then it occurred to me that the White invaders had another perspective as well: they anticipated using the local natives as labourers in their new enterprise of raising cattle. If the natives were used to sitting around plucking fish from a trap rather than being busy all day, then it would be harder to induce them to work for the whitefellas.

This is probably the key to Kirby's perception of indolence. He would have been aware of practices on established properties near Melbourne. He might or might not have been aware that the drafting of local natives into labour on English estates was a feature of the British Empire stretching back centuries. In fact the English had refined their methods on their own peasantry before applying them to the Irish, Scots, Indians and many others. The anecdote leads us into something of profound importance to the predicament we find ourselves in at present.

Suppose you are an English Lord in 1500. You are a Lord because your Norman forebears invaded and brutally conquered the Anglo-Saxons several hundred years earlier. The Anglo-Saxons are there because their forebears invaded and displaced the Celts who were there before them. The Romans had invaded the Celts too, but evidently without wiping out everything Celtic nor displacing them to the hills, as the Anglos did. England was a rather brutal place by our modern (peacetime) standards.

Anyway from your upper-crust mates you've heard of a useful tactic. You 'enclose' a large part of a local common from which many people make a living - by some combination of grazing, farming, fishing and hunting for example. You force the people off the common. Then you allow most of them to return as tenant farmers, but you don't let them all back. You impose two requirements on these new tenants: you require them to pay a tax to you every year, and you require them to increase the yields of their crops, their 'productivity', by a little bit every year. Any who do not meet these requirements can be ejected and replaced by those previously excluded[41].

Any who resort to their old habits of fishing or hunting will be accused of 'poaching', of stealing from your newly-stolen 'estate', and severely punished.

This is an important innovation, an improvement on the old Feudalism. As a Feudal Lord your great grandfather had his castle and he had a deal with the surrounding peasants (whether he asked them or not): he would protect them (from other Lords) in return for a share of their produce. That was fine for him, but he did not have a very strong purchase on the peasant population. He could use threats and punishments to increase his share of the loot, but if he were too severe their production would fall and he would be no better off. By making the peasants tenants with the threat of eviction hanging over them you gain more purchase over them. As one aristocrat remarked at the time, hunger is a great motivator.

Enclosure is actually a revolutionary innovation. If you depend on a wage income, and you do not feel fully secure in your employment, then you are an inheritor of that innovation – from the wrong side. If you are a financier then you are an inheritor of the Lords of Enclosure and you will have every chance of prospering.

Our economic system is ruining our society, our land and the world. If we want to change that we need to understand how to stop its relentless expansion, its *growth*. That means we need to understand *why* it grows.

You can say greed keeps the economy growing, but how is the greed implemented in a modern economy? Feudal lords were greedy too, but their economic system hardly grew at all.

The 'enclosure' mechanism seems to be the fundamental driver of growth. You can see its modern version working throughout modern economies. The modern version is called *privatisation*. When something that was formerly public, like a school or a train service, is privatised the new owners can charge you for what was previously available for free or a low cost. The owners might also offer you employment, but with the threat that if you are not sufficiently 'productive' you can be fired and replaced from the pool of unemployed.

The aged care industry provides some telling illustrations. Even the name is telling. Since when did looking after our parents and grandparents become an *industry*? That is something people just did, back in a simpler age. Granny was often part of a household, living with one of her offspring and with grandchildren. Perhaps there were some adjustments to make and some tensions to deal with, but that was part of life.

This began to change as more women joined the workforce, either because they wanted their own income or career or because the family needed the extra income to pay off the (increasingly large) mortgage.

Various kinds of aged care homes were created, often subsidised by one or more levels of government. Old people traded family contact for contact with other oldies like them, and with 'carers', staff employed to look after them day and night, working in shifts. Granny may or may not have been happier with this arrangement. She traded close contact with family for a more limited and artificial social environment. Commonly there would be a nurse on duty, and they were often called *nursing homes*.

In 1997 the Howard Government cut $1 billion from aged care funding and greatly loosened the levels of care required for operators to qualify for remaining government funding[42]. For example nurses were no longer required, and the service was renamed *aged care*. Howard claimed that higher fees and bonds would provide the incentive for 'consumers' to pressure investors to expand and improve the industry. Instead, conditions in nursing homes deteriorated and average waiting time lengthened significantly. An agency charged with monitoring conditions was severely underfunded.

The government's changes made the industry a more lucrative target for corporate takeovers. American-based corporations moved into Australia to capitalise on a growth industry protected by an assured flow of government funds.

By 2000 horror stories were appearing in the media of care so poor as to amount to abuse. Some tweaks were made to policy, but the complaints of poor care and abuse continued. By 2018, after *twenty one years*, the Morrison Government was forced to appoint a Royal Commission to investigate conditions and recommend changes. A litany of horror stories was unearthed by the Commission[43].

The arrival of the Covid-19 virus early in 2020 then made things worse. The elderly were especially vulnerable, and many residents died alone, isolated so as to try to limit the spread of the virus. It emerged that many aged-care workers were working multiple jobs at different sites because their pay was so poor. This accelerated the spread of the virus from one facility to another.

The Commissioners identified fundamental systemic flaws with the way the Australian aged care system was designed and governed, as well as failures of individual operators. It was common for facilities to be understaffed, for staff to be undertrained, and for basic supplies to be lacking, so residents might have toilet pads changed only once or twice a day. The Commissioners recommended greatly improved regulation, oversight and funding.

Let us look at this from the point of view of the corporate operators. Their first duty is to shareholders, which means they must maximise profits by whatever means they can. If they do not, shareholders will shift their money somewhere else and the company might fail: competitive financial markets impose an artificial scarcity of investment funds. You maximise profits by increasing fees and bonds and by reducing expenses. Competitive pressures mean there is a limit to how high your fees and bonds can be. After that you must cut expenses. You can do this by reducing staffing levels, by employing less qualified people, by minimising their on-the-job training, but cutting pay and by cutting supplies, which would include meals and equipment of various kinds. It seems all those things are exactly what the corporate operators did.

What is the basic problem here? The problem is that the means to increase profit are not aligned with providing quality care. In fact they are opposed: higher profit requires less provision of care. The system, as designed, ensured poor to abysmal levels of care merging into abuse.

The government naïvely assumed that clients would demand the best care for the lowest reasonable price. Why did that not happen? Perhaps because many of the clients' families had little time of their own to monitor the care, and possibly little idea how to deal with such poor conditions they might have seen. Their elderly relatives were in these facilities precisely because families did not have time to care for them themselves, being on their own employment treadmill. Nor could they easily move their relatives to another facility because there was a chronic shortage of places, bonds would have to be reclaimed and so on. Whatever the reasons, it is clear that 'customer' demand was quite insufficient to ensure quality care.

Also, the government almost completely abrogated its responsibility, and declared intention, to monitor the system to maintain quality. It would have done this because it claimed to believe 'the market' would do the job, and because it wished to minimise government regulation and government spending.

This is a classic example of the failure of a 'free' market to deliver a desirable result. If you put aside theories and ideologies about free markets being best and just look at the incentives under which providers operated you see a complete misalignment. Higher profit requires poorer care. The market demands higher profit, so the continuation of the providers' business requires higher profit, therefore the market demands poor care.

This fits with the conclusion of an earlier chapter that the theory that supposedly demonstrates free markets are best is a toy abstraction that has no useful resemblance to real economies. It is irrelevant. There is no assurance at all that a free market will be efficient, nor that it will deliver desirable results. Without that general assurance you have to look at individual markets to see how they behave. If they are behaving poorly, as they commonly are, you might introduce penalties, subsidies and regulations to try to better align their incentives with what you want them to deliver. That is what the Aged Care Commissioners recommended in their final report.

Alternatively you might decide that a market is not an appropriate way to deliver a service. You might have governments of various levels provide the service, or you might encourage local communities, charities, churches and even families to provide the services, perhaps supported by subsidies from the government.

As it happens there is a health care company in the Netherlands, Buurtzorg, that works in a very decentralised way at the community level to deliver government-supported care to homes. It coordinates teams of twelve health care workers that have maximum autonomy. The team decides its own schedules and hires its own co-workers. The headquarters of the company confines itself to looking after the finances and offering help if any team requests it. There are no managers, no planners, no targets or bonuses, no HR. Teams are trusted to be self-motivating. After fifteen years Buurtzorg has over 800 teams working across the nation[18].

Buurtzorg's costs are a little lower than other health care providers and its customer and employee satisfaction is much higher. It has been voted Employee of the Year five times. By getting rid of managers and empowering its employees Buurtzorg is effectively spending public money on the delivery of small-scale care by independent practitioners. The people in charge are the people directly involved with delivery of service.

The most important feature of Buurtzorg is that it is motivated by care, not by profit. The care teams get on with providing care, because that is what they want to do. The elimination of mangers does not just allow them to be more efficient, it allows their *motivation* to remain paramount.

The headquarters does not require them to make profits, it facilitates their caring. The conflict between care and profit of the competitive market approach is removed. The people, working cooperatively, are then free to provide the best care they can. There is no scarcity of funding.

Economist John Quiggin has argued that human services cannot be entrusted to markets[44]. He cites a long series of cases, out of many more that could have been cited, in which 'market-oriented reform' has failed. The failures are documented by enquiries and by company failures of many kinds. Quiggin concludes that market competition is antithetical to 'the professional and service orientation' that is central to human services of all kinds. He further concludes that we should return to having governments deliver human services like education, health and prisons in a non-competitive way.

Human services are not like manufacturing. The point of human services is to have a caring relationship between the service provider and the client. The point of aged care is the caring relationship between carer and resident. You can, if you insist, increase the number of people a carer, teacher or nurse attends to, but beyond a certain small number you degrade the level of care. You cannot use a machine to allow the carer to attend to a hundred people, the way you can use a bulldozer to push a hundred times as much dirt. The whole idea of endlessly increasing 'efficiency' and 'productivity' does not apply.

What about *growth*? We have looked at how a market segment failed to deliver what it was supposed to, but does this tell us anything about the relentless growth of the economy?

The executives of aged-care corporations must maximise profits if they are to remain in business. If they are a 'public' company with shareholders, they live with the threat of shareholders withdrawing their money. Even if they are a private company they will be unable to compete if they are not making substantial profits. Either way the executives' options are limited. They can push up fees and bonds, but not too much. They can cut costs to the bone. This situation is the result of the artificial scarcity of investment funds, the threat that if you do not perform, and perform a little better than last year, you can be discarded.

A common strategy is to get bigger, because then you can find economies of scale on the management side of the business. It may not be widely appreciated that economies of scale are widespread throughout the economy, in management as well as in, for example, assembly lines where they are better known[45]. That is why the world is so dominated by large corporations. To 'grow your business' you might use marketing to induce more people to put their oldies in care, but you might also expand into new places. That, presumably, is why American companies moved into Australia in response to Howard's business-friendly policies.

Market competition thus pressures companies to get bigger. If all the companies in a market segment are trying to get bigger, then the segment will tend to expand. In human services there is not a lot of scope for expansion, beyond persuading people to pay for a service rather than do things for themselves – or get the government to *require* people to pay for a service, as in Australia's health insurance industry.

In manufacturing and retail there is more scope for expansion, by making more stuff and inducing people to buy it. This is the function of the marketing industry. Marketing started to become important in the 1920s, because people in the industrialising nations already had more stuff than their parents had dreamed of – refrigerators, radios, cars, washing machines, their own cottages – and evidently they were not frantic to work harder or longer so they could buy more. The marketers resorted to playing on our emotional insecurities to induce us to want more stuff. It has been working beautifully for a century. We now have vastly more stuff than we really need, and we work much longer and harder to get it. The end result is that we are stuck on the treadmill, the treadmill has sped up and the economy has grown dramatically.

To review, firms must maintain or increase their profit to stay in business. If they fall behind they my spiral down and fail. The pressure to increase profit comes from shareholders: in a competitive financial market they can move their money somewhere else if yields are not high enough.

Everyone, from the chief executive to the cleaner, is on notice to perform or be replaced, just like the tenant farmers after enclosure. The competition is the driver. Where does the competition come from? These days it comes from the financial markets, which are full of people trying to maximise their gains, even if they are already filthy rich. They are like the Lords of Enclosure in the old days.

Jason Hickel[41] explains growth as due to *artificial scarcity*. After enclosure there was not enough land available for all the peasants. The land was there, but the Lord had fenced some of it off so there was not enough left to support all the peasants. Thus was a pool of landless peasants created (or augmented, because loan sharks also cheated people out of their land). The poverty-stricken landless formed a pool of 'unemployed' that then pressured tenant farmers to produce, and to *grow* their production. When the industrial revolution got going a while later they were a ready source of ultra-cheap labor for the *dark satanic mills* of the new industries.

For most people these days there is a scarcity of good employment. Such employment as there is may be very insecure, involving short-term contracts or no contracts. There is plenty of work to do, but it is not shared around. Those who have a job may be overworked, and at the same time others have no work. There is an artificial scarcity of jobs.

A new term has arisen to describe the many people trapped in such jobs: the *precariat,* those whose employment is highly *precarious.* They proliferate in the *gig economy,* that part of the economy in which you are employed for one task at a time, like a food delivery, or a rock band's performance at a pub, or a fruit-picking stint in an orchard. It is a return to the bad old days when wharfies had to line up every morning in the hope of being chosen for a day's work.

The bosses of large corporations are also insecure, because there is an artificial scarcity of investment funds. Investors are not required to leave their money in the firm for the long term, so there is always the threat of them removing it. The primary job of the boss is to ensure substantial quarterly dividends are paid to investors and, even better, to ensure the firm's share price steadily increases. Of course the bosses do not suffer very much for their insecurity, because they may be pulling in millions, in salary and share options. If they lose their job they will survive quite well. The main price they pay is a bruised ego. However they are very likely to move into another job fairly soon, unless their performance was egregiously bad.

Even though the bosses don't suffer too much, their insecurity is not good for society. They are required regularly to extract wealth from the business and hand it over to share holders, whether or not the business is actually doing well at the time. They cannot manage so as to optimise the prospect that new innovations will become more productive over the medium term, they must keep their eyes on next quarter's bottom line. The financial markets enforce *short-term wealth extraction* rather than *long-term wealth creation*. This means modern financial markets are parasitic, just like the old Lords of the Manors were parasitic.

Occasionally you may see it mentioned that in the late Middle Ages the common people of Europe lived quite well. Their incomes were higher than in earlier periods. I had never seen any attempt to explain why this was so, if indeed it was so, until I read Jason Hickel's *Less is More*[41].

In the 1300s the peasants were revolting. Yes it's an old undergraduate joke, but the common people's lives were so bad that rebellions occurred. People demanded a greater share of the wealth they produced. The rebellions were ruthlessly put down, even though some of them were quite large. A rebellion in Flanders in 1323 lasted five years before the nobility defeated the rebels. Other rebellions occurred right across continental Europe and Britain.

The rebels made few gains, and then in 1347 things got worse as the Black Death plague broke out. By the time it subsided a third of Europe's population was dead. This calamity had an unexpected consequence. Labour was scarce and land was relatively abundant, which gave peasants and labourers greater bargaining power. They demanded and got lower land rents and higher wages.

This new circumstance did not simply increase the commoners' share of the wealth for a time. Rather, it showed everyone that the old order did not have to be. The rebellions increased. In England Wat Tyler led a revolt against feudalism in 1381. In Paris a 'workers' democracy' seized power in 1413. In 1450 an army of peasants and workers marched on London in the 'Jack Cade Rebellion'. Entire regions of Europe rose up, forming assemblies and recruiting armies. They were no longer interested in just adjusting their share of wealth, they wanted to put an end to the power of the lords.

Although individual rebellions were put down and their leaders and many followers executed, feudalism disintegrated anyway. Serfs became free farmers and people gained access to commons, forest and rivers. In Germany commoners came to control 90% of the land. Incomes doubled or tripled and nutrition improved markedly. The people began to build an egalitarian, cooperative society rooted in the principles of local self-sufficiency. The period from 1350 to 1500 was a golden age of the European proletariat.

By 1500 the aristocracy was desperate. Its wealth had declined, what it regarded as the natural order of things was disrupted and its existence was threatened. Nobles, the Church and the merchant bourgeoisie united in an attempt to regain power. They did so by forcing people off their land in a violent, continent-wide campaign of evictions. Thousands of rural communities were destroyed. Crops were ripped up and burned and whole villages were razed. Resistance was ruthlessly put down. In Germany in 1525 100,000 commoners were slaughtered. Life for commoners became much worse than in the feudal era. Desperate poverty was widespread, and paupers and vagabonds roamed the land.

Thomas Hobbes is famous for claiming in 1651 that before they received the benefits of civilisation peoples' lives were 'nasty, brutish and short'. He was quite wrong. Such nasty, brutish and short lives were the *creation* of civilisation, as James C. Scott has described in his history of the earliest cities[46]. The problem was magnified by the far-reaching innovation of the enclosures. Hickel observes that at the time Hobbes wrote Europe was one of the poorest, sickest places in the world.

This was the real context of the origin of enclosure. It was part of a desperate and vicious attack by the aristocracy on the common people to regain the power and wealth they once had, and to forestall their own extinction as a class. The feudal system had ended through peasant rebellions, fortuitously aided by the Black Death. The aristocratic counter-attack was a brilliant success, and its methods are still succeeding five hundred years later. The enclosures not only allowed the aristocracy to regain their wealth and power, they began to yield innovations that increased productivity, first in agriculture and later in industrial production.

It's a curious thing, but I don't remember being told any of this in school. Of course we were told about the industrial revolution, which happened because James Watt was clever and invented a steam engine (a *better* steam engine, more accurately). In my school we were also told that there had earlier been an agrarian revolution, which involved turnips and crop rotations or something. I'll give my limited school education a smidgin of credit, I've rarely heard mention of the agrarian revolution since school. We can recognise it now as the earlier stages of a gathering process of innovation.

Three central lessons come out of this more complete history. The first is that the strategy of enclosing commons and creating artificial scarcity generates innovations, increasing productivity and *growth* of economic output. The second is that the strategy can be applied to invaded lands as well as homelands. The third lesson is that growth is done on the backs of the common people – usually.

The European powers took their methods to Africa, North and South America and India, among others. The broad strategy was to seize control of lands, to disrupt the existing systems of production there, to set up your own system of production and to employ some of the locals as slave, servant or wage labour to run it.

A significant additional innovation was to demand people pay taxes, and pay them in the conqueror's currency. This forced people to work for wages, paid in the invader's currency, so they could pay their taxes, on pain of severe punishment. In this way the invader's currency can displace any local currencies and become the dominant currency[47]. Controlling a nation's currency yields a great deal more power over it, as bankers have understood through the ages. The introduction of a foreign currency creates another artificial scarcity.

Even as sophisticated a society as India succumbed to this treatment, although the process was a long drawn out series of incursions and manipulations rather than a single invasion. Shashi Tharoor, in *Inglorious Empire*[48], says India was the jewel of the medieval world. It was looted by the British (and others). Whereas previously there was a stable social order that took care of the basic needs of everyone, however unequally, under the British everything was geared to the extraction and export of wealth. Local production of textiles by traditional methods was banned and Indians were required to buy back cloth, made from Indian cotton, from the British. Even the production of salt was banned. That is why Gandhi chose salt-making and cotton spinning to catalyse the rebellion against the British. The railways were not for the convenience and benefit of locals, they were for the literal extraction of wealth to the ports. Under the British there were severe famines, which there had not been before, and the railways were not used to alleviate them.

The Irish suffered the same lesson. While their potato famine raged and people were dying by the million the English lords who had seized much of their land were exporting food for their own profit.

Jason Hickel makes the observation that there is no difference between colonialism and capitalism, it is the same system whether it operates at home or abroad[41]. The process may be more transparent to us in the colonial context, because we have heard more stories of invasion and brutal repression of other peoples than of the repression of our own forebears.

Capitalism requires the accumulation of a surplus that is then re-invested. The conventional, sanitised story is that the surplus accrues through superior innovation, and it is re-invested in further innovation, to the benefit of everyone. On the other hand the history outlined above says that early surpluses were acquired by seizure, through enclosure and violent eviction, not by innovation. As the aristocracy regained control of much of the homelands they began to seize lands in other countries and continents. Thus surpluses were re-invested in further conquest.

There was also innovation, like steam engines, and perhaps that became more prominent over time, but the goal always was to enhance the accumulation of wealth, not to benefit the welfare of humankind. This is the inevitable result, because the capitalist enterprises will fail if they fall behind in the race for more wealth.

Nor has conquest ceased. One invader, not so long ago, had vastly superior arms to those of the locals. The locals were small of stature and dark of complexion. They fought a bitter guerrilla resistance at great cost in lives and suffering. They resisted the invading forces for several years. One of the invaders' commanders said he was forced eventually to conclude that the resistance fighters had the support of the entire local population. A soldier accused of massacring 11 defenceless locals said he was ordered by his general to kill and burn and to take no prisoners. He could kill anyone over the age of 10. Referring to this and other foreign adventures of the time, a politician in the invaders' home country said 'We want a foreign market for our surplus products'.

The above description, following Howard Zinn[49], refers to the United States' invasion of the Philippines, 1898 to 1901. US behaviour in Vietnam, seventy years later, was nothing new. The invasion of the Philippines was at the time only the largest in an already long series of US interventions in the affairs of other countries, 103 between 1798 and 1895. There have been many more since. So the US was acting like any other imperialist nation, all the while espousing the rhetoric of democracy and freedom.

The grim irony of this push for imperial expansion was that the markets the industrialists craved were right under their noses. If they had but paid a decent wage to their millions of impoverished employees at home, then those employees could have afforded to buy the goods they were producing. Henry Ford was apparently one of the few who understood this.

More recently the invasions of Iraq and Afghanistan have been more obviously for the purpose of seizing wealth, this time oil. The reason for fighting in Vietnam was to resist communism, which directly threatens the power of the wealthy just as the peasant rebellions did centuries ago.

The standard claim for capitalism is that it has, by generating (or extracting) vast wealth, greatly improved the lives of the common people. The simplistic version of this claim is known as the 'trickle down theory', though it is not so much a theory as a marketing slogan: the wealth acquired by the wealthy trickles down to everyone to some degree. A careful study does not support it.[50] History does not support it. There have been times when the common people have demanded and fought for a greater share of the wealth. The peasant rebellions of the late medieval period are one example. The wealthy have rarely volunteered to give away any of their wealth, however illicitly gained.

In Australia in the late nineteenth century the authorities were struggling to maintain control over a settler population that had surged during the gold rushes. They were anxious that the gold-diggers remained, settled and became part of the growing colonies, so they granted many small holdings to commoners (completely disregarding the existing custodians of course). With the continuing influx of commoners the balance of political power shifted from the landed gentry to the commoners[51].

Labourers demanded and got shorter working weeks, men got the vote and many other moves towards more democratic arrangements were made. By the turn of the century there had been Labor governments in several states and soon there were Federal Labor governments. This culminated in 1910 when Labor, led by Andrew Fisher, won majorities in both houses (each the first majority for any party). Through this period many reforms benefitting the common people were made, notably the requirement that employers pay a minimum living wage fixed by a government body. Australia and New Zealand led the world in social innovation.

These moves towards a 'workers' paradise' were brutally interrupted by the First World War, in which Australia suffered heavy casualties fighting in the war among Europe's imperialist powers. The role of the British elite in greatly prolonging the slaughter for their own ends will be examined later.

After the Great Depression and another World War, Australia and much of the developed world emerged into a golden era of prosperity. Material wealth not only increased, it was widely shared. The wealthy had suffered, in relative terms, from the Depression and the war, so their command of wealth and power was reduced. At the same time workers' unions had gained in numbers and power. They demanded and got progressively higher wages. Tax rates on the wealthy were high; in the United States the top income tax rate was 90% for some time after the war. Banks were tightly regulated. Social services were expanded. The material lives of common people improved noticeably year by year. All of this happened because common people organised and struggled to make it happen, even though the period was presided over by the conservative Bob Menzies.

Since the 1970s the wealthy fought back. They misconstrued the problems of that period and claimed free markets were the panacea for economic difficulties, as described in a previous chapter. Reduced regulation allowed them to regain power. The result has been a rapid decline in the share of wealth and the quality of life for many people, as employment became progressively less secure, wages stagnated, social services were cut, stress rose and health declined. The gains made through the great efforts of many people in the twentieth century are being rapidly lost.

There is no trickle down. The system is rigged to pump wealth upwards. Inequality has blown out dramatically, and is still growing.

James Kirby was evincing a well-worn attitude when in 1843 he judged the clever blackfella fisherman to be indolent. The strategy Kirby would pursue had been tested over centuries of practice, in England and then in many other lands. Seize the land. Enclose it, by claiming ownership over it. Hire labourers or capture slaves to work it, requiring of them high productivity for little reward. Enjoy your stolen wealth, and re-invest some of it in further seizures of wealth. If you are a little more enlightened, invest some of it also in innovations that improve productivity.

If Mr. Kirby were a thoughtful man he might have realised that in fact he had little alternative but to pursue this strategy, if he wanted himself or his children to avoid becoming poor labourers themselves. Indeed he might have pointed this out to any bleeding-heart who reproached him for his treatment of his labourers.

So it is in the modern, industrialised and financialised economy. Any boss who wants to care well for his family must cut costs of wages and environmental impacts so as to stay in the race for customers and finance. The effect of all this striving is for the whole economy to grow. If it does not, then more than the usual number of businesses will fail and unemployment will rise. Rising unemployment is every politicians nightmare. The justification for each new destructive enterprise, whether mining or land clearing or using only gig workers, is always jobs, more jobs. By now the quality of those jobs is obviously declining and the prospect for continuing to create jobs at the required rate of growth is becoming more obviously precarious, even apart from the destruction of our planetary life support system. Whether this will change significantly under the Albanese Labor Government remains to be seen. So far they have been extremely cautious, even timid.

In any event the likes of Mr. Kirby prospered in Australia, even though their foreign and thoughtless methods, including the use of foreign species, soon cause ecological collapses that considerably reduced the productivity of the land. Increasingly mechanical agriculture would partially compensate. A century later the problems with this strategy would be further disguised by the advent of chemical agriculture. However this innovation would only postpone the problems following from enclosure and extraction, rather than long-term cultivation, as we'll explore later.

We have made a machine, a system, that is devouring our world. Individually we cannot stop it. Even the billionaires cannot stop it. Simply resisting it will not work. There is no-one actually in charge who might respond to our pleas. There is no driver on the bulldozer, so lying in front of it will have no effect on the bulldozer, only on you.

To stop the juggernaut we have to understand how it works. We have to find the place within it where we can *turn it off*.

I think Jason Hickel is right, that it is the competition for a limited resource, the artificial scarcity, that drives the juggernaut[41]. That is what keeps us on the treadmill, running to stay in place, trying to get ahead, but above all desperately trying not to fall behind and be discarded.

The example of the original commons shows us what we might do. The land was abundant enough to support everyone, when everyone had access to some land, the streams, the forests. Some were quite poor but that was because others were taking more than their share. When the greed of the nobility was restrained the people lived better. After the nobility fought back and enclosed the land's abundance the peasantry were made poorer and more desperate than before, and the treadmill had begun.

The remedy is to allow the Earth's abundance to be available again to everyone. Then everyone may have enough to live as they choose. Any common needs to be collectively managed so it is not abused, and so its abundance continues. The old commons were so managed, and Garrett Hardin's 'tragedy of the commons' was avoided. We are quite capable of collectively managing our lives, if we allow our innate social skills room to operate.

If there is enough for everyone, and everyone has *access* to enough, then we can step off the treadmill.

How do we ensure everyone has access to enough? As usual, plenty of people have been working on this, and showing us how it might work. One way that will not work is to have a great central dispensary. That would be the great socialist dictatorship, much dreaded by libertarians. Its problem, the problem with the Soviet Union's communism, is that the deciders are too remote from the recipients. They do not interact socially. The deciders do not understand all the needs of the people of each community.

The same problem developed in capitalist systems as well, of course. As corporations became bigger, they became more remote from those whose needs they might serve. They serve their own needs, just like a socialist bureaucracy, and not those for whose benefit they supposedly exist.

Much better to devolve the management of abundance to the local level, as much as possible. There is a whole movement promoting *localisation*[52]. Not everything, but much of what we need can be supplied locally. Huge corporations straddling between continents, with long supply lines stretching around the world and back again, were created to serve the imperative of competitive growth, not because it is sensible and efficient to operate that way. Fish caught in the southern hemisphere are shipped to China for processing and then sold in Europe, or back in the southern hemisphere. That is obviously insane. It is based on false economies of fossil fuels that are too cheap and Chinese wages that are too low.

Food, especially, can be grown and delivered locally, with a minimum of processing. It is much healthier. Communities are more resilient. Wealth remains in the locality.

5

Housekeeping

Some years ago I read of a woman, an immunologist, who came home from a conference of immunologists and wept. She became depressed. At the conference it had become evident that chemical pollution is harming our children, starting from the moment of conception. It is hard to become aware of an important truth that is not widely recognised, and that you know will be resisted by powerful interests.

Minute amounts of artificial chemicals can change the course of the development of a foetus. The result can be major physical deformities, as were caused by the notorious drug thalidomide in the 1950s. But there are many more industrial chemicals now, and so-called hormone disruptors can be particularly insidious. The effects may not show up for a long time, and they may be much more subtle, such as a deficiency in the child's immune system, or infertility when they mature, or a greater propensity to depression[53].

The load of toxic chemicals has only grown since then. There are 350,000 artificial chemicals permeating everything, including babies in utero. Many disrupt our nervous system, including our brains and intelligence, others disrupt our endocrine systems, including the hormone disruptors.[54]

Over the past few years pictures have appeared in news media of beaches strewn with plastic and other human rubbish. The startling thing is that some of these pictures are from remote islands, very far from any human habitation. They portray compellingly that our industrial civilisation pollutes the world from one end to the other.

A campaign is under way to reduce the production and use of discardable plastic products, particularly of single-use plastic bags. However this approach will make only a marginal difference. Even if discarded plastics were reduced by 80%, something industry and politicians are unlikely to be willing to contemplate, there would still be far too much of it in the world. Regulating waste does not get to the core of the problem.

The core of the problem is that our present industrial system uses material resources only once. It is a once-through system. Resources are extracted, manufactured into a product, the product is used once and when it is worn out or its use is no longer desired it is discarded. It is then supposedly put into landfills, which only pollutes the world less obviously than throwing things onto the beach. The system's logic is *extract, use once, dump*. A proper system, a system that observed the imperatives of the biosphere, would recycle all materials, excepting only a small percentage lost within each cycle. It would also avoid producing toxins that persist in the environment.

The word *economy* derives from the Greek *oikonomia,* meaning the wise management of a household for the benefit of all its members. We are instead practising *chrematistics,* short-term exploitation. We are fouling our nest.

An important part of why we make such a mess is in the way we count the benefit of our activities. Much of the mess is just ignored, so there is no incentive to do anything about it. But a lot of the mess is counted as a positive contribution to our welfare. No, this is not a joke.

If a chemical factory sells $3 million worth of chemicals in a year, but creates pollution that costs $1 million to clean up, then, in dollar terms, how much better off would you say we are? You would say, I expect, we are only $2 million better off. However economists and politicians say we are $4 million better off. Instead of *subtracting* the $1 million cleanup cost from the $3 million production, they *add* it.

Why do economists add a cost as though it is income? Because they rely on the Gross Domestic Product as a measure of wellbeing, and that is how you calculate a GDP. The GDP is essentially the sum of all those things we do that are bought and sold. It is the sum of all our activities that involve the exchange of money.

Calculating a quantity like GDP would not necessarily be much of a problem if the GDP were just an obscure thing used by economists to measure total economic activity, so long as they were clear that's all it is. The problem is the GDP has become the dominant measure of wellbeing. It is the goal of almost every government in the world to keep the GDP increasing. When the GDP increases, politicians and economists say 'the economy has grown', and this is universally considered, within mainstream political discussion, to be a good thing.

It is claimed that a growing GDP means we are becoming richer. It is assumed that if we are richer then our wellbeing is improved. Neither claim is necessarily correct. Over the past half century or so the GDP and wellbeing have become less clearly related. It is quite possible that GDP could increase while both wealth and wellbeing were static, or declining. Some argue that is already true, especially for wellbeing.

There are in fact *several* fundamental problems with using GDP as a measure of overall wellbeing.

- One is that costs like pollution are added rather than being subtracted.
- Another is that many of our beneficial activities do not involve the exchange of money, so they are not counted.
- Another is that GDP is not a measure of wealth, it is a measure of income.
- Another is that it is a purely material measure.
- Another is that no account is taken of the state of our communities and society as a whole.
- Nor is any account taken of the state of the Earth.

It is quite possible to use more sensible measures of our state of wellbeing, or even just of our material net incomes and wealth. Such measures have been developed and are being improved all the time.

However they do not dominate the headlines the way 'growth' (of the GDP) dominates the headlines.

The heavy reliance on GDP severely distorts our priorities, and our view of ourselves. Anything that falls outside the materialist and very blinkered purview of mainstream economics is regarded as secondary, irrelevant, or an expensive luxury to be attended to only as and when we become richer. That dismisses a mother's love, healthy families, healthy communities, a tolerant and safe society, and the health of the Earth, our sole and irreplaceable life support system.

***Why* do economists *add* the cost of** cleaning up pollution to the GDP? It is because the GDP is defined as the sum of all activities involving money, regardless of the desirability of those activities. It came to prominence during World War II in the USA. At that time the government was heavily involved in directing the economy to support the war effort. It might therefore have been presumed that most activities were contributing to the overall effort, and the GDP was helpful in informing the government on overall levels of production.

However once the war was over, what assurance was there that most activities were beneficial? Pollution was already an old phenomenon, associated especially with the industrial revolution. An even older problem is the presence of people who sell shonky goods, or who practice other kinds of fraud. Then there is the occurrence of accidents and disasters, and the necessity of maintenance and replacement of equipment and infrastructure.

A sensible way to deal with such problematic activities is to set up a balance sheet, as a shop-keeper would do, with income on one side and costs on the other. You then add up both sides, *subtract* costs from gross income, and arrive at net income, or profit.

One version of this approach is the Genuine Progress Indicator (initially known as the Index of Sustainable Economic Welfare[55]). As an example, the calculation of the GPI for Australia in 1996 is shown in Table 4.1 below. We don't have to worry about the details here. The point is just to show it is possible to put gross income in one column, estimated costs in the other, and subtract costs from income. You will see that various kinds of pollution appear in the Debit column. There are also things related to the state of society (unemployment, crime) and other aspects of the environment. Commuting is considered a cost. Illness is a cost. Accidents are a cost.

Table 4.1. Australian Genuine Progress Indicator, 1996[56,57]

Credit		Debit	
[Personal consumption]	[260.9]	Unemployment	19.76
[Income distribution index]	[107.87]	Underemployment	2.02
		Overwork	10.09
Weighted personal consumption	281.43	Private defensive expenditure (health and education)	12.19
Public cons. expenditure (non-defensive)	25.35	Commuting	5.44
Household and community work	155.08	Noise pollution	2.40
Services of public capital	6.09	Transport accidents	5.01
Net capital growth	5.87	Industrial accidents	7.63
		Irrigation water use	0.64
		Urban water pollution	3.58
		Air pollution	9.42
		Land degradation	4.51
		Loss of native forests	4.81
		Depletion of energy resources	42.59
		Climate change	22.90
		Ozone depletion	0.00
		Crime	9.94
		Net foreign lending	21.10
Total Credit	473.82	Total Debit	184.03
Net (Credit *minus* Debit)	**289.79**		

(Amounts in billions of 1990 Australian dollars. Income distribution is an index used to adjust personal consumption.)

Long ago Ralph Nader noted that every time there's a car crash the GDP goes up. A few years ago when bushfires raged into Canberra, then my home town, and destroyed about 500 houses, the local economy was boosted, according to economists. The cleanup of the huge oil spill resulting from the 1989 grounding of the oil tanker *Exxon Valdez* in Alaska noticeably increased the US GDP. This is the same nonsense as the chemical pollution example. Accidents, pollution and natural disasters make us worse off. We may have to work harder to repair the damage, and thus be more economically *active*, but that keeps us from doing more productive things, or from enjoying our lives.

So the first fundamental problem with the GDP is that just adding up activity takes no account of whether the activity is useful, useless, harmful, or repairing previous harm. To an economist it's all just *activity*.

Why did economists continue to use GDP as a measure of wellbeing, or at least of what used to be called *standard of living*? I make no claim to understand the minds of mainstream economists. My best guess is that it's because free markets are supposed to ensure that all activities are useful. During World War II, government direction was intended to play this role. After the war, the government withdrew from such direct central management, but markets are supposed to play the same role.

However this still doesn't explain why the cost of cleaning up pollution or repairing damage from accidents and natural disasters would be considered as contributing to the benefit of the economy. There has been a failure to think properly about how to do accounting in a national context. Well, that's putting it mildly.

Some economists may say, at this point, they *know* the GDP is only a measure of total activity, not a measure of quality of life, or even of net material benefit. It's not their fault if politicians mis-use the GDP. In fact the inventor of the GDP, Simon Kuznets, specifically warned that it should not be used as a measure of the quality of life of a nation.

However I haven't heard a sustained campaign by the economics profession to get the GDP replaced by a proper balance sheet, one that shows incomes and costs and calculates the *net* benefit of our activities. Using the GDP to measure our 'standard of living' or national income violates the most elementary requirement of accounting - that costs are subtracted from gross income.

Economists crow about being the superior social science because it is quantitative. They use a lot of complicated mathematics. We noted in a previous chapter that in fact they get some of their fancy mathematics wrong. Here, they can't even do arithmetic.

A second fundamental problem with GDP is that the it doesn't count anything that does not involve money. Not everything we do deserves to be counted as contributing to national production, it's true. Playing in the back yard or attending a concert is how we enjoy our spare time, and does not contribute to national production. However growing vegetables in the back yard arguably does contribute, since it substitutes for something that would otherwise be bought, involve the exchange of money, and count towards both GDP and GPI. Exactly which things ought to be counted may be debated, but what about volunteer work for charities, or raising children?

Marilyn Waring came up with the example of six mothers who stay at home caring for their babies[58]. The mothers' loving care doesn't register with the GDP, because they are not paid for it, so their loving care has no value according to our national accounting. However if each mother were to hire the next to baby-sit her child, then money would change hands and the GDP would go up.

Thus having someone else care for your baby is implicitly regarded as more valuable than caring for your own baby, in the sick world of our national accounting. Governments anxious to see the GDP rising have little incentive to encourage mothers to stay home and care for their babies. However governments have a real incentive to see mothers out working, because then their paid work and their child care costs both add to the GDP.

This kind of problem is even more important in poorer countries, in which much more activity may be at the local village scale and fail to register in the GDP. This means, on the one hand, that some such countries may not be quite the 'basket cases' some economists describe them as. On the other hand if people are displaced into cities to work for a pittance as land is taken over for cash cropping, then the people have to pay for things they formerly did for themselves, or obtained from the local village. The shift from growing vegetables to buying fast food adds to the GDP and thus counts as progress, whereas it commonly represents a significant regression in the person's health and happiness, and in the health of the nation's social fabric.

Table 4.1 includes the item Household and Community Work in the Credit column. This is the estimated value of activity that contributes to national productivity but does not involve money, things like volunteer work for charities. It is a very large amount, 55% of Weighted Personal Consumption (basically everyone's personal monetary income), and over half of the net GPI. So this item seems to say that over half of Australians' net wellbeing came from unpaid activities in 1996.

There seems to be a rather dramatic implication here. It is that all of the frenetic activity of the monetary economy contributes only about half of our net wellbeing. Much of the total of productive and beneficial activities, monetary or not, is cancelled out by the negatives in the Debit column.

Australia's GDP for 1996 was $432 billion (in 1990 dollars). But according to Table 4.1 over 40% ($184 billion) of the activity that might have counted towards the GDP were actually costs that reduced our wellbeing. Perhaps some of these activities were what David Graeber called *bullshit jobs*[59].

Now the GPI includes some important items that are estimated with varying degrees of confidence, and it is appropriate to debate how such things should be counted. Therefore the specific numbers I have just noted should not be taken too literally. However the numbers certainly raise important issues. The most important issue is that the GDP may be extremely misleading, even as a measure of material standard of living.

One manifestation of this is that the relationships between GDP and wellbeing, and between GDP and GPI, seem to have changed over time. In the post-war decades, until roughly 1970, most people would not have disputed that their wellbeing was rising along with material wealth and the GDP. Since then, many people are not so sure their wellbeing is really being served by a 'growing economy'. Figure 4.1 compares the changing GDP *per capita* (i.e. per person) with the GPI per capita for both Australia (left) and the US (right).

In both cases the GPI has risen by a smaller proportion than the GDP, even declining for a time in the US. In Australia GDP increased by about 2.9 times, whereas the GPI increased by only about 1.8 times. In the US GDP also increased by about 2.9 times, whereas GPI increased by only about 1.7 times. So GDP suggests we were three times better off in 2000 than in 1950, but GPI suggests we were less than twice as well off. If GPI is a better measure of quality of life than GDP, the implication in both cases is that since about 1970 growth in the GDP has not resulted in much improvement of quality of life.

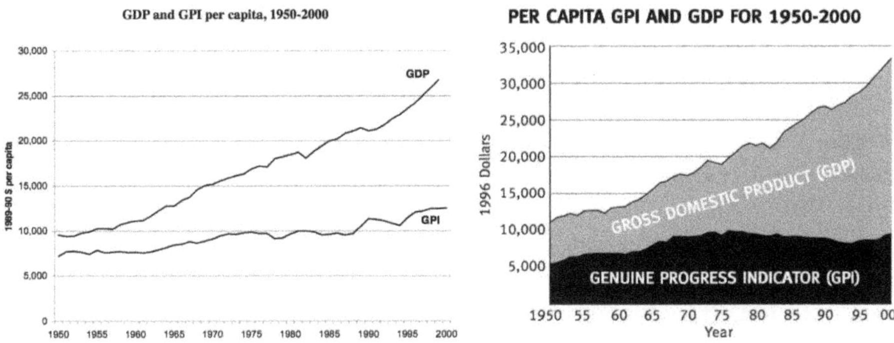

Figure 4.1. Comparison of GDP and GPI *per capita* over time for Australia (left)[57] and the United States (right)[60].

As already noted, the precise value of the GPI is not to be taken as highly accurate. Yet it corroborates the qualitative evaluation of many that increasing monetary wealth is not yielding an unalloyed increase in wellbeing. For many people work hours have been increasing, their income is insecure, the pace of life has become too stressful, suburban backyards are being built over, the natural world they used to value is retreating, and they worry about the global threats of pollution and destruction of forests, soils, and habitat.

One measure of this disaffection is that remarkable numbers of Australians have *downshifted,* as mentioned earlier. This means they voluntarily took a reduction in income so as to improve their quality of life[7]. Comparable numbers downshifted in the UK[61].

These thoughts bring us to a third basic problem with GDP, its failure to take any account of the state of society. The difference between the GDP and GPI is not just because of more sensibly accounting for material problems, it is because the GPI also takes account of some social factors, including unemployment, underemployment, overwork, crime, and an adjustment for inequality (through the Income Distribution Index). Inequality has a significant effect not just on the quality of a society but even on economic performance[62]. More unequal societies are more conflicted, and income is not spent or invested as wisely as in more equal societies.

A striking portrayal of a dramatic increase in inequality in the US is shown on Figure 4.2, which was compiled by Robert Reich[23]. It compares the steady rise in productivity, 1947-2009, with the income of ordinary people. Productivity is the value of production per hour worked. Income (hourly compensation) closely followed rising productivity until the 1970s. After 1980 (the start of the Reagan years) there is a sharp break, and income rose by only 8% thereafter, compared with an 80% further rise in productivity. Most of the extra wealth generated in the neoliberal era has been creamed off by the very wealthy.

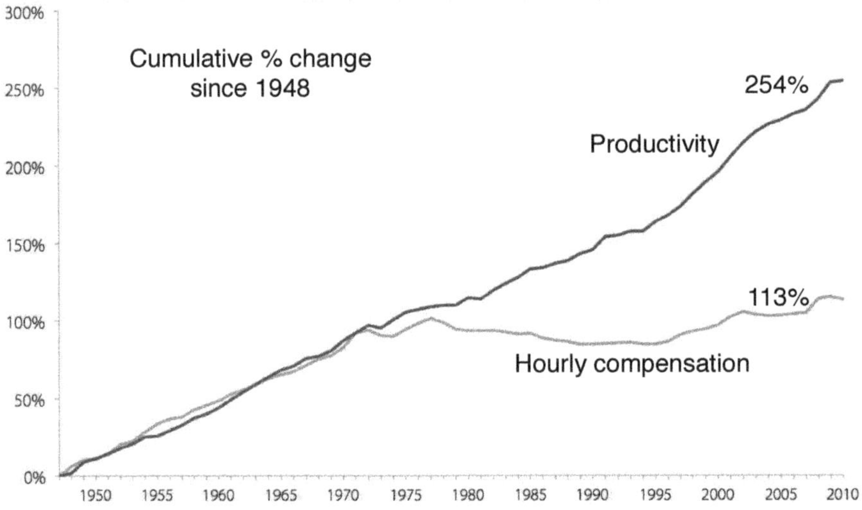

Figure 4.2. The Great Regression of the neoliberal era, compared with the post-war Great Prosperity. From Reich[23].

There are other social factors that make a difference to our quality of life. If work hours have increased, both because people work longer and because two adult partners of a household feel the need to work, then families are more stressed. Employment has become less secure, because neoliberals regard employees as just another disposable commodity, and that increases stress, along with unemployment. With greater inequality, those at the bottom are more resentful, and that feeds into both ill health and crime. If people are working more, then they have less time for community activities, so they don't have as much social support as they used to, which compounds stress and ill health. Neoliberal hostility to governments, and particularly to social programs, has resulted in cuts to community and social services, along with infrastructure, so people receive less 'in-kind' income and have less social support as stress levels rise.

A problem with both GDP and GPI is that they try to capture the state of society in a single number. At least the GPI tries to take some account of some social factors, but how do you compare the effects of crime or ill health with the value of a new car? In the GPI they are compared by using some documented costs of crime or ill health. But the negative effects of crime and ill health go well beyond their immediate cost. They raise personal angst and they may permanently reduce the quality of someone's life. On the other side, how to you value a mother's love for her baby? It is certainly extremely valuable, because the quality of our whole society is improved as we learn to raise children more lovingly and effectively[19]. There is no dollar measure of such qualitative things. So they are left out of the GPI, and the GDP.

The same thing can be said about the state of the Earth. You can put a dollar value on the timber in a forest, but you can't put a dollar value on the healthful and aesthetic experience of being in a mature forest, nor on its biodiversity, without which the Earth would be a less effective life support system. Nor can you put a dollar value on the medicines that might at some future time be discovered in plants that grow in the forest.

For these reasons an alternative approach called *Triple Bottom Line*, has been developed for measuring our overall wellbeing. It separately evaluates the economic, social and environmental areas. In this approach, some of the things in the GPI might be reassigned to other categories, or might appear in more than one category. Thus crime does involve financial costs that could be counted in the economic category, but it also indicates that a society is less cohesive and peaceful than it might be, so it would also appear in the social category, also as a negative. Similarly the loss of timber in a degraded forest would have an economic value, but a forest provides us with many other 'services' like clean water, better rainfall, a refuge for biodiversity, potential but undiscovered drugs and aesthetic and spiritual nurturing. Thus the health of a forest might be listed in appropriate ways in all three categories.

There will be no 'best' way to summarise the wellbeing of a whole society, and many other variations and elaborations are possible. In a sensible world, the Triple Bottom Line would be better than the GPI, because it gives us more complete information with fewer debatable assumptions about whether things have dollar values.

However in the superficial and sensational world that passes for political discussion and reporting, politicians and media would rather reduce everything to a single number. Thus if the GPI were adopted as a primary measure we could expect it to be reported prominently, whereas a Triple Bottom Line might be relegated to page 6 of a newspaper, and might not appear at all in the infotainment that TV executives are pleased to call 'news'. For the time being, if we're stuck with a single number, the GPI is of some use, whereas the GDP is highly misleading and we'd be much better off without it.

It's worth saying a little more about GPI *versus* GDP. The GPI makes quite debatable assumptions, for example including a dollar measure of the negative effects of global warming (included through the euphemism 'climate change'). I would agree with some critics that you could put almost any number for the 'cost' of global warming. If it will result in the collapse of global industrial systems, the loss of major agricultural production, epidemics and flooding of half the world's cities and all of its harbours, what is the dollar cost, now?

So I agree the GPI is an approximate and imperfect measure. However I do not agree we should just leave important things out of our assessment of the state of our society. So the GPI is approximate and imperfect, but it is based in a sound approach, that we *add* benefits, *subtract* costs, and arrive at a *net* evaluation of our condition.

The GDP, on the other hand, is not based on a sound approach to evaluating the state of our society, even the material parts of our society the economics profession chooses to focus on. In no defensible form of accounting would you put all your transactions, incomes and costs alike, in the Credit column of a ledger, add them up, and proclaim that your shop is thriving because your Gross Shop Product is increasing. As a measure of our overall state of material wellbeing, the GDP is deluded and indefensible.

Using GDP to measure our wellbeing is not just a minor detail, it seriously distorts our society's priorities, as some of our examples illustrate. Consider the opening example of the polluting chemical company. Because the pollution reduces the GPI, a government anxious to keep the GPI increasing would have an immediate incentive to stop the chemical company from polluting. In the present situation, however, the $1 million cost of cleaning up the pollution is merely added into the GDP as 'activity', so the government has no incentive to stop the pollution. In fact the incentive is to allow the pollution to continue. The flood of artificial toxins grows.

Similarly, unsustainable clear-cutting of Tasmanian forests would reduce the GPI but increase the GDP. Our national accounting actually encourages governments to ignore over-exploitation of natural resources. In fact, since exploitation of resources and of people (through overwork and low wages) simultaneously increases corporate profits and the GDP, there is a clear incentive for an unholy alliance between unscrupulous corporations and unscrupulous or stupid governments.

What about the things GDP doesn't count? In Marilyn Waring's example of the mothers who stay at home to care for their babies, their loving care doesn't register with the GDP. However if each mother hires the next to baby-sit her child, then the GDP goes up. Governments anxious to see the GDP rising have little incentive to encourage mothers to stay home and care for their babies, but they have a real incentive to see mothers out working, because then their paid work and their child care costs add to the GDP.

We can now see that the familiar refrain 'the economy is growing' carries a quite deceptive message. It doesn't mean what it seems to mean and it won't accomplish what it's supposed to accomplish. It doesn't mean our quality of life is improving. It doesn't even mean we're getting richer. It means we're busier. It means the dollar value of our paid activity is increasing, but it takes no account of whether that activity is useful, useless, harmful or attempting to repair some previous harm. It ignores unpaid activity and so undervalues or ignores and implicitly discourages many valuable things, including mothers' care of their children.

Even if we understand 'the economy is growing' to mean 'the GDP is increasing', unemployment and poverty will not be eliminated. They will, in the long run, still obstinately persist, as they have through decades of

GDP growth. The factors controlling unemployment and poverty evidently must be found elsewhere.

A bizarre outgrowth of the obsession with keeping the GDP growing is a recent obsession with keeping Australia's population growing rapidly, through high rates of immigration. Several lines of argument are involved, and none of them withstand cursory examination.

The most immediate concern is that the Government has to be able to say 'The economy has grown', otherwise its economic management is considered to have failed. Simply by cramming more people into Australia the economy (i.e. the GDP) can be made bigger, so long as our net income per person does not actually decline too much. Before the pandemic, the total GDP growth rate had dwindled to only a couple of percent. In fact the GDP *per capita* was stagnant or shrinking, and that should have concerned everyone, because it implied our incomes were falling. Some economic commentators noted this situation, and some called it a 'per capita recession', or something similar. However this never made the media headlines, because virtually all the mainstream commercial media did not want the Coalition Government to fail so they only mentioned the misleading growth of the total GDP.

A second factor was that the government was keeping the big end of town happy by bringing in lots of new workers. This keeps downward pressure on employment and wages[63]. Many of the immigrants are brought under the excuse of a *skills shortage* of one kind or another, though others are low-skilled people willing to do the tedious jobs like picking fruit. If there are skills shortages, this reflects on our education system, which for decades has been run down for lack of investment. We thus fail our young people by not properly educating them, but this is rarely noted. In any case importing skilled migrants has only a minor effect on the level of skills in the country[63]. At the unskilled end, employers complain there are plenty of jobs but our pampered young city dwellers are not willing to take them. There is supposed to be a free-market remedy for this condition: you raise wages until people come. It means that the employers really want *cheap* labour, an inference supported by recurring stories of workers being illegally underpaid, working in very poor conditions and not uncommonly being abused as well.

A third factor is that mainstream economists claim immigration is good for the economy. You might wonder about this, because more people will get more work done but they will need many facilities, including not only public infrastructure like roads, hospitals and schools but also private infrastructure like homes, shops and cars. Those facilities all have to be paid for one way or another. Every year before the pandemic we had about 400,000 new people (net of immigration and more babies). Every year the equivalent of a new city like Canberra had to be built and made functional. Jane O'Sullivan, an ecologist, did some calculations and concluded that it costs about $500,000 to set up each new person[64]. That comes to *$200 billion* we were paying each year to enable the new people to function and to keep our infrastructure working - sort of. Have you tried travelling across Sydney or Melbourne lately? The conclusion is that there is a large net cost to having high immigration rates. The cost is carried either by diverting spending from other things or by degraded services if spending does not keep up with demand[63]. The cost is invisible to the GDP, which doesn't care whether we spend money on making our lives better or on things we do not or should not need, it just counts the amounts spent.

A fourth factor is the claim that the average age of our population is increasing, and as the baby boomers retire they will become a large burden on the working population, which will decrease as a proportion of the total. It turns out that immigration has only a minor effect on age distribution and this is well recognised among the experts[63]. Other countries with higher mean ages have not suffered a drop in the working population and, as O'Sullivan points out, if there are relatively more old people then there are relatively fewer children, whose support is also expensive[64].

We can step back and look at what economists are implying here. They are saying we can't afford to take care of our elderly, even though we will supposedly be richer. They are saying that the present population of Australia can't properly take care of itself so we need to import more people to keep the economy functioning. These are fatuous claims.

The problems with GDP outlined in this chapter are of a quite different kind than other criticisms of conventional economics, some of which we have discussed, or will discuss later. There is no obscure theory to be debated. There are no strange assumptions, nor even basic ignorance about banking, money and debt. One might simply have thought the business of counting our income and wealth was fairly straightforward, at least conceptually, whatever the practical difficulties, and would be in basically reasonable shape.

However it is clear that even at the level of elementary accounting mainstream economics is astonishingly deficient. Even to refer to 'elementary accounting' is to understate the problem. Adding things that should be subtracted does not qualify as even the beginning of accounting.

How do we describe such a deficiency of thought? As monumental stupidity? At the very least it involves a fundamental lack of attention to the task at hand. Current practice is highly misleading, distorting our view of our present condition and distorting our priorities.

6

Working together

What has until now passed for 'civilization' might in fact be nothing more than a gendered appropriation – by men, etching their claims in stone – of some earlier system of knowledge that had women at its centre. – **David Graeber and David Wengrow**[65]

As Tyson Yunkaporta tells it, the biggest crime in the cultures of First Australians is to be a narcissist, to think you're better than anyone else[66].

We Whitefellas have heard of men's business and women's business. There is secret men's business and secret women's business. Not everybody is allowed to know everything. But did you realise that *all* the knowledge is parcelled around? Everyone has a role, and part of that role is to carry the knowledge that goes with it, and some of that knowledge is secret. Putting everyone's roles together, all of the knowledge is carried, but no-one knows it all.

Perhaps this arrangement makes it easier to carry the vast knowledge accumulated over thousands of generations. In the old days, before we invaded and messed a lot of things up, there would have been redundancies, multiple carriers of overlapping knowledge. If someone was lost others could share the knowledge back to appropriate people in a local group so the knowledge was restored.

I heard first hand a story of a bloke who was visiting others quite far from his home Country. An Elder approached him and said 'I've got something for you'. In due course they got together and the Elder told stories that belonged in a certain section of a songline, stories that had been lost to the visitor's people. In this way the knowledge was retained and restored, even in this deeply disrupted time of the First Australians. As Elders progress through stages they learn stories from further afield so that, as I understand it, knowledge is backed up and can be recovered.

There is another implication of parcelling the knowledge around, and keeping some of it secret. It is that no-one can hold all the knowledge. Knowledge is power, in any culture. No-one can have too much power. This is my interpretation.

Yunkaporta writes about violence. There was a level of violence among First Australians, as there is in any culture. Anyone is allowed to be violent. My first reaction to reading this was to be a bit repelled. Perhaps you are too. However you can't be randomly violent. There are strict contexts within which it is permissible to use violence. The violence is channelled so it is consistent with the law, so it reinforces the law, and the law has been refined to foster the survival of the people. Not that people follow the law perfectly, no-one ever does, and the disruption of invasion means it may only be followed erratically these days.

This arrangement has an effect that is analogous to parcelling out the knowledge. It ensures that violence is not monopolised. No-one can try to dominate others using violence. It also ensures that, in contrast to knowledge, violence is out in the open. In White society much of our violence is hidden away. Official violence is mostly hidden in places like prisons. Military violence is conducted by specialists, often far away. In this way most of us are oblivious to the violence conducted in our name. We can pretend to be peace-loving non-violent citizens without thinking about the underpinning of violence, and the threat of violence, that is used to maintain our society in the structure that those in charge desire. Sadly, a lot of violence is also hidden away in people's homes. So in White society a lot of violence is random, borne of passions, and a lot more is wielded by a state monopoly. The former disrupts order, and the latter maintains an order that may or may not be in the interests of all of us.

In First Australian cultures there were law men whose job was maintain the law and to deliver punishments when laws were broken. The deed may have been done in secret, but everyone knew the deal. If someone was speared in the leg it was because he transgressed.

No-one is better than anyone else, but some are accorded more respect because of their knowledge and their role. It doesn't mean they are a more deserving person. It doesn't mean they can tell everyone else what to do, beyond the requirements of the law they maintain. A new initiate from youth into womanhood or manhood has much less knowledge but they are respected and nurtured as the valuable people they are, and will become. If you persisted in acting as if you were better than others you could end up stopping a spear.

We humans are more social than our close animal relatives, according to anthropologists. Male chimpanzees and male gorillas use more violence to dominate their group. Chimp troupes have a dominant male who will fight to maintain his position. An alpha gorilla does not tolerate any other males in his troupe. In both species males dominate females through their larger size and greater strength. Bonobos, that used to be known as pigmy chimps, are more egalitarian. Males are less dominant, and if a male starts making trouble several adult females may gang up on him to pull him into line. Bonobos are also noted for using sexual contact, everyone with everyone else, to lubricate relations in their troupe. Even so bonobos are still said to be more violent than humans in traditional small bands[18].

Human males seem to have undergone a process that has tamed them, compared with their near relatives. In fact anthropologists use the term *domestication* to describe the process. It's a shame they did not find another term, because it also seems to apply in a more literal sense to most humans these days: we have undergone a second change over the past ten thousand years or so. To distinguish them I will call the earlier process *ape domestication*.

Ape domestication has produced less aggressive human males, with an accompanying suite of physical changes. Some of the changes have occurred in females too. For example our faces are foreshortened, more child-like compared with ancestors of a million or three years ago. Males are smaller and have smaller brains.

How this change came about is the subject of conjecture, but it seems that one way or another the most aggressive males were discouraged or prevented from being so violent or threatening. Evidently our ancestors found advantage in being more cooperative, and a too-aggressive male could inhibit cooperation. Natural selection might have played a role, as groups with domineering males might have fared less well and been slowly weeded out. A more conscious process might have been involved, for example other males might have ganged up on a disruptive male to subdue him or kill him.

One theory is that the mechanism was simply that over-aggressive males were killed. Richard Wrangham favours this idea[67], but it need not have been such a brute process. One might dismiss Wrangham's idea as crude and overly dramatic (he had published an earlier book called *Demonic Males*), but the example of First Australians suggests it plausibly had a role, as one of several factors. Wrangham's thinking may still be a bit limited though, because he cites murder as the only mechanism. Presumably some combination of natural selection among groups with varying levels of cooperation, conscious discouragement of aggression, and killing slowly changed our ancestors.

Anthropologists called the physical changes *(ape) domestication* because analogous changes have been observed in domesticated species such as dogs and pigs. Compared with wolves, their wild ancestors, dogs have foreshortened faces, smaller brains, floppy ears, and they wag their tails. They are friendlier. In a famous breeding experiment, aggressive wild foxes in Siberia gave rise over some decades to friendly tame foxes with floppy ears and that wag their tails. The key feature they were bred for was to be friendlier, and the physical changes simply accompanied that behavioural change, evidently because of incidental genetic connections.

Anthropologists have made the reverse inference, that fossil evidence showing foreshortened faces, smaller size and smaller brains than, for example, Neanderthals, reflects selection for human males becoming friendlier. This is consistent with the evidence recounted in Chapter 2 for us being innately social, within our in-group.

Rutger Bregman[18] proposes that the key innovation of *Homo Sapiens* (us) was to become more social, more cooperative within our group. Our species survived while other species did not because we were better cooperators.

So why is written history such a catalogue of tyrannies and wars if our original, innate nature is to be friendly? Three possible reasons. First, we don't live in small groups anymore, within which our innate friendly responses are readily triggered. Second, we are still indifferent to those we regard as strangers. Third, our inner 'demonic males' have not been eliminated from our makeup and can still be triggered.

Before we dig into those issues, we need to digress into civilisation. Ideas about what it is and how it came to be have been shifting rapidly in the light of new knowledge from archaeology, anthropology and other disciplines. Let's recapitulate a couple of versions before getting to the latest.

Civilisation, Version 1. When agriculture was developed, first in Mesopotamia and then in a few other places, it created a surplus that enabled people to specialise into various trades and social roles, like craftspeople, administrators, soldiers and priests. As settlements became much larger than the forager bands or small part-time villages people had lived in until then, there was a much greater need for coordination and planning, and someone needed to be in charge. So hunter-leaders and village chiefs evolved into kings, and eventually emperors.

As these new cities grew in size, experience and sophistication they allowed the arts and sciences to develop to new levels. Architects created grand monuments and palaces, metals were smelted and worked, ceramics and art became more refined and eventually literature took flight. Such civilisations developed in a few places like China, India and, belatedly, Central and South America, but it was the earliest in Mesopotamia that fed into the Mediterranean and eventually gave rise to the jewels of the ancient world, Greece and Rome, each of which took things to new levels. Greece gave us democracy and great art. Rome bequeathed its law, administration and other sophistications to Europe.

By the nineteenth century the British Empire was the largest ever. At the time colonial Australia's national-anthem-to-be was written, the British regarded themselves as the pinnacle of civilisation, and of human evolution. Former Prime Minister Tony Abbott is a big fan of Western Civilisation, and presumably it is something like this version he has in mind. It is a good story, but it is very incomplete and fundamental aspects of it are contradicted by clear evidence.

Civilisation, Version 2. This version is recounted by James C. Scott[46]. Agriculture developed about 10,000 years ago in Mesopotamia. This gave rise to some larger towns and some scattered monumental architecture, but nothing resembling a city developed until 6,000 years ago. The 4,000-year gap between agriculture and the first cities suggests that it was not a particularly obvious or easy step. This is supported by the facts that many foraging and herding people have resisted taking up agriculture, that farming is much harder work than foraging or herding, farmer's diets were much more limited and the concentration of people and animals gave rise to many new diseases, so people's stature and health suffered. Early cities only lasted a century or two before falling apart for reasons not usually obvious. It is not really obvious why people kept trying to live in cities, if it was such a bad deal for most of them. Anyway they persisted and eventually developed the basis of civilised, i.e. citified, living: organisation, administration, writing and a command structure dominated by men. This is regarded as the origin of 'the state'. It was not a good deal for women, because they were valued mainly for breeding and arduous craft work. It was not a very good deal for most of the men either, because they did not have much say in anything and they were required to help to build the grand monuments and palaces as well as growing the food.

Civilisation, Version 3. This is a new synthesis presented by David Graeber and David Wengrow[65] based on a lot of recent archaeology and anthropology not previously well known outside specialist circles. The overall message is that things were much more heterogeneous both before and after some centralised cities were developed. People very consciously developed a range of ways of organising themselves, some top-down and others bottom-up. Cities did not inevitably follow from agriculture nor require agriculture, and did not inevitably become hierarchical and patriarchal. We have more choice in how we organise our societies than is commonly believed.

Agriculture developed as a supplementary activity in many parts of the world: the Middle East, North and South America, West Africa, China, India and New Guinea. Some practices may not have involved systematic tilling and planting, yet cultivation of some kind and harvesting still occurred, one possibility being flood-retreat cropping. Much of the work and innovation involved would have been by women. Only in a few places and after the passage of considerable time did this 'play' activity progress to full-scale agriculture, and even then hunting and foraging may have continued in parallel. Some foraging societies explicitly avoided agriculture though they would have been well aware of its practice by neighbours. Some even tried it for a while and then dropped it.

First Australian practices of managing the landscape and resources, as described by Bruce Pascoe in *Dark Emu*[35], fit comfortably within this spectrum. (A critique of it by Sutton and Walshe[68], to the effect that it is unprofessional and riddled with errors, is itself poor scholarship, misunderstanding key aspects of Pascoe's argument and raising irrelevant examples[69]. There is significant evidence for Pascoe's broad thesis. A more discerning and constructive debate is needed.)

Some foraging societies show little sign of any hierarchy whereas others developed obvious signs of big chiefs. Graeber and Wengrow describe in some detail the cultures of the Pacific Northwest of North America, which featured extravagant posturing by chiefs and a stratified society including slaves. Their immediate neighbours in California seem to have explicitly turned away from such display and lived a more frugal, hardworking and egalitarian life. Some societies alternated seasonally between strong hierarchy and little or none. Graeber and Wengrow's larger point is that foraging societies came in many forms and that those forms were a conscious choice, where sufficient evidence, including historical accounts, is available to tell.

Even in earlier, ice-age times in Eurasia when settlements were smaller and commonly temporary or part-time, people were trading and travelling over very long distances. Cultural elements were shared over very wide areas, even across diverse languages, to the point that Graeber and Wengrow suggest there was, in effect, an 'imaginary city' involving large numbers of widely-scattered people – not that they would have thought of themselves that way. The development of more concentrated populations after the ice age (i.e. after about 10,000 BC) might have brought together people already sharing cultural elements. Cultures seem to have diversified more as populations increased and settlements developed.

First Australians also developed such shared cultural elements, possibly even earlier. Bill Gammage's *The Biggest Estate on Earth*[34] documents a common 'template', with local adaptation, across the entire continent for comprehensive management of the landscape. The same template applied in Tasmania, which implies it had developed well before the rise of sea level at the end of the ice age, about 11,000 years ago. (Graeber and Wengrow have little to say about Australia, except for a rather obvious misinterpretation of custodianship and initiation based on an early account by Lutheran-raised anthropologist T.G.H. Strehlow.)

Another surprise is large Eurasian settlements, big enough to be called cities with perhaps more than 10,000 residents, that clearly lacked any central monuments, statues or other features that would indicate the presence of a hierarchy with a king. In southern Ukraine is a series of these 'mega-sites' (the academics don't have a good terminology) in close proximity and dating from 4,100 to 3,300 BC. Each has a double concentric ring of dwellings, and in the middle of the rings is ... nothing. Perhaps the space was used for meetings, festivals or penning animals, but it was not used for grand and permanent gestures of power.

In Mesopotamia a different kind of shift took place in the so-called Ubaid period, roughly the fifth millennium BC. Villages across a wide area, most of the Euphrates catchment, became more standardised, for example in household plans, and craftwork became less ostentatious or individual. It was a period of important innovation in metallurgy, horticulture, textiles, diet and long-distance trade, yet in social terms everything seems to have been done to prevent such innovations becoming markers of rank, individual distinction or status, within villages and between villages.

Even when cities with a distinct centre did begin to develop in Mesopotamia, with grand central platforms or monuments, there was still a conspicuous absence of the markers of hierarchy, such as lavish burials, palaces and royal inscriptions like those that appeared half a millennium later (around 2,800 BC), along with city walls. How did the grand architectural statements come to be, without kings? Evidently through voluntary labour (so-called *corvée*) and bottom-up organisation.

These examples indicate that some large settlements developed without top-down governance, presumably with women and men both prominently involved in running things. This seems to have been true in Central America as well, at Teotihuacan 300-800 AD, which grew to more than 100,000 souls. Graeber and Wengrow cite modern examples such as surviving traditional Basque villages in which there is a quite complex decentralised system of assigning mutual support to handle seasonal and other contingencies, a system that could be scaled up without centralised authority.

On the other hand in North America the first identified large settlement, at Cahokia across the Mississippi River from modern St. Louis, early on became highly centralised and brutal, with mass sacrifice and other clear evidence of tyrannical hierarchy. It seems that Cahokia and satellite centres declined, around AD 1400, because people could and did abandon the tyranny. There followed a period of conscious turning away from top-down governance, across a wide area of central and eastern North America, and a search for more equitable arrangements.

This shift to bottom-up thinking came to have a large influence on the world, according to Graeber and Wengrow. It gave rise to what they call the *indigenous critique*, when French Jesuits reported the thoughts and arguments of people of northeastern North America over quite a long period of the seventeenth century. Though the Jesuits were horrified by many aspects of those indigenous lifestyles, including the freedom of women to choose partners, they were intrigued by arguments put to them that they were too subservient, that the French were also intolerant, quarrelsome, envious, covetous, deceitful and violent. They encountered people capable of eloquent and sophisticated debate on the subject of governance, people arguing for much more individual freedom than anybody in Europe had at that time. These arguments fed into, even possibly sparked, the Enlightenment that in turn fed into the American and French revolutions and a turn away from autocracy that had not been seriously questioned until then by European thinkers.

This much less simple version of history raises the question of why, despite the many options created before and in the earlier stages of city living, we seem to have got stuck in hierarchical versions that commonly were quite tyrannical through subsequent history. Graeber and Wengrow pose the question and eventually offer an answer, but their answer does not seem to be very compelling. Pre-dynastic Egypt had herders who became hierarchical, and the hierarchy took on a mixed role: on the one hand the rulers issued the orders and on the other hand they offered care to some of the unfortunate, some of whom were taken into what became royal courts. The rulers pitched themselves as benefactors, and this supposedly persuaded people to tolerate them. Well, rulers always pitch themselves as benefactors, because they are sure they know what is best for us. Perhaps Graeber and Wengrow's thinking was constrained to stay close to the evidence they could assemble, though they seem to be willing to offer hypotheses on other topics.

A rather obvious possibility emerged in their story. As the early Mesopotamian cities developed, evidently fairly egalitarian, there were different cultures among the hill people of nearby Turkey, cultures featuring ostentatious chiefs competing for prestige. The developing lowland cities would plausibly have been ripe targets for raiding, yielding both loot and prestige. Eventually some raiders might have decided to stay and take over, setting themselves up as king, courtiers and soldiers. This, after all, is a common pattern of later history in which barbarians repeatedly swept in and conquered cities, sometimes founding new dynasties.

A basic factor here, not featured by Graeber and Wengrow, is that the bigger the city the greater the reward to a tyrant. You might lord it over 1,000 people and be the big chief, but if you can lord it over 100,000 people you can be mystical ruler on high, either anointed by the gods or a god yourself. The greater social distance would have allowed the ruler to be more indifferent to his subjects. These conditions would encourage the re-emergence of inner demonic male behaviour. As tyrannies became larger and people more docile they would probably also have become harder to dislodge.

There are serious questions about why people ever thought living in a city was a good idea, and how the change affected people. In earlier times when farming was a supplement that groups were less dependent on, and there was less compulsion, people evidently found that the trade-off could be worthwhile. The later intensification of farming is less obviously worthwhile for most individuals. Perhaps the issue was forced by invading barbarians.

Farming is much harder work than hunting and gathering, as emphasised by James C. Scott[46], and the drawbacks of farming become stronger as it becomes more intensive and people more dependent on it. Crops are prone to failure. Monoculture crops are a magnet for many other 'pest' species happy to have a free feast. Crowding of people, livestock and crops create ideal conditions for diseases, including diseases passed from animals to people. Diets are much more limited and monotonous. Nutrition and general health are correspondingly poorer.

Because barbarians might attack, soldiers would be required. Soldiers can be used for defence or attack, or to keep an unruly citizenry in order. Battles and wars might be enabled. Because of greater losses to disease, domestic animals are required to breed faster than they might have in the wild. This would apply to people too: women would be required to produce more children. Once a tyrant was in charge, everyone in the lower orders would be required to be more obsequious.

Because life for the lower orders was hard there would be a tendency for people to abscond. This would have been countered in two ways. One would be to have a city wall, and soldiers to chase absconders – so a city wall may have been as much to keep people in as to keep enemies out. The other way would be to emphasise how dangerous it is away from the protection of the city, with desolate wastes, dark forests, wild animals, barbarians and probably demons and monsters as well. Life out there would be nasty, brutish and short. Best to stay within the benevolent confines of the city, the civic, the civilisation.

It is not hard to identify some features of this description that could effect some important changes in people and their behaviour. There would be a hierarchy. Innate social responses would not work between the king and the common people, because they do not make eye contact. The king would be detached and less caring. Even among the common people divisions might arise, because you can't personally know 10,000 people, so internal fractiousness and crime might arise. The hierarchy would place the common women at the bottom, valued mainly for their breeding and their domestic labour.

For most of recorded history, 'civilised' people have been smaller, with poorer nutrition and poorer health than our 'wild' ancestors and cousins. When Europeans arrived on the shores of North America the Native Americans found them to be dirty and smelly runts and, to their great cost, diseased. Jared Diamond is of the opinion that an average person in the New Guinea highlands, where Diamond worked as an anthropologist, is more intelligent than your average modern city dweller because the highlander has to know and contend with a far more complex environment than a city dweller[70].

We don't have tails to wag but we do tend to be more obedient than 'uncivilised' people. The role of the common people in the early hierarchical cities was not so different from the role of the cows, sheep, goats and pigs. It was to support the continuance of the larger entity, the city, with food and labour. We have already encountered stories of 'uncivilised' people, including North Americans and First Australians, regarding civilised (i.e. city-dwelling) people with contempt for their subservience. So as well as a more ancient 'ape domestication', we seem to have been domesticated in the more immediate sense of being tamed to support settled agriculture.

Autocracy, war, hierarchy, patriarchy may not necessarily be intrinsic to this strange new way of life, but they did come to dominate, even if we're not sure why.

Despite their early ephemeral nature, new cities kept popping up, in new places or on the ruins of a previous one. The early cities seem to have been a marginal proposition, but people kept giving them a go, for whatever reasons. Over time they became more stable. Presumably people got better at running them, and immunities to diseases would have slowly built up. Perhaps the people became more domesticated too.

Even if hardly anyone within a city really liked the life, the city as a unit became a potent force. It could displace people living traditional lifestyles through a combination of greater concentrated force, greater food production and, perversely, new diseases. Jared Diamond argued that the spread of European empires was aided as much or more by the diseases carried by Europeans as by guns and technology, and that would have been true from early on[70]. Lethal new diseases, caught from domestic animals, would have spread through surrounding regions and depopulated them.

Although there was a diversity of forms of society in both foraging societies and early cities, hierarchical cities do seem to have become the dominant form, for reasons just suggested, and perhaps other reasons as well.

Hierarchical cities have tended to bring out the worst in us. Our social reflexes and other inducements no longer worked well within larger concentrations of people. Those (mostly) men inclined to dominate and bully would have encountered fewer restraints and greater rewards as towns and cities grew. Thus perhaps the inclinations to bullying that had not been eradicated from our nature over the previous hundreds of millennia got a new life, in the form of tyrannies.

War would have been facilitated by our indifference to those we regard as strangers, as emphasised by Joshua Greene[16]. Cultural diversity seems to have increased in Eurasia since the ice age, so outsiders may have seemed more alien. Such indifference can turn into cooperation or conflict, depending on circumstances and depending on our collective choices.

It does seem to be easy to trigger fear of strangers, to turn indifference into hostility. Sadly it is a standard ploy of autocrats to concoct an external threat to frighten people so they put aside internal squabbles and the autocrat can retain his power over them. Currently we are being told that China is a threat to Australia, when in fact China always moves cautiously and would have no interest in open conflict with us if we stopped our provocative behaviour.

Occasionally there are leaders who do the opposite: they sooth fears and bring groups to better understanding and perhaps to peace. Nelson Mandela was one such, who soothed the fears of white South Africans and persuaded everyone the best way forward was to work together (though his successors have been less skilled and conflict remains severe).

First Australians may give us a salutary example. Conflict was not absent between various groups: some neighbours were friendly whereas others were regarded as enemies. Yet the conflict evidently was managed and kept within bounds prescribed by the law. The simple fact that there were hundreds of languages in Australia, and that they were rather more diverse than the languages of Europe, for example, implies that there were no great invasions. If there had been invasions then a few languages or language groups would predominate, as is true in Europe today. It seems the various 'nations' kept to their own Country for very long periods.

A crucial part of this relatively peaceful arrangement was an elaborate system of diplomatic protocols for relating to or visiting others' Country. One White explorer with a native guide recounted moving into a new Country. The guide slowly approached a group of locals. Quiet words were spoken by both sides, all with eyes cast down. After a time all raised their eyes. More quiet words were spoken. Eventually there was a shift in energy and everyone relaxed. The guide explained that he had sought permission to enter their Country by the required process and all were now satisfied. They were welcome to travel through the new County. Clearly a part of this sort of protocol is to avoid any impression of aggression, even to the point of not making eye contact.

Although we humans lack innate responses to strangers, we still have the choice to be friendly or hostile. Being friendly need not imply letting your guard down – you don't know how a stranger might act or react. But you don't have to approach with weapons drawn and displayed threateningly (literally or figuratively), you can instead speak quietly and carry a big stick, as Woodrow Wilson advised. If you are threatening you are very likely to provoke a defensive and threatening response and any prospect of a friendly interaction may be lost. If you demonstrate your willingness to make connection then you keep open the possibility of friendly interaction that would likely be of mutual benefit.

At bottom it comes down to a choice we have in all facets of our life: a choice of acting from love or from fear. To act from love in the deepest sense is to hold open the possibility that the other person is human like you and would welcome being treated generously. It means being self-aware enough to recognise when your own fear is triggered, and to override the fear and act from love anyway. People who allow themselves to be driven by fear will react defensively, close down and quite likely be threatening, whether they consciously mean to or not.

Many times in my personal life I have realised too late that I reacted defensively, wanting to justify myself, rather than acknowledging what was said to me and exploring why it was said. Commonly a defensive reaction will lead to a dispute in which hurtful things may be said or done. On the other hand many comments that may sound like criticism turn out to be due to misunderstandings, or to be more about the other person's fears than your own behaviour, if you are able to remain open and explore. It requires a willingness to be open about your feelings and wants so the other person may recognise you are a person just like them; this can lead to a meeting of minds and feelings and to unexpectedly positive results. This is not mere wishful thinking, I have experienced it many times and it is the basis of conflict resolution processes (as distinct from mere mediation). Often there really can be a win-win resolution that surprises everyone.

Obviously it is not so straightforward to bring together large groups of people or nations in this way, but that is the genius of people like Mandela and Gandhi. On the other hand it is extremely easy to provoke fear and the consequent destructive reactions between large groups. Media do it all the time and far too many politicians do it too, because they are scurrilous or because they lack the personal self-awareness to know they are being driven by their feelings, especially by fear, rather than by the rationalisations they use as a cover.

Even though we now have examples of non-hierarchical cities from our history, in the modern world we have still mostly submitted to hierarchies of varying degrees of tyranny. We have thus failed to organise ourselves in a fair and peaceable way. In a few times and places we have managed something a bit better than endless tyrannies and wars, or at least toned down the level of tyranny. Conventional democracy sounds nice in theory, and for a time the Greek and American versions were not so bad, but they were subverted by other forces. Europe and Australia, since the great conflicts of last century, have fared a little better but they are still dominated by the wealthy and powerful, and those interests have been rapidly gaining the upper hand in Australia. Whether we have begun to reclaim our democracy remains to be seen.

We have learnt a few things over the millennia. We perhaps know our own nature a bit better, though wise elders through the ages have known most of it and tried to enlighten us. Lately there have been some novel ideas and trials that make use of a better understanding of systems. Novel structures have been developed that allow our innate cooperation to function and still permit informed decisions within large organisations.

One of the most promising is *sociocracy*[71]. It was developed in a business setting and has been taken into other contexts. It takes the novel approach of alternating between discussion circles and a production hierarchy. Any governance process can be broken into three stages: information gathering, decision and execution. The first two stages are conducted in circles of no more than twenty or so people in which everyone's voice is equal. During the information gathering stage, people directly involved can report how things are functioning. Decisions are taken by a modified consensus procedure in which discussions continue until no-one feels they cannot live with a proposed decision. Objections need to be backed by clear arguments and evidence. Once a decision has been reached the circles dissolve and people revert to a hierarchy for the execution or production stage; if everyone has agreed to the decisions made, they can just get on with doing things. A hierarchy may be the most efficient arrangement for the production stage, but it is very inefficient at transmitting information, especially upwards. That is why circles are used in the information gathering and decision stages.

If the organisation is large, there may need to be a hierarchy of circles. In this case each circle includes someone from the circles above and below, whose job is to pass information as well as to partake as an equal member in the circle's deliberations. At first people find it a strange arrangement, because they are made responsible for keeping track of their part of the larger operation. It was pioneered among Quakers and in the Netherlands, where consensus procedures are more familiar. A startling feature of sociocracy is that leadership becomes distributed through the organisation. The top level may be keeping the overall operations on track, but they are dependent on everyone else and everyone has a role.

Sociocracy could be an aspiration, but it would not be a simple transition from the hierarchical and commonly autocratic cultures we are used to in Australia, and which keep the lower orders disempowered, disengaged and often apathetic or alienated.

In the meantime there are many good and sensible people who know how to work constructively with people who have a diversity of views. People do it all the time, in social welfare groups, in the better businesses, in many clubs, even in some local government councils. With a bit more conscious cultivation our state and national affairs could be conducted more in this spirit. A crucial step is to go around the old political parties. They are the focus of a century of entrenched influence and corruption by selfish interests, and they have the ingrained habit of confrontation rather than cooperation. Perhaps they can be reformed, but we can't wait, and anyway the best way to force them to reform is for them to see their vote shrinking away. Meanwhile there is nothing to stop us continuing to elect sensible Independents, and others who will work constructively within the arrangements we have now, as happened in the 2022 election.

The quest for a fair society is often framed in terms of *freedom,* but this is not a very useful way to come at it. We noted in an earlier chapter that there is an irreconcilable tension between the demands of a group and the wish for individual autonomy. If you want absolute freedom (from other people) you must live as a hermit. If you live in any kind of community you must surrender some of your autonomy for the sake of the group, otherwise the group will disintegrate. So the cries of libertarians in the street for 'Freedom' and 'Liberty' are simplistic and unhelpful. Freedom from what?

Graeber and Wengrow make some useful distinctions. They propose three kinds of freedom.

- Freedom to leave.

- Freedom to disobey commands.
- Freedom to find new ways to relate.

When the world was less populated with humans it was more feasible for people to move away from an oppressive leader or culture. This seems to have happened to the Cahokia society, for example.

French Jesuits were surprised by and disapproving of Wendat (northeast North American) people who insisted they could and would ignore any directive from one of their fellows. Even the women insisted on this right! Such autonomy may have been a continuing reaction to the excesses of Cahokia, which were widely known even among those not subject to Cahokia rule. First Australians also insist that no-one can boss anyone else around.

There is an important qualification to First Australian's freedom that very likely applied also in other non-hierarchical societies. People could ignore 'orders' from each other, but they lived in close accord with the strictures of the 'law' inherited from the ancestors. That law is very prescriptive about many aspects of life and relationships, and seems to have been well refined to ensure the survival of the people and to avoid serious conflict. So there was an important qualification to their freedom that kept them from degenerating into chaos.

The third freedom implies the freedom to defy current norms of behaviour and to set up a new social order. The American and French revolutions partly involved exercising this freedom. Even clearer examples have been the many social changes in our own society since the nineteenth century: voting rights, women's rights, gay rights and so on.

Historical movements to liberate people have commonly been movements to escape particularly oppressive regimes. The answer to 'Freedom from what?' was obvious. In the current ferment to break away from corporate plutocracy we need to be more discriminating.

A central lesson from the new history of civilisation is that we do have choice. Cities (and nations) are not inevitably hierarchical and patriarchal, nor inevitably oppressive. Greater care may be required to restrain tendencies to dominant behaviour, but the potential is there: in our innately co-operative nature and in historical examples of quite large societies governing themselves from the bottom up.

7

Pulling apart

Australian Liberals are not the exponents of an open go, for if we are all to have an open go, each for himself and the devil take the hindmost, anarchy will result and both security and progress disappear. – Sir Robert Menzies, 1970, quoted by Senator Ron Boswell[72]

We can reject everything else: religion, ideology, all received wisdom. But we cannot escape the necessity of love and compassion. – the Dalai Lama

The contest between our innately social, cooperative nature and the imposed requirement to be selfish and competitive has wrought deep changes in Australian society. We feel more isolated and insecure. Economic policies implementing the neoliberal selfishness doctrine have compounded that insecurity.

The severe Keating recession of the early 1990s created high unemployment. Older white men were among those hardest hit, as many of them became long-term or permanent unemployed. Their bitterness gave rise to scapegoating, and immigrants are always an easy target. This gave Pauline Hanson a constituency for her xenophobia, directed at that time against Asian immigrants who were blamed for taking Aussie jobs[25]. (It is not unusual for immigrants to be blamed simultaneously for being dole bludgers and for stealing jobs from real Aussies.) For a time many other politicians decried Hanson's racist divisiveness and worked to counter her influence, not least because she was taking votes from the Coalition.

That changed in 2001 when Prime Minister John Howard took over her policies and blocked the entry of boat-borne asylum seekers, even though they have a legal right to enter under Australia's international obligations. Background to this development was that Howard was under pressure from big business to increase the rate of immigration, which he had held back to around 70,000 per year. Rapid population growth is not popular among Australians[73], who recognise the stresses it creates, not least on city infrastructure, especially transport. Howard proceeded to increase immigration rates to around 200,000 per year while at the same time, as a distraction, vilifying asylum-seeking 'boat people'. Right up until the pandemic closed our borders asylum-seekers continued to stream in by plane, but the media ignored them even as they sensationalised 'illegal' boat arrivals.

These moves by Howard were completely cynical, reclaiming racist votes for the Coalition and delivering high immigration for big business and thus keeping downward pressure on wages and job security. They turned Australia from misguided policies to deliberately divisive policies, from the well-intentioned but foolish policies of Hawke and Keating to fostering the dark side of our nature. It was clear at the time that Howard's appeal to fear would need to be continually escalated to retain its potency. That has been our history ever since.

Howard's move was soon reinforced by the '9/11' attacks in the US. We were required to be fearful of Islamic terrorists, though our putative ally Saudi Arabia seemed to be involved in ways that have never been clarified. The US, predictably, responded with brute force by invading Afghanistan (to remove terrorist bases) and Iraq (to remove alleged weapons of mass destruction). Howard enthusiastically took Australia into the invasions, which had no international mandate. He dismissed warnings that it would increase the terrorist threat to us, which it did. The usual imperial motivations were behind the public justifications, namely territory and oil. We eventually withdrew in disarray, having been defeated at enormous cost to locals, to our credibility and to our reputation among neighbouring nations. Almost immediately we are being plunged into a confrontation with China which has no prospect of any kind of 'success'.

Through all of this our civil liberties and human rights have been curbed by so many new laws it is difficult to keep track, mostly in the name of guarding against the terrorists we have antagonised and to a significant extent helped to create. Asians have been vilified, then Moslems, then Lebanese, then Africans, now Chinese in particular. The restrictions imposed to limit the pandemic generated a US-style libertarian movement in Australia featuring large demonstrations against infringements on 'freedom' and 'liberty'.

There has also been a long-term concerted campaign to place far-right people in strategic positions throughout our society, in the media, the public service, semi-government bodies and politics. They have basically taken over the Liberal Party. This is the way the Right has operated for a long time here and abroad. They are well funded and that is why they have become so powerful.

The epidemic of fear and divisiveness has still been running out of control, fanned by right-wing politicians and media. Labor, in opposition, wavered between being mute and complicit. The 2022 election featured a distinct shift of voters' sentiments away from such negativity. Labor has the opportunity to reinforce the trend by playing to our better angels, something that Prime Minister Albanese has said he wants and expects. So far there has been little beyond lip service by way of restoring a trusting society.

The role of government has been denigrated, and the poor performance of governments has generated cynicism, so the validity of government is in question. We need to look again at some basics about ourselves and our societies.

Small groups, like a village or a group of hunter-gatherers, can function well without much formal structure. Traditions, respected elders and perhaps a chief who is more advisor than ruler tend to suffice. As we have seen, foragers nevertheless might become hierarchical. As larger settlements grew, both egalitarian and hierarchical forms of organisation developed. Only later, and for reasons not fully clear, did hierarchies tend to be the more common form. Thus for much of citified history the default form of organisation was an autocratic pyramid, though this form is not necessarily the most functional nor the most healthy. The much-lauded episode by the Athenean upper class to conduct a limited form of democracy, and the Mediaeval regional councils, did not last very long and are much in the minority through history.

In eighteenth-century Europe there was a debate, amplified by the indigenous critique discussed earlier and by the American and French revolutions, concerning the form of government and the desirable degree of democracy. Edmund Burke famously argued that there was, or ought to be, a compact between the governing elite and the people. He argued this was for the best, as it put the most capable in charge while supposedly imposing on them a duty to govern for the best interests of all.

Burke was disputed by Thomas Paine, most notably in *The Rights of Man*[74]. At issue was the source of a government's authority. Many autocrats had claimed their authority derived from the gods, or from God. Paine dismissed the divine right, and Burke's argument was an attempt to replace it. If government were a pre-existing separate entity, Paine argued, then there might be a logical basis for proposing that it had a compact with the people. But from where else were governments derived than from the people? From nowhere else. Elites and governments had no separate existence. They could only arise when a sufficient number of people joined together into a society. If a government's *existence* depended on the people forming a society, then necessarily its power derived from the people who formed the society. Paine argued very clearly that sovereignty resides ultimately with the people, and they delegate their sovereignty to a government. This is so whether the government is nominally a democracy or has a more authoritarian form. The autocrat's power still derives ultimately from the people, and he governs only with the implied consent of the people.

If the people grant the government power then they ultimately have the right to withdraw that power. If a government abuses its power, or it becomes dysfunctional for any reason, then the people have the implied right to remove it and replace it with a government that serves them better.

Australian governments over the past couple of decades have been progressively less responsive to the people, more corrupt, less competent and less functional. The major institutions of politics, the media and the old political parties, have become less responsive to the people. The decay reached the point where the Morrison Government ignored protocols of governance that were inconvenient to it, and sometimes was contemptuous of the law and of court rulings. Ministerial responsibility was almost lost, except for temporary removals of Ministers and one particularly flagrant case of failing to reveal the source of large donations. Boards and semi-government bodies were stacked with partisans who may or may not have had any relevant competence. Public money was used for partisan purposes. In the context of removals of many civil and human rights because of alleged terrorist threats, the substance of representative democracy was in peril.

There is, at last, a growing grass-roots movement to counter this decline and get Independent or new party representatives into parliament. The *Voices For* movement was pioneered in the Victorian rural seat of Indi[75], and it has now won three elections for its nominated candidate. Several other wins in other electorates inspired more groups to form in as many as forty electorates[76]. Six new community independents were elected, along with more Greens to both houses and independents of other stripes. The community independents, who defeated moderate Liberals, are a clear threat to the Liberal Party. The other parties ignore their potential at their peril.

The Liberal Party was formed from the fragmented conservative side of politics by Robert Menzies in the 1940s. He expounded a liberal philosophy of tolerance of a diversity of views and, as a matter of practicality and the common practice of the time, a mixed economy with a substantial government presence and a vigorous private sector. According to Donald Horne in *The Lucky Country*[4], he soon drifted into more conservative practices, though putting more attention into acquiring and retaining power than in actually governing the country. Menzies had large doses of luck, along with political cunning, in surviving so long in power.

Since Menzies the Liberal Party has changed several times over and now has little resemblance to its early form. Malcolm Fraser projected a stern and rather dictatorial air, but according to friends and foes was less effective. He was reasonably socially liberal and moderately conservative in economic policy. The Hawke Labor Government that took over in 1983 also took over the newly fashionable neoliberal policies to which Fraser had been somewhat resistant. In moving decisively to the right Labor pushed the Liberals even further to the right. During the long Hawke-

Keating years, until 1996, there was a struggle for control of the Liberal Party between the 'wets', like Fraser, and the 'dries' – neoliberals like Margaret Thatcher. The dries ultimately won, in the person of John Howard. Howard was not a dedicated ideologue but he was very right-wing in his instincts, to the point of embracing racist and divisive policies as described earlier.

There was also a growing rump of social reactionaries within the Liberals, to which Howard played in the so-called 'culture wars'. Since Howard lost in 2007 the party has been strongly influenced by vested interest like mining, arms, gambling and finance, to the point of being virtually captured by them, as many Ministers and senior staffers came directly from those industries. *Michael West Media* has documented these cases in its *Revolving Door* series[77].

Most attention in the past has been focussed on the way retired politicians quickly transition into lucrative jobs with major companies. Less attention is paid to the more serious threat of company people moving into government. Former Senator Scott Ludlam has been one of few commentators to call the situation *state capture* – capture of the state by special interests[78]. Through special interests combined with some increasingly zealous ideologues, the party clung to unrealistic policies, being pro-fossil fuels, highly resistant to serious action on global warming, and handing Australian sovereignty over to the US.

The Liberals' coalition partner the Nationals has also morphed from its old Country Party role, being even more captured by mining and also a haven for social reactionaries. It is losing support in its rural strongholds. It was challenged by the Shooters, Fishers and Farmers party, Pauline Hanson's One Nation and Clive Palmer's United Australia, though their influence is waning. Now, on the other side, it is being challenged by a rapidly rising movement of farmers for climate action.

Labor has also largely deserted its origins. Formed late in the nineteenth century, Labor was described as socialist without ideology. It worked to improve the lot of 'the working man', and it was quite successful until 1914. World War I broke that progressive and reformist momentum and conservatives have been ascendant ever since, with only brief interludes. Even so Labor's presence, and the strong union movement, significantly advanced the lot of the workers, despite the Party's incoherence, muddling, corruption and frequent internal wars, especially during the years after World War II. The Curtin and Chifley governments navigated the country through the war and set it up postwar with clear Keynesian economic policies, an arrangement that Menzies was content mostly to continue.

Two big changes occurred later. Gough Whitlam set about making Labor a reformist government, mainly promoting the 'social wage', removing some highly discriminatory practices and responding to shifts in social attitudes. Whitlam was, in a sense, the opposite of Menzies. Menzies specialised in retaining power and was less interested in governing. Whitlam wanted to govern, and neglected the politics of power. His changes challenged the power of the mediocrities who had comfortably run Australia for decades and who felt they had a natural right to govern, and they fought back viciously, eventually getting him sacked without legitimate cause[79]. This has become clear, because the Governor General was talking with the Royal family about sacking Whitlam even before Opposition Leader Malcolm Fraser used the Senate to block 'supply' (of bills to fund government operations).

The next big change was the takeover of Labor by the 'right', led by Hawke and Keating. It has been a mystery why they chose to so completely take over the neoliberal ideology that would obviously disadvantage employees relative to bosses. Lech Blaine's portrait of Bob Hawke makes clear that Hawke and his associates were phonies whose main interest was power[80]. Keating was also highly ambitious, uneducated and evidently misguided in how to achieve what he wanted. They seemed determined not to suffer Whitlam's fate, so rather than challenging the powerful they sucked up to them.

The Hawke-Keating era undermined and diminished the union movement and unleashed a destructive financial sector. Rather than setting Australia up for decades of prosperity, as the common myth would have it, it hollowed out the economy, disempowered the people and set us on course for the enfeebled, sycophantic and corrupt state we find ourselves in. Since they lost power in 1996 Labor has drifted, its old purpose gone and its interest apparently confined to regaining power by being not quite as nasty as the Coalition. It has been a notably unsuccessful strategy. The Rudd-Gillard period accomplished some useful things but failed to address the major challenges we face and failed to develop any coherent vision. The one accomplishment on a major issue, the carbon pricing scheme, was forced upon Gillard by the Greens. It was very poorly sold to the people and soon abolished when the Coalition returned to power.

Labor's shock loss in 2019 was due to incoherence and trying, far too obviously, to be different things to different people: against coal mining in Victoria and for coal mining in Queensland. Labor continued to follow a 'small target' strategy through the subsequent parliamentary term, which deprived the country of an effective Opposition. If it had a big vision it might have been able to carry some bold policies into the next election without fear of being shot down by the first volley from the Murdoch snipers. In the event, it won power in 2022 with a record-low primary vote of less that 32%. Perhaps it will become a little bolder if it consolidates itself in power, but there are few signs of that happening.

It seems that the old parties have lost most of their purpose apart from power and corruption, and that they are so gridlocked by special interests, ideology and factions they are unlikely to reform soon enough to matter. If that is true then they deserve to wither and die.

There is another political force in Australia, more powerful and more regressive than the old parties.

Language is one of the defining human characteristics, as we looked at in earlier chapters. Talk is a big part of what binds a community together, a central part of our intensely social nature. Talk serves this purpose in small communities, communities up to one or two hundred people, communities small enough that we can know everyone and meet them eye to eye.

In large modern societies we cannot talk directly with each other so we use technology. Over the millennia we have used writing, printing, broadcasting and the internet. These technologies do not completely fulfil the role that talking does in a small community, but they do go a long way towards allowing us to communicate across our large societies. They play the same role, however imperfectly, of binding our societies together. They are therefore a very special, critical part of our society. Ask any systems analyst and she will tell you that the nature of the signalling mechanism within the system critically determines the system's behaviour. A sensible society would therefore do its utmost to ensure its media function as well as possible, and in the interests of everyone.

Instead, we have allowed a few powerful people to control much of our media. Australia has had the great privilege and benefit of a publicly funded broadcaster which has played a role much closer to facilitating society's conversation. However for some time now the ABC has been bullied and undermined by those, on both sides of politics, who wish to control our conversation. Lately this has amounted effectively to occupation of management by the Liberal Party. The commercial media have required no such bullying, their proprietors have ensured only an approved range of communication occurs. To be approved, such communication must not threaten the profits and power of the proprietor. The best way for a reporter to advance his career is to provide material that startles or alarms us, so we break into a frenzy of chatter.

Commercial media's first requirement is to make a profit. The surest route to profit is to cultivate outrage and fear. They want conflict, colour and movement. They are not informing, they are entertaining. They are not interested in the truth, they just want drama. If what they report is shown actually to be a lie they are studiously silent, or they feign outrage and threaten legal action. If innocent people get hurt by what they report, they deny it. If vulnerable groups are maligned, they're not interested.

On the other hand if the commercial media are challenged they are the most thin-skinned of all. When it was suggested the existing voluntary code of conduct should be marginally improved, and actually made enforceable by an independent, non-government body, they went into paroxysms of betrayed innocence and outrage that anyone should question the integrity of the 'quality press', and at the supposed threat of a police-state ban on freedom of expression.

Rupert Murdoch owns around seventy percent of Australia's newspapers, a growing TV network and a huge global media empire. His tabloids regularly splash gross distortions and inflammatory exaggerations across their front pages. His flagship, *The Australian,* indulges in self-proclaimed political campaigns (such as to 'destroy' the Greens) and regularly conducts personal vendettas against anyone who attracts its disapproval. It so freely mixes editorial comment with its so-called reporting that it gives the impression of no longer understanding the difference. Much of its commentary comprises fact-free rants. Robert Manne in 2011 undertook the thankless task of documenting hundreds of its abuses over a period of months[81]. Of course *The Australian* says he's a biassed lefty who is the one who commits all the things he falsely accuses them of. Like all the shock jocks, attack dogs and internet trolls of the reactionary right, it cannot perceive the difference between a gut-fuelled, fact-free rant and an informed, evidence-based commentary – or perhaps it chooses not to.

There are a few rather basic requirements before media can think of describing themselves as *quality*. News reports must not contain editorial comment. That means they must not even contain judgemental terms, such as 'leftist' or 'radical', terms that were routinely applied for example to Yanis Varoufakis, the short-lived Finance Minister of Greece, though he was only proposing actions that were normal a few decades ago.

It should not need stating that reporting should not be persistently incorrect or significantly misleading. Yet *The Australian* in particular is persistently incorrect and misleading on the matter of global warming. I do not mean that aspects of global warming cannot be debated. I mean that if a sceptical point of view is reported then it should be made clear that only a tiny minority of climate scientists think humans are not causing global warming. By omitting this perspective, *The Australian* persistently and deliberately misrepresents the balance of scientific opinion.

Far-right commentators are thickly sprinkled throughout all of our media. Many of them have connections with the Institute of Public Affairs and other right-wing think tanks, which are conduits for rich vested interests. Even the ABC has IPA people as commentators. Why? There are plenty of those in the commercial media.

By traditional measures there are no really left-wing commentators in the mainstream media. As with our political parties, there are a few in the centre and a lot on the right. There are others who merely give informed commentary that does not have much overt political flavour, but they are still often portrayed as left-leaning. It is only the right-wing extremists who perceive everybody else to be leftists.

The idea of informed balance is largely absent from the commercial media. Robert Manne, in his 2011 essay on *The Australian*, documented hundreds of items that were misleading, incorrect, or, through selective publishing, giving an unbalanced impression of important issues. If newspapers were required to have a licence, the way electronic broadcasters are, then there would be ample grounds for withdrawing *The Australian's* licence. Perhaps a general licence, for any news and commentary site commanding a large audience through any medium, would be a useful innovation.

The rest of the media are less blatant in their biases, but they still misrepresent the balance of scientific opinion on global warming, by insisting on giving sceptics nearly equal time, and thus creating the false impression that the climate science community is seriously divided.

The media's use of a simplistic notion of balance is quite inappropriate when technical subjects are being reported. The 'balance' conveyed should roughly reflect the balance of the weight of evidence, as interpreted by specialists. A favourite trick is to take a scientific estimate of uncertainty, such as 10 plus or minus 5, and report only the upper limit: could be as much as 15! Anyone is free to disagree with specialists, but the interpretations of the specialists should not be misrepresented, as they routinely are when the media treat them as just another group demanding attention.

Even in reporting politics, the media should use a more sophisticated interpretation of balance, instead of just lazily serving up the views of the two major parties, which anyway are not so far apart in their world view. The views of independents and minor parties are only sporadically represented. The media would serve us better if they went beyond the political fray and reflected the range of views in the community. Even better would be to convey some historical perspective, which could convey how the present range of political views is well to the right of where they were several decades ago.

This pervasive bias has an obvious effect on our politics. It is harder for the left or centre to win elections. Julianne Schultz[82] recounts that eminent journalist David McNicoll, in retirement, allowed that 'All those seats would have gone to Labor ... without our right-wing influence ... There's no doubt about that at all.'[83] Australians are claimed to be conservative, but we don't know really know that. What would our attitudes be if reporting was balanced and comprehensive? Certainly more compassionate than recent governments. It is our media that are conservative.

Our media inflame divisions and insecurities in our society, as their core business model. Combined with our tribal political culture and adversarial legal system it is no wonder we are riven. We cannot work together constructively, as our innate propensities might urge us, while we are continuously being alarmed and divided. Relating constructively to other countries is even more difficult.

How might we improve the quality of our media? An obvious start is to restore the ABC. Regarding the commercial media, we could make some improvement through regulation, though regulation is a blunt instrument and its effect would be limited. A better approach is to look at ownership. There are many more options than ownership by government or rich people.

We need to restore the independence and funding of the ABC. Simply by pursuing a policy of balanced news and informed commentary, the ABC used to help to balance the routinely right-wing commercial media, and without having any explicit left-wing or socialist point of view. However that was not good enough for the radical Right, whose plans were impeded by the informed populace that followed the ABC. The Greens have long had a proposal for a Board at arm's length from politics, comprising representatives from the community and with political hacks excluded. It is hard to tell how much the ABC's funding has been cut over the decades, as reporters usually only tell us how much it has been cut over the last year or two. A funding boost by at least 50% would seem in order. That way the ABC might be able to provide Australian programming to replace some of the endless parade of English murders, English renovations and English antiques, and SBS might be able to get past its obsessions with trains and obscure branches of the English royal family. Paraphrasing Phillip Adams from decades ago, we need to hear our own voices, see our own places and dream our own dreams.

Regarding commercial media, first, there could certainly be more effective regulation of the media. A licence for major media is an idea worth considering. Anyone who wants the right to broadcast (by any means) to large numbers of our citizens also ought to have responsibilities. Those responsibilities ought to include not being consistently misleading or factually incorrect, clearly distinguishing opinion from reporting, and not systematically promoting discord. Such requirements would not be simple to police, but even some modest restraint on the present excesses of irresponsibility could be a considerable improvement. There would certainly need to be care not to over-police and unduly restrict discussion. That of course is the difficulty of this approach. It is also why the ownership approach is more promising.

In the meantime a public internet campaign calling out the worst of the distortions and lies of the media could be useful. Former Prime Ministers Kevin Rudd and Malcolm Turnbull have taken to speaking forcefully that there needs to be an inquiry into the Murdoch media, and their abuses need to be curbed. A campaign to boycott the Murdoch press might also have a role. It might not have a large overt effect, but the Murdoch press is already struggling financially so even a few percent of sales lost might get their attention. More importantly, both actions could create a little more room for politicians to advocate progressive policies with less fear of being isolated and attacked in a Murdoch vendetta.

One thing progressives can do anyway is to subscribe to those outlets, mostly online, that offer more balanced news and informed commentary.

Regarding ownership, at a minimum foreigners should be excluded from owning our media, and empires should be broken up. Our media are for our society to have its conversations, and we must be firmly in control. Media ownership is more concentrated in Australia than almost anywhere, and everyone agrees it is unhealthy, it is just no-one has the guts to do anything about it. There should, perhaps, be at least two major independent centres of editorial control in each major city. Of course that doesn't work for internet news, because it is available everywhere, so the limit would be on newspaper, radio and TV editorial control. Therefore a national minimum number of editorial centres above a certain size would also be needed. Such limits would not be simple to determine or enforce, but any fairly simple scheme would still be a big improvement on the present oligopoly that reigns over both print and internet, with broadcast forming a parallel oligopoly.

A quite different approach would be to require ownership to be distributed among large numbers of people. For newspaper and broadcast media, each outlet could be owned by the people it serves, with no-one permitted to own more than a small fraction of the business. In the big cities, one could require at least 10,000 or 100,000 owners, so no individual or small group could gain control, and there could be a residency requirement to ensure ownership is within the community served. Clear rules to ensure democratic control among owners would be required, unlike present corporate governance rules. For the internet, analogous limits, depending on size of audience, could apply, with no-one being able to hold shares in more than one news organisation.

I wrote about distributed ownership of the media nearly two decades ago (in *Economia*, 2004[84]), and had never encountered any real-world interest. It is heartening to learn, therefore, the UK magazine *Positive News* has moved to become a cooperative. As they say, '*Positive News* will be owned by hundreds or thousands of people with an equal say on important matters, meaning it is a more democratic form of ownership. We will then be ultimately accountable to you, our readers, ensuring that we always report in your interests.'

The collective ownership approach would still allow some large organisations, required for comprehensive news gathering, to exist, but it would be much harder for individuals or groups to dominate or control them. Some charter limits could be mandated to ensure an appropriate kind of service was provided, so an organisation did not drift away from its purpose, such as news, commentary, analysis, with social and entertainment news.

Nothing is perfect in this world, and neither would such media avoid management and operational issues, but they would move us away from domination by big government or big money, and this would be a vast improvement. It would be so different it might perhaps be hard to imagine. Hopefully our grandchildren might find it hard to imagine why we allowed ourselves to be browbeaten and deceived for so long by a handful of the rich and powerful.

The social media are different, important and more challenging. People obviously want to use them, and they do serve some useful purposes by enabling people to communicate and to share material much more readily than used to be possible. A central problem is that they are private monopolies that are globally so big they have largely escaped national regulation. Their business model is to cultivate addiction so they can sell eyeballs to advertisers. They tailor the options people see so as to maximise their advertising revenue and the number of people using them.

A second major problem is that people spontaneously divide into interest groups, and because the social media have become so pervasive and penetrated so deeply into our lives it means people live in bubbles of like-minded people, with little awareness of, interest in or concern for other people and their needs and preferences. This cultivates social division, including the growth of extremist cults that now pose substantial threats to societies.

It would be possible to create public, open versions free of advertising's distorting influence. Open-source versions of many kinds of software exist, and that probably includes social media models. Nations could, with the will, converge on one or a few inter-operable open models that would give people the benefits without such a grave threat to global society.

It is less obvious how to deal with the silo effect of social media. At present the algorithms that the big companies create and rely on tend to aggravate the growth of conspiracist groups, so it would be possible to use more benign algorithms to reduce that tendency. More active means might also be needed. As with the old media, even some basic changes could reduce some of the worst trends and abuses, and that would already by well worth while. Beyond that the contest between operators and the public good is likely to be a long one, perhaps never ending. At the moment there is very little will in our political culture to enter the contest, though China and Europe are showing it is possible. So the first requirement for Australia is to create the political will.

It is sometimes said we get the politicians we deserve. That cannot be true if the candidates on offer were chosen by small cliques that have captured the old political parties, and if the information we are fed about them and the state of the nation is highly incomplete and often misleading.

The Liberal and Labor parties used to have large memberships, and could more plausibly be said to represent significant segments of the people. Over the past four decades their policies became more extreme and the memberships correspondingly dwindled. This made them easier targets for takeover by interested parties. There are regular branch-stacking scandals, as the parties are manipulated by unscrupulous operators with selfish or ideological objectives. The systemic corruption, through which much of their funding is obtained and that obviously determines many of their policies, further distances them from representing what most people want. The mainstream media collude by failing to portray this situation, by downplaying embarrassing news, by excluding the voices of serious critics, by failing to report candidates they do not favour, by being increasingly partisan and more broadly by conveying a quite distorted picture of the world.

It turns out the old parties have no legal standing. They are unincorporated associations. This emerged recently in the course of lawsuits against both Liberal and Labor for imposing candidates against the wishes of memberships. The courts declined to intervene because the parties have no legal standing. So they are just irregular gangs of bullies and conspiracists who can operate in any way they like.[85]

Australia is a land of smart, inventive, industrious, creative, talented people who regularly produce remarkable achievements in all sorts of ways. (This is not to say we are any better than others, just to emphasise we are not stupid and heartless drones.) We still have a large streak of decency and caring, despite the fetish of selfishness foisted upon us, as the 2022 election has shown.

It might be said we have allowed this situation to develop, so it is our own fault. But most people are busy keeping their lives on track, a task made more difficult by the present regime. The present form of politics is distasteful to many people, and that is not discouraged by those in power. The situation has developed by degrees, and the operators are skilled at manipulating appearances.

Our mainstream political culture, comprising the old parties and the mainstream media, is the main reason Australia has never reached its potential, and is now falling even further short. It has been divisive, petty, nasty, selfish, deceitful, mendacious and above all fearful. It has betrayed the trust of the people. The politicians it has produced are unworthy of Australians.

The emergence of the community independents and the greater success of the Greens in 2022 is a promising development with the potential to challenge and reverse this destructive trend. Let us hope it succeeds.

I once started writing a manuscript entitled *To Parliament with Love.* Were I a best-selling author a publisher might perhaps have taken it on, as an indulgence. A decade ago it would have been mostly laughed at. Hopelessly soppy and idealistic. By now it is not so ludicrous, as the venal, corrupt, sexist, brutal culture of our national parliament has been exposed, mostly by brave women who have suffered it and called it out.

The word love carries many meanings in our culture, from lust through infatuation to sentimental attachment, and on to deeper kinds. At its deepest, I have come to believe, acting from love means not being driven by fear. It means being aware of fear, feeling it, and choosing anyway to act calmly, believing that there is a vulnerable human being inside whoever it is you are addressing.

The Dalia Lama says that the best kind of relationship is one in which your love for each other exceeds your need for each other. If you *really* love someone you can choose to let them go, if that is their wish. You refrain from trying to control them. You allow them to live their life of choice We have many kinds of relationships in our lives, from intimate partnerships through family, friends, work and those we see mainly from a distance. In all these relationships, we can regard the other with a basic respect. We may try to persuade, but we refrain from trying to control. We can ask the same in return.

There is an important distinction to make here, between the person and their behaviour. We may object to a person's behaviour if we think it is harmful, but we can still choose to believe there is a vulnerable, well-meaning person inside who might behave better if they were not driven by their own fears. I don't claim to be very good at this with people whose behaviour I detest, but I get the distinction. So, if we come from a place of generous and respectful love we can call out bad behaviour without labelling the person *bad*. They were once an innocent little kid, like all of us.

This kind of love is very little in evidence in our political culture, which reeks of acrimony with little room for generosity. It is about me winning and, perforce, you losing. The notion that we might both win, if we find out what each other really wants and look for a different path forward, that notion is little in evidence. It is why the recent movement of *Voices For* Independents is such a hopeful development. The better candidates give evidence of being willing to deal with each other as human beings, looking for a better way forward.

There is yet a deeper reason for wishing for a parliament in which love can manifest. It is that love is essential to our being. As the Dalai Lama has said, we cannot escape the necessity of love and compassion. If we don't get love, and give love, we wither as human beings. Some of the most powerful people in our politics seem to be almost devoid of compassion for the people they are supposed to be serving. That would make them sociopaths. Our political culture is a dry and withered thing, perpetuating fear and dysfunction.

Trent Dalton, in his book Love Stories[86], tells of his grandfather, who was a Rat of Tobruk and whose life was probably saved by his best mates, one of whom did die in the course of rescuing him. The men who survived that war, and others, returned traumatised, and guilty for the mates left behind. Trent spoke with Gordon, another Rat:

> Gordon and I had no doubt between us that the blood-pool ripples of war and coming home from war stretched for the next eighty years through my family, sure as they stretched through eighty years of Australian domestic and cultural and social life, generation to generation, husband to wife, father to daughter, father to son.

We have had a century or more of political acrimony. It exacts a heavy price on our whole society. It will perpetuate itself, fear stoking fear, until we put enough people in our parliaments who can act from love, and break the cycle.

8

Too many promises

What is fragile is their economic status and self-worth, teetering on the brink of downward mobility. Living in today's financialized economy creates stresses that seem more damaging emotionally than living in a poor country. – **Michael Husdon**[87]

The first house I ever bought cost $17,000. It was in 1975 in the United States. My annual salary was also about $17,000. It was quite a reasonable house in a reasonable neighbourhood, if a little old and quirky.

In 1983 I moved my family back to Australia. We bought a house for about $55,000, and my salary might have been about $35,000. Granted prices and dollars were not the same in the two countries, but that does not matter much for these comparisons. When seeking a mortgage loan we were annoyed to be told that it could not be immediately granted because there was a 'credit squeeze' in operation, which meant the government limited the rate at which banks could issue loans, otherwise the economy would 'overheat'.

By 1997 I bought a house for about $220,000, when my salary might have been around $55,000. My salary was rising because my career was progressing and because wage levels were allowed to increase modestly by a percent or two each year, supposedly to keep up with inflation. This would have been the 'best' house I owned, a good upper-middle class house in a good neighbourhood but nothing lavish. That house sold five years later for $375,000 and I downsized to a townhouse for about $280,000, when my salary might have been $65,000. In 2010 it would have cost $700,000 to buy a reasonable house, but we moved to a small town and got a well-renovated older house for $535,000. By then I had retired. Ten years later it might sell for around $850,000.

You can see the obvious trend. The cost of a house rose by about 50 times in my experience, while my salary rose by 5 or 6 times. Even in the Australian part of the story my house price increased by about 15 times relative to only 2 or 3 times for my salary. The rise in my salary was due to my career progressing as well as to inflation or to a broad increase in wealth across society, so the increase in house price was even more marked relative to inflation and general wealth.

Anecdotes from a single life do not prove anything but official statistics support the trend, if less dramatically. The ratio of median house price to median income in Australia increased from around 3 in the early 1980s to around 7 in the 2000s, according to a Reserve Bank study[88]. Prices have rocketed up even more during the pandemic. The mean price of homes reached $835,700 in June 2021, up from $689,400 a year ago, more than 20%.

In the big cities $1 million will buy you a fairly ordinary house in an ordinary suburb, and prices have climbed more rapidly in the past year of the pandemic, as much as 20%, than for many years previously. Many younger people can no longer afford to buy a house. It is harder to afford a house now than it was in the 1950s during the postwar boom. That boom benefitted a lot of ordinary people, bringing a house and a car within their reach for the first time. A lot of that benefit is now being wiped out.

Economic managers have since the 1980s prioritised keeping inflation low, and have largely succeeded, according to the official measure of inflation. It's a curious thing though that the price of a house has increased much more than the general wealth, as measured by the GDP, and much more than official inflation, yet for most people it is a major expense, manifest either through a mortgage payment or rent. Why doesn't the increase in house prices show more in the inflation figures?

I have seen some explanations but they're unconvincing. Basically, someone, somewhere decided housing is a separate category from groceries and cars, perhaps because it is regarded as an asset, and it was left out of the international standard index of inflation. Our economic managers have been proudly proclaiming their success at 'taming inflation' (though they don't remind us that it took a draconian recession around 1990 to complete the job). Official inflation was then held more or less in the range 2-4%, and lower until very recently, when pandemic disruptions and war in the Ukraine pushed prices up significantly.

On the other hand a price increase from $55,000 to $850,000 over the 38 years since 1983 amounts to an average increase of about 7.5% per year. In other words house prices have increased much faster than official inflation. They have also increased much faster than average incomes. We could be honest and just say housing prices have inflated by around 7.5% per annum over four decades. Hold that thought, we'll come back to it.

Inflation occurs when the amount of money in circulation outruns the supply of goods and services. The dollar cost of things rises because people have enough money to pay higher prices. However the change is just in prices, including the 'price' of wages, so long as the rate of inflation is moderate. Things might cost twice as much but if your income is twice as great then you can still buy the same amount of stuff.

Where inflation does make a difference is if you have a savings account, or a contract written in dollar amounts. Then inflation will cause the purchasing power of your savings to decline. This is of concern to the financial sector because contracts commonly apply over years. A home mortgage loan is a good example. In the 1970s when inflation was quite high the lucky people who already had a mortgage loan saw their repayments decline, relative to incomes, until they were quite small. Banks were not happy with this, because they were not getting back the value they had loaned out. On the other hand the banks were receiving interest payments that typically doubled the ultimate cost of a house, so they were still making money. The banks are careful to make sure their interest charges are higher than the rate of inflation, so usually they still come out ahead.

OK, but what determines how much money is in circulation? If you ask an economist you will commonly get a long and confusing lecture about interest rates and reserves and different measures of how much money there is. Money I is the sum of notes, coins and reserves. Money II and III and so on include other things like futures contracts that can be traded around as if they are money. It's all very complicated and managing 'the money supply' is quite tricky, which is why you need clever economists to look after it all for you.

There is a simpler answer. Money is created by the Reserve Bank and by the commercial banks. Our economist lecturer might say well yes, and the commercial banks are restrained by the money multiplier and the Reserve Bank must be very careful not to create too much money, otherwise inflation. The behaviour of the money multiplier is governed by the quantity theory of money, so we don't really have to worry about the commercial banks. It's all very complicated blah blah blah. Well that part is true, it is all very complicated. Perhaps that's not by chance.

Some years ago a few economists set about finding their way through all the complications. They found that what the mainstream economists and economic textbooks say about where money comes from is wrong. The stuff about the quantity theory of money is wrong. Rather, the commercial banks just create money as they need it. The mainstream story about where governments get their money is also wrong. When governments need more money, they have the Central Bank create some for them. The new story is called Modern Money Theory (MMT), and it has been catching on over the past year or so. It is a shame though that they called it a Theory, because really it's just a description of how the system works, so it might better be called Modern Money Practice. Much the clearest account of the new story is in *The Millenials' Money* by J.D. Alt[47]. J.D. is an architect, not an economist, which helps to explain why his account is much easier to follow.

So money is created by the Reserve Bank and by the commercial banks, and the Federal Government gets its money from the Reserve Bank.

You won't hear many people state the situation in such simple terms. Even though, below the surface, it is that simple, the bankers still manage to make it pretty complicated, and the complications feed misunderstandings and fuel arguments.

I'm driving towards answering two big questions here. The first is why house prices have inflated so much. The second is what role government deficits and taxes play in the economy, and how much we have to be concerned about them.

When you get a loan from a bank, the bank creates the money and puts it in your account. It does this by using a keyboard to write the numbers in your account, and a balancing entry in its own accounts. It really is that simple. As you pay off the loan the money is 'uncreated', by subtracting your repayments from your account until it reaches zero. However you will also have paid interest, which you will have to scrounge from somewhere else and which the bank puts in its 'income' account and keeps.

Statements like those commonly provoke furious arguments, because there is a widespread misconception that the bank loans you money that someone else has deposited with them. Economists' *quantity theory of money* is a more complicated version of this. The implication of the misconception is that your mortgage loan does not change the total quantity of money in circulation. Therefore most economists think they can safely ignore bank loans when considering inflation. Unfortunately bank loans can cause big problems, like market crashes and recessions.

In settled times bank loans need not be a problem. As new loans are created other loans are being paid off. New money is being issued into circulation, but other money is being paid back and removed from circulation. The amount of circulating money is fairly stable, there is little inflation and the economy can hum along nicely, facilitated by the money that's going around. The trouble is this situation is unstable: if loans start increasing they can keep spiralling upwards, and if they start decreasing they can spiral downwards into a crash.

Suppose Joe Goldwatch is very keen to buy a certain house. Because he has plenty of assets the bank is pleased to loan him some money. Using some of his own money as well as the loan, Joe offers more than the asking price. The sellers are pleased to get more than they expected and Joe is pleased to get the house he badly wanted.

The real estate agents and the bank are also pleased. Because Joe bid up the price, it becomes the new benchmark for that whole neighbourhood. Agents recommend higher asking prices as other houses come on the market. The bank is willing to make bigger loans because the market value of the asset has increased, so their loaned funds are safe. Both the agents and the bank make more money because they get a percentage of the transactions, and such transactions are their main source of income.

One such sale is not going to trigger a spiral on its own, but if enough such sales happen then the process can continue: prices rise a bit more, loans get a bit bigger, and prices rise more again. A self-reinforcing upward spiral sets in. We can import a term from the inflation that *is* considered by economists, inflation of the general cost of living. They say that if a cycle of price rises and wage rises gets going then it can become self-sustaining because *inflationary expectations* have been triggered. Then other factors can accelerate the cycle. 'Investors', who are really speculators, buy second, third or fourth houses expecting to profit by selling at a higher price in the future. People thinking of buying a house decide they had better do it soon, before the price goes up more.

A crucial step in the process is the bank's ability to make a larger loan because the market price has increased. If it could not make a bigger loan then most buyers would not be able to bid more and prices would remain more stable. This point was made by renegade economist Steve Keen[30]. He has suggested that mortgage loans be limited in some way, such as being scaled to expected rental income, as we'll look at later.

Remember I complained earlier that we could not get a quick loan for our first house in Australia because there was a credit squeeze? Banks could only issue loans at a certain rate, so the level of household debt did not rise too much and so the economy did not 'overheat'. That was standard practice in the postwar decades. All through the Menzies years and up until Hawke and Keating the banks were much more tightly regulated. There was no simple formula for how much credit to allow, but limiting the amount of credit was a standard tool, like adjusting the interest rate. It was the job of the economic managers to monitor the economy and make adjustments to keep the economy running smoothly. Their management was not perfect, there were still mini-booms and recessions, but overall the economy performed very well, with minimal unemployment and a general increase in wealth that was widely shared, as described in Chapter 3. That all changed when Hawke and Keating deregulated the financial system.

Before exploring that, let's complete the discussion of house prices. Many economic commentators will allow that there is a housing 'bubble' in Australia that has increased prices much faster than incomes. However very few blame it on the lack of controls on commercial bank lending.

Instead they will say interest rates are at historic lows, which is true, and that makes it possible for people to borrow more and still afford the repayments. They will also mention low tax on capital gains and negative gearing.

Low interest rates are a factor, but borrowers still have to repay the principal. If they borrowed a million dollars at 2% interest then the interest will be $20,000 per year, less than if they had borrowed $300,000 at 10% interest twenty years ago. But the repayments of the principal, the million dollars, are 3.3 times larger. Buying a house still takes a bigger bite out of income in spite of lower interest rates.

Capital gains tax reductions and negative gearing are tax breaks that tend to favour 'investors', and they certainly do bid up the price of housing. Another factor is first-home-buyer schemes, in which a panicked government subsidises people buying their first home. At least these schemes are directed at people who need the most help, rather than being captured by speculators, but their main effect is to further bid the price up.

But underneath these factors is still the ability of commercial banks to make bigger loans. We could change the tax incentives and raise the interest rate but the problem would persist. Much the largest portion of the money used in most house purchases comes from a bank 'loan'; it is new money created for that purpose.

In terms of the basic recipe for inflation, the problem is not *too few houses*, the problem is *too much money*. Tax breaks and subsidies allow more of the existing money to be diverted to the housing market, but the biggest source of excess money is still the commercial banks: they just keep pumping out more money.

Governments tend to like debt bubbles. At the moment there is a bubble in household mortgage debt. In the 1980s there was a bubble in business debt. If there is a lot of borrowing then there is a lot of money sloshing around the economy. People have plenty to spend, the GDP goes up and the economy booms along. Whoever is Treasurer at the time is feted by business groups. In the 1980s Paul Keating was called the world's greatest Treasurer, or the Placido Domingo of Treasurers as he modestly put it. In the 2000s Peter Costello was similarly feted, although his 'success' was substantially due to a mining boom. The present debt bubble has not generated a boom, but it has disguised how poorly the real productive economy was performing, before the pandemic.

The problem with debt bubbles is the same problem as trying to live off your credit card. Eventually the bills come due. If you can't pay off your debts you go bankrupt. If too many people in an economy are carrying too much debt then the economy is vulnerable to small shocks. If the economy slows a bit, some people's income may fall, and houses may be sold for less than the previous market value, which lowers market values all around. Just as a rising market can become self-reinforcing, a falling market can become self-reinforcing: the more prices fall, the more people want to sell so they don't go 'underwater', owing more than their property is worth.

If enough debtors default, then the banks lose money, and each default reduces the amount of money in circulation, so the economy is slowed. As the economy slows there are more defaults. Even people who are not in danger of defaulting on a loan will tend to slow their spending, because they can see hard times approaching and they want a cushion of savings. The economy slows more. Left to itself the economy may pause, or there may be a recession, or in the worst case a depression.

We suffered the process in the 1980s. The Hawke-Keating deregulation of the financial sector led to a big build up of business debt, and the economy boomed through rest of the 1980s, until the bills came due. The whole debt house of cards collapsed in 1989 and we sank into the Keating Recession, the worst since the Great Depression.

Around year 2000 the US had the dot-com bubble and crash, when people threw money into new internet companies, many of which never accomplished anything useful nor made any profit. The financial sector's attention then shifted to real estate. They pushed mortgage loans onto people who were unlikely ever to pay them off, on the expectation that rising prices would allow them to sell higher and make a profit. That works so long as prices are rising. Worse, the financial technocrats created all kinds of clever financial 'instruments' that shifted the risk off those who were issuing loans. This neutered a fundamental market mechanism, that investors should bear risk as well as collecting profit. Risk was spread through the global financial system. Inevitably the mortgage market became saturated and prices stopped rising. A cascade of defaults and bank failures began and the worst global financial crash occurred since the Great Depression – the Global Financial Crisis of 2008. Australia escaped the worst only because the Rudd-Swan government temporarily dropped its neoliberal obsession and spent money.

The commercial banks' major incentive is to make loans, to push debt onto people and businesses. There are requirements that banks should not issue loans unless they assess that borrowers are reasonably able to repay the loans. In normal times those requirements might be enough, but 'normal' does not seem to have occurred much lately. Clearly banks have been pushing too much debt and destabilising economies. Politicians like it as long as the economy booms, so they don't do anything about it, and anyway most of them don't understand it. Economists ought to know better, but they have been taught that loans do not increase the money supply, they just shift existing money from one person to another. The Bank of England is among those authorities that have clearly spelled out the error of this belief[89]. Mervyn King, a former governor of the Bank of England, concurs[90]. King goes so far as to say that our present system of providing money to the economy is about as perverse as one could imagine.

So the ability of commercial banks to create money, almost without limit, is a big problem. After the Great Depression some stringent regulations were imposed on banking. Recessions still occurred, but nothing like the Great Depression (and many depressions before that). In the 1980s those restrictions were loosened, and the US loosened its regulation of financial dealings even further in the 1990s. The result has been the re-emergence of boom-and-crash economic instability.

There is another aspect of housing bubbles still to be looked at. Why should the price of a house just keep going up? The cost of building a house does not increase that much, because the cost of materials and labour only rise about as much as general prices and wages. The official inflation rate, which excludes house prices, is only about 2%, but property has been inflating sometimes more than 10% in a year.

The answer to this puzzle is that it is really the cost of the land on which the house sits that inflates. If you want to build a new house, the price of the land might well exceed the cost of the house itself. There are a couple of things to separate here.

The price of a piece of land, an area of the surface of the Earth, legitimately depends on where it is. You could buy a block out in the desert for not much money at all, but of course you probably would not want to live there (I'm talking here about city and town dwellers, not farmers). You would rather live close to shops and schools and within reasonable range of your work. Accordingly there is a premium on land in a good location, because you buy not only the bit of space on the planet but the services available to it. I call that premium the *emergent community value,* because it depends on the community around the land, not on what is on the land itself.

However the price of land is also subject to speculation. If land prices are rising, some people will buy it with the intention of selling it later for a higher price. Because the land price may rise because of increasing community value, it is a tempting target for speculators. Then the speculation can cause the price to increase faster than it otherwise would have. If the speculative bubble pops, the price of the land will fall back towards the community value, plus whatever dwelling may be on it.

Now there is a crucial difference between land and the house that sits on it. There is a known cost of building the house, and that cost will to some extent anchor the price of the house, in the same way that the cost of any manufactured item will reflect the cost of its production, plus a margin of profit for the producer. However there is no cost of production of the land, it is just there. I'm not talking here about whether it might be fertile land and useful for growing food – land in a city is valued as space, not as a means of production. If the space was just there, there is no cost of its production to anchor its price. It could cost anything, or nothing. It might seem to be a radical thought, but why should something that was just there cost anything?

So the price of city land is the sum of its emergent community value and a speculative cost that could be anything, or nothing. Something like these thoughts were expressed by Henry George over a century ago[91]. He proposed that land should be taxed, so the community value is recovered for the community and speculation is discouraged. He was quite influential for a time, and the rates we pay to our local council are a residue of his thinking. Canberra was initially set up with a leasehold system, the idea being that you could lease the space for the cost of the services provided, and any increase of community value would be captured by the local government and used to benefit the community[92]. However this system was soon subverted by allowing the price of a lease to be determined by 'the market', so speculation was allowed in.

Both parts of the cost of city land are mishandled by conventional economists. Henry George's ideas were ridiculed, possibly because they could get in the way of speculators, and also because economists like to pretend that all things can be exchanged for all other things at a price – everything is fungible. Without that, their theories don't work, rich people would not sponsor them as much, and their influence would wane.

The emergent community value of a plot of land should belong to the community, not to the owner of the plot, because the owner of the plot does nothing to create it. It ought to be held by a local land trust, and the increasing value used to provide facilities for the community. The land could be leased out by a land trust for the cost of the services provided, like water and electricity[93].

The mishandling of land has large consequences. The emergent community value of land is routinely captured by 'developers', for whom it is a pure windfall. If there is a speculative price rise as well, then they capture that too. This is a major source of inequality and corruption. Those who can get on the escalator of rising land prices gain large unearned income, and those who miss out pay them rent or exorbitant purchase prices, as is the case at present.

Most governments have the whiff of corruption from the influence of 'developers', and sometimes it is a stench. Things can get very nasty if anyone tries to interfere in the plans of developers. There is currently some revived interest in the fate of journalist Juanita Nielsen, who disappeared in 1975, presumed murdered, while campaigning against the 'redevelopment' of her Kings Cross neighbourhood in Sydney. Such investigations and enquiries as occurred made little progress in obtaining information, a strong indication of the corruption of both police and politicians.

Now let us return to the other source of money, the central bank. In Australia it is the Reserve Bank of Australia, in Britain it is the Bank of England and in the US it is the Federal Reserve. Central banks have the power to create money. Some of that money goes into 'reserve' accounts that commercial banks are required to hold at the central bank. Some of it funds government spending. According to the Modern Money theorists, the government, with the automatic support of the central bank, can create and spend money virtually at will. That is how the Rudd/Swan government was able quickly to spend money into circulation and thus compensate for the fall in money supply caused by the GFC.

That is not the usual story you will hear from the media. The usual story is that the government can only spend what it receives in taxes plus what it chooses to borrow from the private sector. If it borrows money then it is in deficit. Until the pandemic, deficits were widely decried, especially by right wingers, even though they were routinely and constructively used in the prosperous postwar decades.

There was a time when the usual story was closer to the truth than it is now. In former times the values of currencies were tied to the price of gold. It was called the gold standard. The amount of money a government could spend was restrained by how much gold it held, and if the government wanted to spend more it had to borrow it. It was supposed to be possible to exchange government-printed money for gold, although governments had long since stopped providing that service. But the idea continued that money was 'backed' by gold. This gave everyone the reassurance that the fancy piece of paper that had Fifty Pounds written on it could actually be exchanged for something of real value, like gold. In fact it was never that simple, and anyway the value of gold fluctuated rather wildly, depending on gold mining, speculation, hoarding and international power games.

In 1971 US President Nixon, struggling to pay for the expensive war in Vietnam, detached the US dollar from the gold standard and left its value to fluctuate according to the whims of international currency markets. This changed a lot of things, but some of the practices from the previous era have continued, even though they don't make much sense anymore. One thing that changed is that money has value only because the government says it does. In effect the government guarantees to back the value of a bank note. As the government is acting for all of us, this guarantee has credibility, though there are those who are not convinced and pine for the days of the gold standard.

In fact the government still does borrow from the private sector, even though it creates its own money. Why would it do that? Because that's what has always been done? Because the private sector gets free income from loaning money back to the government? It turns out that most countries have a law that the government cannot carry an overdraft with the central bank, according to Steve Keen[30]. This would be a hold-over from earlier systems, but evidently no-one thinks to remove it, either because they don't know about it or because it would set off howls of protest from those who profit from the present system, or who don't understand it, or both.

As a result there is a rather bizarre ritual, which I have called *the dance of the government bonds*[94]. The government has the central bank create some money. The central bank does a 'swap' of that money for some bonds that certain privileged money traders already hold – it is called a swap, not a trade. The Treasury department then offers some more bonds for sale, and the privileged dealers buy them, using the money they just got from the swap with the central bank. In this way Treasury ends up with new money and the dealers have some new bonds that they can sell 'on the open market'. The government pays interest on the bonds, so they are useful to the private financial sector because they are a secure way to hold wealth. In effect they are like a savings deposit. The central bank also has some bonds, which is like borrowing from yourself.

Well, something like this transpires, and it is true that the Australian government converts the money it creates into bonds that are then the vehicle for 'borrowing' from the private sector, with interest due. The charade is justified, if it is addressed at all, with the claim that it is necessary so the central bank can control interest rates.

Do interest rates need to be controlled? Wasn't this supposed to be free-market capitalism? Why does the government centrally control one of the key factors in financial markets? Well, in practice, because it is one of the few ways it can exert some influence on how the economy is working, or more specifically on how much debt there is. It could go back to regulating credit with credit squeezes, but that is against the current ideology.

Let's summarise this confusion. The Federal Government can create any money it needs. It disguises this, for reasons both historical and obscure, by issuing interest-bearing bonds instead of money, and then spends the money it just needlessly borrowed.

Thus right-wingers can still maintain that the government is in debt, debt is a bad thing and so there will come a time when all that debt has to be paid back, and our grandchildren will be burdened by our profligacy. No good household would be run this way, they will say, so the government should not run this way either, except, it turns out, when there is an emergency like a pandemic.

You may have been wondering, through this rambling confusion, what about taxes? If the government can, in effect, print its own money why does it need taxes? The answer used to be that the government had to tax before it could spend. Since 1971 the answer has been that taxes are the means to control inflation, according to MMT. Taxes can be used to control the amount of money in circulation. If there is too much money circulating there may be inflation, and so higher taxes may be needed *to remove some of the money from circulation*.

Some people are alarmed by this news. If the government can just print money, what is to stop it from printing so much we end up with hyperinflation? At this point they will mention the Weimar Republic, Zimbabwe and the new favourite, Venezuela. The answer is nothing, but the answer is also that this is not a radical new proposal – it is a description of how things have worked since 1971. Somehow most governments have continued to budget more or less responsibly, and hyperinflation has not eventuated.

If you have not come across this story before you may well be confused and unconvinced. It contradicts so much of what is said in mainstream political discourse that it can take time to digest and to decide it has its own internal consistency and does make some sense. It is very important though. It affects the fundamentals of how government can proceed, and thus of how our society can proceed.

Government debt is not really a debt in the normal sense of the word, or at least it need not be. To understand this we need to look at another topic that abounds in confusion: what is money?

The money we commonly use is just a token. It has little or no intrinsic value of its own, it is just a small sheet of paper or plastic, a small amount of metal or a number in a computer. You can't eat it, or drive a nail or chop some wood with it.

Your token money carries an implicit agreement. Your $10 note may be exchanged for some goods or services: a loaf of artisan bread or ninety minutes of entertainment on your screen. Your $10 note carries an implicit *promise*, from your community, that you can exchange it for something of real value, like bread that you *can* eat. There is an implicit contract between you and your society that your money token can be exchanged for something of real value to you.

Token money is a very useful invention. I could dig a garden plot for you and you could give me two loaves of bread in return. That would be barter. But what if I don't need bread and would rather have a newly published book? If you can give me a $20 note in return for digging your garden, then I can go to a bookstore and buy the book.

In the words of a smart but obscure thinker, E.C. Riegel[95], token money allows *split barter*[96]. By breaking the barter transaction into two parts, token money allows exchange to be much more flexible. In part one, I exchange my digging for a token. In part two I exchange my token for a book. Of course you will have had to earn the $20 note from a previous transaction, and the bookstore has to be willing to accept it in exchange for the book. You already know how that works.

Token money has allowed the amazing proliferation of our economies into doing and making all sorts of things, but there is a catch. It is a token of a promise, and a promise is an insubstantial thing. Suppose I dig your garden in exchange for your promise to give me a share of tomatoes when they ripen, but your tomato crop is destroyed by a big hailstorm. Then you can't keep your promise.

Suppose, if we did not know each other well, you had given me a note that said 'I owe you $20 worth of tomatoes', just as an assurance of good faith. The note is potentially worth $20 to me, but after the hailstorm there are no tomatoes, so it is worthless. Even though you made the promise in good faith, not all promises can be delivered on. Of course there are also those who will deliberately break a promise.

The big catch with token money is that the value of the promise it carries depends on the future unfolding as we expect and hope it to unfold: there will be a bountiful crop of tomatoes that we will share. But the future may unfold differently: a hailstorm and no tomatoes.

I may borrow money from a bank and promise to repay the money, with interest, over the next twenty years. But if I lose my job I may be unable to keep that promise. The bank may force the sale of the house so it can recover its money.

A bank may make mortgage loans to a lot of people, but if the economy goes bad and the price of housing suddenly starts to fall then the bank may not be able to recover all the money it loaned out. In the worst case the bank may fail.

A clever Wall Street operator may bundle a lot of mortgages into a 'derivative' and sell it to a retirement fund. The bundle will carry all the promises of borrowers, but it may become worthless if the borrowers cannot repay. The retirement fund may lose money, but the bank that made the loans is fine because it offloaded the risk when it sold the bundle. A lot of that sort of thing happened during the Global Financial Crisis.

Because a promise involves the future, and because the future is uncertain, a promise involves *risk.* Token money involves risk. The derivative bundle involves risk. All financial agreements involve risk.

If we get to the essence, *the whole financial system is about promises, and promises involve risk.* The financial system is a house of cards. If we are smart we will manage the financial system very carefully so the house of cards does not collapse. Clearly we have not been very smart. Especially since the financial deregulations of the 1980s, too many promises have been made.

Money is said to be many things. It is said to be a store of wealth, but token money is only a token of wealth. To be sure you may accumulate a lot of tokens, but they are only promises, they are not the wealth itself. Money is said to be a unit of account, and it is true that the value 'one dollar' allows the relative value of different items to be counted, but that only accounts for the values that we have already decided. Being a unit of account is a useful secondary property. Some people want gold to be money, but the value of gold is unreliable, and really rather arbitrary, depending a lot on speculation. Bitcoin is not really money because it does not carry an implicit agreement and its alleged value is due entirely to speculation.

The fundamental purpose of money is *to facilitate exchange.* The other properties follow from the promise it represents. Its ability to facilitate exchange follows from its ability to split bartering into two parts, making exchange vastly more flexible and powerful.

If the Federal Government has the Reserve Bank create some money that the Government then spends into circulation, what is the nature of the transaction involved? You and I cannot just print up some money and buy things with it, that is called forgery and severely punished. We would have done nothing to 'earn' the money, so the transaction is unbalanced, stealing really. So how can the Government get away with printing money. Is the Government making a promise?

The answer is that the Government promises to discount your tax bill when you pay some of its money back. There is a law that says taxes can only be paid in currency issued by the Reserve Bank. This is invisible to most of us, because the commercial banks are intermediaries. We pay the bank in bank money and the bank pays the Reserve in Reserve money. Yes, it's as though there are two kinds of money, even though they look the same.

According to the MMT researchers[47], requiring taxes to be paid in government-issued money is a long-standing tactic to ensure the circulation of government money. It was used in India by the British, for example, to displace local exchange systems. The government backs its demands for tax payments with the threat of force. This means you have to scramble to earn some of its money so you can pay your tax bill. On the positive side, this system also ensures the government-issued money retains its value, so long as it is reasonably managed. This is why the government-issued money carries the promise to reduce your tax bill by the designated amount.

This understanding also makes clear that government spending comes before taxing. If the government did not spend, there would be no money with which to pay taxes. In fact the whole money system would stop, because Reserve money underpins the commercial banking system. Commercial banks are required to hold accounts with the Reserve Bank. The Reserve Banks uses these accounts to manipulate interest rates and the commercial banks use them to settle debts among themselves.

In effect the commercial banks are franchised to issue money under some rules, one of which is they maintain a Reserve account. To clear up another fairly common misconception, they used to be required to maintain a percentage of their total money 'assets' in the Reserve account. The percentage was around 10% and the system was called fractional reserve banking. It was supposed to ensure that banks had enough cash available to meet customers' demands to convert their deposits (numbers in a deposit account) into cash, so if there was a 'run' on a bank it would not go broke. That system does not apply any more. If there were a run, the

Reserve Bank would loan them emergency funds to cover all demands (at least up to the total capitalisation of the bank, but that's another matter).

Let us return to government 'debt'. If the government creates and spends money, then in principle it owes us. It does not owe us bread or work in our garden, rather it owes us forgiveness of our tax bill, which will happen when we hand some of the money back. So technically there is a debt, as with all legitimate token money, but there are several things to say about that 'debt'.

First, the government does not have to pay anything back. It does not have to supply us with bread or digging services. It can just leave the money circulating. There is no interest due on this money, so it will not be a burden on our grandchildren. Certainly some of the money is returned when we pay our taxes, but the government can be spending more money at the same time. Now of course it is not quite so simple, although it could be. Instead, the government converts its new money into a bond and sells it, thus incurring a real debt, with real interest due. It could stop doing this tomorrow, but everybody is used to doing things the old way and besides, big business likes being able to buy government bonds and receive free interest payments. For them it is like a savings account – they could just as well have a savings account with a commercial bank, but they feel more secure with a government account. We don't owe this free ride to big business.

The second thing to say about government spending is that as the government is acting on our behalf, the debt carried by Reserve money is, in effect, to ourselves. If the government did not convert this 'debt' into bonds, that would be the end of it. It would not be a burden.

Third, some Reserve money is required to be issued because it underpins the larger system of bank money. That is the money we use every day in our normal transactions. The entire money economy depends on the bank money, and bank money depends on Reserve money. Back in the early eighteenth century the English government foolishly decided to pay off all its debts to the Bank of England, but BofE notes had come to be used as security for regional bank money. The money supply shrank drastically and the economy was thrown into depression. The US Government tried the same thing after the civil war and provoked a severe recession there.

There is a modern equivalent of this folly, called 'austerity'. Right-wing governments, until the pandemic, extolled the virtues of balancing the government's budget. If the government restrains its spending to be no more then it is currently receiving in taxes, then there is less money available to the private sector, and business will slow. It turns out there is a simple accounting identity that says a government debt creates an equal surplus in the private sector. A government surplus creates an equal deficit in the private sector. This is one basic fact explained by the MMT people[47]. This budget-balancing fetish is one reason the modern economy is only sputtering along. (Actually it is a little more complicated than this because there is also the foreign sector, manifest through the 'balance of payments', but it is still true that a government surplus subtracts from the other two sectors.)

Right-wingers (I am not calling them 'conservatives' because the neoliberals are not conservative, they have tried to radically transform our society) often invoke the analogy of a well-run household. This mythical household only spends as much as it earns, so it will never get into ruinous debt and it will as well be very *virtuous*. Of course modern households commonly carry quite a lot of debt. So does modern business, it is considered routine and sensible.

More basically though, the 'virtuous household' analogy gets things exactly backwards. A government that issues currency does not have to earn the money it spends. Rather it spends so the economy can function and it can 'earn' back the taxes it imposes on people. First it spends, then it taxes. *First* it spends, *then* it taxes.

It is important to say that governments that do not issue their own money, like our state governments, *are* more like households, real households. They have to raise money through taxes and then they can spend money. They can also, like sensible households and businesses, borrow money. One always needs to be careful not to take on too much debt, but there is nothing wrong in principle with carrying some debt. The founder of the Liberal Party, Bob Menzies, was happy to continue borrowing money (as they did in those days) to pay to finish the Snowy Mountains Scheme, to build universities and other such infrastructure. So the household analogy *does* apply to state and local governments, and to the countries in the Euro zone that (foolishly) gave over their money creating powers to the European Central Bank. Greece, especially, has paid a very high price for this move. Even so, these governments can sensibly be in debt, they do not have to be obsessive about 'balancing the budget'.

It is time to pull all this together. We started on the topic of house prices. Most of the money in our system is issued by commercial banks, in the form of mortgage loans with interest due. They have issued far more money than is wise, and the result has been inflation, just as right-wingers claim to fear. The inflation has been in house prices and, less obviously to most of us, in stock market prices. (Tonight when you watch the finance report on the TV news and they tell you the stock market just broke another record, do not celebrate. They are parasites, and they have just sucked more of our wealth away from us.)

There has been no fuss at all about *inflation* of housing and stock market prices; there is a fuss, but the housing bubble is not called inflation. This is partly because it is not counted in official inflation figures, and partly because neoliberals don't care about banks issuing money. What neoliberals care about is the *Federal Government* issuing too much money because, they claim, this will trigger disastrous inflation (Zimbabwe etc.). The reality is the other way: the Government is not spending enough money, and the economy is only sputtering along, with a potential threat of *deflation* and a serious recession.

But neoliberals don't really care about Federal Government debt either. This has been made clear by the huge deficits they suddenly ran up in response to the pandemic. It was an emergency and they spent, though not enough and with many groups conspicuously omitted from government support.

There is a quite different agenda behind the debt-and-deficit mantra that has been evident ever since Reagan and Thatcher came to power. First, they say Government spending must be cut to balance the budget, and also because government is inefficient and burdensome. So they cut into spending on social services and infrastructure, things that benefit the common people. When the economy slows as a result they say taxes must be cut to stimulate the economy, and the best taxes to cut are taxes on the rich, so they can get on with investing and creating wealth. This, they claim, will invigorate the economy and the newly generated wealth with *trickle down* to everyone.

The experiment has been running for forty years now and it is clear it hasn't worked, as we saw in Chapter 4. The rich have got richer, the economy has sputtered along, government services have shrunk and most people are no better off, or worse off. So the agenda is really to transfer wealth to the already-rich. Why to they always want more? Because wealth bestows power, and the more power you have the more you are afraid you might lose it, so you always want *more*. Uneasy lies the head that wears a crown.

The wealthy don't use their money to invest in wealth creation so much as use it to speculate, by buying property and stocks. So they drive up the price of housing and make people poorer, because people can't afford a good house, or any house. President Trump's tax cuts for the rich did not much stimulate the US economy, as has been documented[97]. Rather they boosted stock buybacks, which enrich shareholders and executives.

Most of what has been said in this chapter is quite contrary to what you hear in conventional political discourse. If we rid ourselves of the misconceptions, myths and lies about money we could quickly make a great deal of difference to the sad state of the world.

We could, for instance, have the Federal Government make full employment a top priority, as it was in the postwar decades. It could implement this by spending on things our society needs, be they infrastructure or services, until the unemployment rate dropped to one or two percent. It could also implement a job guarantee, which means to back any useful job that can be created for someone. The job might be in a public service, but it might also be a local job repairing community infrastructure or delivering meals to the incapacitated. Such a job guarantee would function as a buffer stock of people who could move into other jobs if the economy speeded up. It has been advocated in detail by economist Bill Mitchell[98], one of the founders of MMT.

Mainstream people may say that such spending will trigger inflation if unemployment falls below about 5% (Zimbabwe!). They choose to ignore the low unemployment rates of the postwar years. Their claim reflects a simplistic understanding of inflation. The usual explanation of inflation is that it happens when there is too much money chasing too few goods. That is basically correct. But 5% unemployment represents a big slack in the economy, reflecting a deficit of money to lubricate transactions. If the government increases spending it will stimulate the economy, which will encourage businesses to hire more employees who will be able to produce more which will increase the goods being chased by the extra money. If you do it at a moderate pace, the money need not get much ahead of the goods and you should be able to soak up the unemployment without triggering serious inflation.

This can continue until unemployment is very low. At that point an increase in the money supply will not be as readily able to stimulate production, because it will be hard for firms to hire extra people. Some inflation could then result. This strategy has been spelled out by US economist Stephanie Kelton, who has had some success in getting the MMT message finally to penetrate mainstream perceptions through her book *The Deficit Myth*[29].

Is there anything to be done about absurdly high housing prices? The huge accumulation of mortgage debt is an ever-present danger to the economy, because it might collapse and tip us into a severe recession. Inflated house prices are also a huge component of inequality, and injustice to the young and the poor. However we are in a trap of our own making, because if housing prices just collapsed then we would have a severe recession. As well, those who owned their homes would suddenly lose a lot of equity they will have been counting on; that's not really fair either, it's not their fault the system got out of kilter. One remedy might be to allow other prices to inflate until they are back in proportion to house prices, but that would be a dicey operation, it would need to be done over many years, and the debt mountain could collapse at any time anyway.

Steve Keen has come up with an ingenious fix that would bring house prices down and keep them there[99]. It would still be a delicate operation but it would be fair to everyone. There are two parts. First, a *monetary reset* to deflate the debt bubble, that I will explain shortly. Second, a change in banking regulation to limit how much private banks can lend out, so the debt bubble does not just re-inflate. It's easier to explain them in reverse order.

Part Two: regulate bank lending. Keen proposes that mortgage loans be capped at a multiple of what the property could be rented for. At present that multiple is about 20. It could be brought down over time to about 10. With less loan money available, prices would also come down, to around half of their present level. This proposal is analogous to the credit squeezes of the postwar decades, when the rate of loaning was restrained until private debt came down to a more sustainable level. However capping loans, on its own, would do a lot of people out of the equity they hold in their home as prices came down, so we need a way to sort that as well. It could also trigger a collapse anyway.

Part One: the monetary reset. Remember that the Reserve Bank creates and issues money, which is called *fiat money*. The private banks also create and 'loan' money that I have been calling *bank money*. Bank money exists because people are in debt to the private banks, and it is that debt that is the big problem. So Keen proposes a way to convert some of the equity of home owners into government bonds, and at the same time pay down mortgage holders' debt to something more reasonable. There would be care required and details to work through but we'll just look at the broad approach here. It goes like this. (Most of the transfers could be done by the banks on behalf of the government and customers, so most people would not have to do anything.)

The government creates fiat money equivalent to about half the total mortgage debt. This is paid into the bank accounts of every adult resident. Anyone who has a mortgage loan must use the money to pay down their debt, so their debt might come down by half or more. Anyone who already owns their home must use the money to buy government bonds (which the government will already have sold to the private banks); the equity in government bonds will replace the equity their house loses as prices come down (because of Part Two). Those who have fiat money left over from paying down their mortgage will use the balance of the money in the same way as home owners, which they now are, i.e. to buy bonds. Renters and others who do not own a house must also buy government bonds: they end up with an asset they did not have before, and this (partly) compensates for them having been effectively shut out of the housing market.

Requiring all the fiat money to be used to buy government bonds ensures that none of the extra money ends up circulating in the economy, so inflation will not be triggered. You would be able to sell your bonds if you wanted, but that would require a buyer who already has money, so again no new money would be added to the economy. I will leave out the changes for the private banks, their operations would be changed but they would remain in business and they would return more to facilitating useful investment, as they are claimed to, instead of facilitating property speculation.

The end result of this scheme is that present home owners would have some of their home equity converted into government bonds and they would be no worse off. Holders of large mortgages would have their debt reduced by half or more. Renters and others would have an asset they did not have before.

Would the latter be a handout? Yes. Is that a problem? Well, big businesses get handouts all the time (tax cuts and billion dollar gas pipelines anyone?), the wealthy have been benefitting from a highly skewed economy that channels more than their fair share of wealth to them, and the poor have been screwed. For a small precedent, the Rudd Government put money in the accounts of pensioners as part of its successful counter to the GFC in 2008, so Granny and Gramps could go on a shopping spree to help save the economy. The right wingers squealed loudly, but the sky did not fall and neither did the economy. For a larger precedent, at the onset of the pandemic the Morrison Government paid billions into employer bank accounts with no requirement to justify their need, and many large companies kept the money even though their business did not decline in the pandemic.

What about government debt? Well, the government sold bonds to the banks to get the money to give to people to buy the bonds. As we've already discussed, it can always pay the interest due and it could buy the bonds back if it wanted, because (effectively) it issues the money, and it does not have to pay it back if it does not need to. Their is no burden on our grandchildren.

This scheme seems to be an ingenious way out of the trap we've been steered into by incompetent economic management. It certainly needs to be carefully examined and debated, but that debate needs to involve people who properly understand the money system, as well explained by Stephanie Kelton in *The Deficit Myth*[29]. To the many at present who do not have that understanding, it will look outrageous and highly irresponsible, but perhaps this is a teaching moment for them.

9

Growing Up

The success of Australian industry in most significant sectors has been that of an advanced colonial society, with overseas capital and enterprise employing intelligent native labour. - **Donald Horne**, writing in 1964.[4]

Events in August and September 2021 starkly portrayed Australia's place in the world. Our last military forces left Afghanistan, along with those of the US, amid a chaotic collapse of the local government after a twenty-year occupation. Then the Morrison Government announced that Australia would acquire US nuclear-powered submarines as part of a new alliance of the US, UK and Australia, awkwardly known as AUKUS. In the shadow of that announcement it emerged that the US would be given virtually unlimited access to use Australia as a staging ground for its growing military confrontation with China, our largest trading partner.

There was a brief episode of agonising over our undignified withdrawal from Afghanistan and the government's failure to ensure the safety of many of those who had worked with our forces, and whose lives were therefore at risk under the new Taliban regime (at least three have since been murdered). Then there was a big diplomatic fuss because Australia cancelled a major contract with the French to build conventionally-powered submarines, and the French were not pleased. Mainstream media and Labor quickly got on board the submarine decision, in principle. The need for a close relationship with the US was mostly taken as a given.

Neglected, except in secondary outlets, were the facts that we are unlikely to be militarily threatened by China if we don't interfere in its affairs, that the few nuclear-powered subs would be less effective than more numerous conventional subs for the defence of our marine approaches, that the nuclear-powered subs were therefore intended to be part of the US military confrontation with China, that the US does not have a good track record of reliability as an ally and that its allegedly liberal democratic system is far from liberal and in serious danger of being overrun by anarchists.

It was claimed that Australia would not need to develop an on-shore nuclear power industry, so as to have the facilities and expertise to maintain the marine nuclear power plants, because the latest US nuclear technology allows the nuclear power system to last the lifetime of the submarine, so it would effectively function as a sealed unit. This would only make Australia more dependent on US expertise. Also the nuclear fuel is highly-enriched, weapons-grade uranium, which would undermine non-proliferation agreements. One requirement of non-proliferation is that nations declare any fissile material in their possession, but the US would not divulge that information to us even though we had 'purchased' it.

The nuclear-powered subs are complex, aside from their power plant, and there is a substantial industrial complex in the US involved with building, supplying and maintaining them. Australia has none of this industrial capacity and any it developed would be subsidiary to US industry.

The withdrawal from Afghanistan was extremely reminiscent of the chaotic US withdrawal from Vietnam 46 years earlier, even to the detail of pictures of helicopters lifting desperate people from rooftops. The invasions of Afghanistan (2001) and Iraq (2003) were widely predicted to be counter-productive and un-winnable, like the invasion of Vietnam, but those objections were brushed aside in the rush of hubris leading to the so-called *war on terror* declared by US President George W. Bush. The US record is of blundering into military actions that not only end in failure but are counter-productive.

Historian William Blum has documented that since 1945 the US has destroyed or subverted more than 50 governments, many of them democracies.[100] It has supported mass murderers, like Suharto in Indonesia, Mobutu in the Congo and Pinochet in Chile, so as to dominate by proxy. In the Middle East, almost every dictatorship and pseudo-monarchy has been sustained by the US. Historian Alfred McCoy describes the US surrogates as autocrats, aristocrats, and uniformed thugs.[101] The US has been at war during every decade of its existence.[102]

Those are harsh claims, and so contrary to the official lines we are fed that perhaps we need to hear it from the horse's mouth. In 2005, the US was annoyed with the rule of President Mubarak in Egypt, so it thought to threaten to promote democracy. This was done by Secretary of State Condoleezza Rice in a speech in Cairo: 'For 60 years, my country, the United States, pursued stability at the expense of democracy in this region here in the Middle East, and we achieved neither.'

Among the better-known examples of the US aiding the overthrow of democratic governments are Salvador Allende in Chile (1973), Patrice Lumumba in the Congo (1960) and President Sukarno in Indonesia (1965). Nearly forgotten now, apparently, is the overthrow of Prime Minister Mohammad Mossadegh in Iran in 1953, a collusion of the US and Britain, because Mossadegh proposed to nationalise Iran's oil industry. It was Iran's oil, one might have thought, but he threatened the profits of the precursor of British Petroleum and the flow of ultra-cheap oil to the West. The oil would still be available, but at a more reasonable price, still very low by current standards.

The overthrow of Mossadegh and his replacement by the Shah of Iran was a fateful action. The Shah ruled with an iron fist, became extremely rich, kept the masses poor, served his foreign masters well, and promoted the flow of Western culture into Iran. The resulting discontent was exploited by conservative Moslem clerics, who succeeded in overthrowing the Shah in 1980 and establishing a repressive Islamic theocracy. Iran is now considered to be perhaps the biggest threat to Western designs on the Middle East as it has threatened to develop nuclear weapons and supports various insurgencies through the Middle East.

Afghanistan also has a significant back story. A socialist government was established by a popular coup in 1978.[103] It began a progressive social reform program that included the abolition of feudalism, freedom for all religions, equal rights for women, social justice for ethnic minorities, and a mass literacy program. For women, the gains were unheard of. These reforms were bitterly opposed by some of the conservative, mostly-Moslem population, particularly in rural areas. The rebels, known as the Mujahideen, were given aid and training by several countries including the US, even though there were severe tribal rivalries among them and opium smuggling was a mainstay of their economy. The Government appealed to the Soviet Union for help, which led to the Soviet occupation of Afghanistan from 1979 to 1989.

This program of backing anti-socialist and anti-Soviet rebels was expanded and repeated in other conflicts. Recruits were trained by the CIA and by the UK, and among their number have been Osama bin Laden. He and other recruits fed into the formation of al Qaeda, the Taliban and later Islamic State[103,104]. The program thus fed into the 2001 attack on New York's twin towers, and thence to the so-called war on terror, which continued to exacerbate animosities. At every stage the US and its collaborators were warned they would only enhance the radicalisation and recruitment of Islamic extremists, and so it transpired. In terms of power, Osama bin Laden and George W. Bush fed off each other.

The US and Britain have been indirectly supporting Islamic jihadists through their support for states like Qatar, Kuwait and especially Saudi Arabia, as much of the funding of jihadists in Syria comes from these states. The most fundamentalist Moslem sect, Wahhabism, is aggressively exported by Saudi Arabia, and inspires most of the calls for the imposition of Sharia law and the persecutions of other Moslems and other religions.

Such is the blundering folly of the United States. The proposed AUKUS arrangement would ensure not only that our military-industrial capacity is highly dependent on the US, but that strategic and operational decisions would necessarily be ceded to the US. With high-value US ships, planes and bases in Australia we would be a target. Our interests will never be the same as US interests, so we cannot assume our interests would be protected, even if the US did not fail. On top of a high proportion of our mining, industry and other key economic sectors already being heavily foreign-owned, it is hard to see how Australia could be described as anything other than a colony.

Of course Australia began as a collection of British colonies, most of them penal colonies. The main colonies were given a measure of self-government in the mid-nineteenth century, but they remained colonies until they federated to form Australia in 1901. Australia's status was then said to be a dominion, meaning the head of state and some high-level constitutional roles remained in the UK. This is symbolised by the UK flag occupying a corner of the Australian flag.

The earliest enterprises in settler Australia were necessarily funded by wealth brought from the UK. By late in the nineteenth century Australia was reputed to be the richest country in the world, *per capita,* but the mentality still was that major projects needed British investment funds. This thinking continued through Federation and World War I. Debts to 'English bond-holders' were a major point of contention during the Depression in the dispute between NSW Governor Jack Lang and the Federal Government – in modern terms, Lang wanted the debts rescheduled.

Although Australia was socially highly innovative early in the twentieth century, that ceased in 1914 and by 1950 our attitude was described as a 'cultural cringe'[105], an inferiority complex that assumed we were always second best to overseas talent and expertise, except in sport. Australia remained, culturally and financially, trapped in a colonial mentality. Bob Menzies described himself as 'British to the boot-heels'. In 1964 Donald Horne described our leaders in all spheres as second rate, lacking in curiosity about the larger world and the near future, running on their luck.[4]

After studying and working in the US for fifteen years, I returned to Australia in 1983. It was culturally a more vibrant place than when I had left in 1968, a legacy of the brief Whitlam years. The cultural cringe was proclaimed to be dead and our best arts talents strutted the world. But the breakout was confined to the arts. Politically the mentality was in stark contrast to what I had seen in the US. If the Americans decide they want to do something they don't look to see if someone else has tried it out, and they don't ask the world what they think, they just do it, for better or worse. Politically, and financially, the cultural cringe was still dominant. The mentality was still colonial.

Whitlam challenged the mentality, but his leadership was quickly snuffed out and most of what he attempted has been wound back. Curtin and Chifley had entertained an independent foreign policy in the nineteen forties, but Menzies ended that.

The US undoubtedly helped to prevent an invasion of Australia in WWII and Prime Minister Curtin was sensible in turning from Britain to the US as an ally in that dire time. Australia's population was still only seven million and it was also sensible to have a loose arrangement for the US, Australia and New Zealand to 'consult' about coming to each other's aid in the event of any military hostilities, which is all the ANZUS treaty specifies. Evidently Menzies took this as an opportunity to take care of our defence on the cheap, and to channel funds into domestic needs for domestic political purposes. By 1964 Donald Horne was warning about the long-term underfunding of defence[4].

That changed at about that time as Menzies suddenly decided to send Australian troops to Vietnam and to introduce conscription into the services. Without notice or consultation he broke the long-standing requirement that only volunteers could be sent overseas, a requirement that had been reinforced by the two bitterly fought referenda of WWI. Thus began a quite new phase of Australia's foreign and defence policies: we were to play the role of faithful ally to the US, in hopes that if we had actual need the US would come to our aid.

The *American Australian Association* was formed, dedicated to 'deepening and strengthening cooperation and understanding between the institutions and people of the United States and Australia'. Despite those nice words, 'the people' don't seem to be of much interest, and the Association quietly focusses on institutions and politicians. Politicians of both sides are feted by the US, and the US world view is maintained in their minds. In the old days, when politicians went 'home' to London to be feted there, it was called *duchessing*[106].

We can be sure the US view is underscored by more than friendly chats over dinner. Former diplomat Bruce Haigh reminds us that the standard US approach to diplomacy is coercive[107]. After Mark Latham became leader of the Opposition in 2003 he was indiscreet enough to remark that the United States was a rogue nation and the greatest threat to world peace, sentiments that many Australians would not disagree with. Evidently something happened behind the scenes because very soon he was on TV wrapping himself in a US flag and declaring his undying dedication to the US alliance. Perhaps he was reminded of the presence of US bases in Australia, and of US dedication to maintaining one of its chief satellite surveillance posts at Pine Gap in central Australia, as well as a naval communication base in Western Australia. Gough Whitlam is reported to have been considering re-negotiating the Pine Gap arrangement at the time of his dismissal[104].

One of Whitlam's first acts was to get our troops out of the Vietnam debacle, but since Whitlam was removed Labor has been dedicated to the US cause. John Howard had us follow the US into the Middle East debacles and now we are to tie ourselves even more firmly into the US military machine as it embarks on a futile quest to retain or regain its slipping dominance over China.

Our role has not just been military. It has recently emerged that Australian agents were used to destabilise the democratically-elected Allende government in Chile, in preparation for its overthrow in the military coup by Augusto Pinochet in 1973.[108] Reportedly it was Whitlam's discomfort with this role that contributed to a reassessment of ties with the US. Bob Hawke's later passing of industrial relations intelligence to the US was mentioned earlier.[27]

Only once has Australia actually been threatened with military invasion, and the bellicosity of an Australian Prime Minister played a significant part in bringing on that threat. Now other Prime Ministers' provocations threaten to put us in harm's way again.

At the 1919 Paris peace conference Australian Prime Minister Billy Hughes argued loudly against a Japanese proposal to insert an anti-racism clause into the charter of the League of Nations. Its rejection ensured the League would be a white man's club, which suited the European powers whose dirty work Hughes was unwittingly doing. Humiliated, the Japanese declined membership of the League and began to prepare for war[109].

Over the past year or two there has been talk that 'the drums of war' are beating and we must prepare for military conflict – with China. The drum beating has mostly been on our side. That provocative rhetoric, followed by the sudden announcement of the AUKUS arrangement, is playing the same role as Billy Hughes' racist rantings. It antagonises China. Australian ships have also sailed through the South China Sea, as a clear provocation of China. The response from China has been angry rhetoric and the curtailment of trade in a number of commodities, even coal.

Former Liberal Prime Minister Malcolm Fraser warned in 2014 against being drawn into a confrontation between the US and China.[110] He advocated even-handed relationships with both countries. The immediate issue is the relationship between Taiwan and mainland China. Both sides regard Taiwan as part of China. In that sense it is an internal issue. The trouble is that the US backed Chinese nationalist forces that lost to the communists in the 1949 revolution. The nationalists withdrew to Taiwan. It then became a cold war issue between communism and 'capitalism'. The US still views the issue in cold war terms, even though most regard the cold war as long over. It is now a matter of US prestige, both national prestige and 'free market' prestige. On the other side Taiwan is a continuing reminder of humiliations China endured during the colonial era. Pride on both sides does not bode for a rational resolution.

It is hard to see how the US can gain anything from this confrontation, except that President Biden dare not be seen to be 'weak' in foreign policy. Even less is there any potential benefit for Australia. We have no direct interest in the Taiwan issue. That may seem to be a callous attitude, to leave the prosperous and notionally democratic island to its fate with the mainland, but we tolerate far worse among alleged allies – Saudi Arabia, for example, funds terrorism through the Middle East and is currently engaged in brutally bombing Yemen with great loss of civilian lives. Foreign policy employs the rhetoric of freedom and democracy, but in reality it is about power, pure and simple. In a longer perspective, the future of Taiwan is an internal Chinese question.

We don't need foreign investment. Foreign debt is the other primary way we are kept subservient to foreign interests. We are and always have been dependent on foreign money, but we do not need to be.

That may be a startling thought, but let's think it through. MMT advocate Stephanie Kelton repeatedly stresses that the limitation on enterprise is not money, it is people and resources[29]. The question is not 'How do we pay for it?' The question is 'How do we provision it?' Do we have the resources to do it? If we have the people and materials to do something, then money can be issued to facilitate the project. The purpose of money is to facilitate exchange.

Of course we might not have all the needed expertise or devices within Australia, and there might be foreign patents we need to licence. In that case we can throw up our hands and beg some foreigners to do it for us, or we can hire some foreign experts, buy the required devices and buy the required licences. We need foreign money to buy foreign things, but we can obtain that by selling things to foreigners. In other words getting what we need can be part of our trade with the rest of the world. Nothing has to be borrowed from foreigners. We can retain complete ownership of and control over our own enterprise.

There may be some novel or very specialised things that we don't have enough knowledge to tackle, in which case we might have foreigners manage it for us. But those could be exceptions. We really should not need foreigners to dig up iron ore and ship it overseas, we've been doing it for a long time, even if a lot of it is foreign-owned. The Chinese have been smarter than us. They have invited foreigners into joint ventures, for example to build airliners, with requirements to share technology, so that by the end of a project they know how to do it themselves. It's not clear whether in the long run it's a good deal for the foreign company, but they have done it anyway. So foreign trade is useful but incoming foreign investment is not required.

Foreign trade is useful, but it has become a fetish in the neoliberal, globalised world. There are many examples of a country simultaneously importing and exporting the same thing or of, say, fish being caught in Australian waters, processed in China and imported back to Australia. Such practices waste energy, produce excessive greenhouse gases, deprive locals of employment and allow extra profits to be skimmed off. We can help 'developing' countries more by buying their products at a fair price than by taking advantage of underpaid and exploited labourers in their own country. We can help them by teaching them how to do things for themselves. We can help the planet more by avoiding transporting stuff all over the world and back when it could be made and used locally. A certain level of trade is useful. The neoliberal 'free-trade' mentality, that all trade is good and more is better, is nonsense.

Donald Horne lamented in 1964 that much of our industry is foreign-owned and foreign-directed. The situation has only got worse. Not only is foreign ownership still the norm in larger industries but foreign corporations are now much larger and more powerful. Australia is still a colony industrially and financially as well as politically.

The financial sector comprises banks, insurance companies, superannuation funds, investment funds and the financial markets. Its role is supposed to be to supply money where it is needed and to provide insurance against loss and growing old. The financial markets are supposed to ensure that invested money is used the most efficiently, by going into companies with the best returns, taking account of risks. They used to serve that role more closely, when they were strongly regulated in the postwar decades.

Internationally, through the 1970s and early 1980s, restrictions on finance were rapidly broken down. The US dollar was removed from the gold standard, major currencies were 'floated', so their exchange rates were determined in financial markets instead of being fixed by governments, and restrictions on cross-border movements of money were removed.

After deregulation the rate of transactions in financial markets jumped by around *a factor of fifty*. Not 50%, 50 times[94]. There were fifty times as many transactions per day as there had been before deregulation. The reason was a rapid rise in speculative transactions. In the postwar decades regulations were deliberately tight to keep the financial markets focused on investing in productive enterprises. It means that these days only around one in 50 financial trades serves the productive economy. The other 49 are speculative trades.

In other words the financial markets are completely dominated by gambling. However, unlike a casino, the odds are not stacked in favour of the house. Rather the odds are stacked in favour of the gamblers, who have much more inside knowledge than most of us. The objective is to siphon wealth into their own pockets. Where is that wealth coming from? It can only come, ultimately, from the productive economy. It means the productive economy is being hollowed out by a parasitic financial system.

But that's not the end of it. The frenetic rate of trading, combined with the common strategy of betting on trends, means the market speculation greatly magnifies market fluctuations. Rises are driven too high, then the following falls are driven too low. Long-term 'bubbles' are inflated, and when they burst they turn into a crash.

Thus not only are the unregulated financial markets parasitic, they destabilise the whole economy. The rapid fluctuations in share prices makes it harder for managers of actual productive activity to optimise their operations, so the efficiency of the whole economy is degraded. Then, if the financial markets crash, they bring the whole economy down with them, visiting great tribulation on the world.

Even that is not the end of it. Financiers have amassed so much wealth they have bought the US Congress. Despite grossly negligent and allegedly criminal behaviour on a grand scale, in bringing about the Global Financial Crisis and the ensuing Great Recession, Congress fought to prevent even moderate regulation of the finance industry. Allegations of similar criminality and pliability of our own politicians go un-investigated, according to Philip Soos[111] and Ian Verrender[112].

Then, just to add insult to all that injury, some of these Wall Street gamblers (think Donald Trump) stand up and claim they contribute great wealth to the nation. The word *hubris* doesn't really capture the gall of this claim. One definition of *chutzpah* is the man, convicted of murdering his parents, who pleads for mercy because he is an orphan.

The true role of the financial markets is also revealed by what they do. A good account is given in *The Big Short,* a book[113] and movie. Financial traders build towering houses of debt cards, deceiving themselves and many others that their gambling systems are sound, and legal. They bundle speculative 'products' into packages and then speculate on those in turn. The tower of debt gets higher, until it collapses.

The mentality of the financial markets is hollowing out productive enterprises in a more direct way as well. The managers of big corporations have been learning they can make quicker profits, especially for themselves, by playing financial games than by actually making stuff. Many of their lurks are spelt out in depressing detail by Rana Foroohar in her 2016 book *Makers and Takers.*[114] Foroohar is a business journalist, and she's no slouch, having worked for *Time* magazine, CNN, MSNBC and others.

Some of the practices she describes have been around for decades. Corporate raiders buy struggling companies, strip them of assets, including employee pension funds, break them up and sell them for a tidy profit. Or they run them for a short while with costs cut to the bone and then sell them before their growing dysfunction becomes obvious. Tax avoidance, using offshore tax havens and so-called transfer pricing has become routine.

The hyperactive financial markets had already shifted the focus of business from medium-term productivity to next quarter's bottom line. If the quarterly report is not as positive as shareholders like, they can bail out and put their money somewhere else. The productive economy was already being greatly harmed by this short-term focus of financial markets. Now that managers also have a greater personal stake in the quarterly bottom line the problem is worse. Regulations could go some way to ensuring corporate managers' incentives are less conflicted, but a transaction tax might be a more comprehensive reform, as we'll get to shortly.

Foroohar recounts the story of General Electric, the iconic company founded by Thomas Edison and the only company to remain in the Dow Jones Industrial Average since the Dow began 120 years ago. In the 1980s under Jack Welsh GE turned to financial manipulation. Its financial arm, GE Capital, became its biggest earner and eventually America's biggest non-bank financial institution. In her words, it was a taker, not a maker. It crashed and burned in the GFC and had to be bailed out with $139 billion of taxpayer-backed loan guarantees. Unusually, GE seems to have learnt a lesson. In 2015 GE announced it was getting completely out of finance and henceforth would return to focusing just on being a maker.

Foroohar begins her book with the words 'It wasn't the way Steve Jobs would have done it'. She then recounts how in 2013 Apple, under new CEO Tim Cook, borrowed $17 billion for a share buyback. It did this even though it had $145 billion sitting in offshore tax havens and $3 billion in profits flowing in every month. Interest rates were at record lows, and blue-chip companies can issue bonds at very low rates, so it can borrow cheaply, jack up its own share price, reap some unearned profit for managers and shareholders, and look very good on paper.

Foroohar asserts, plausibly, that Steve Jobs never worried about the share price. Rather, he focused relentlessly on creating the next amazing product, and figured the share price would look after itself. Certainly Apple would never have become the world's most valuable company if he had focused on playing money games instead of creating the iPod, the iPad, the iPhone and so on.

We don't have to put up with such crazy and parasitic financial markets. A key regulation in the postwar era prohibited deposit-taking institutions from also being investment banks. In simple terms, they could not gamble with other people's money, unless it was explicitly allowed by its owner. Remember, the underlying purpose of a commercial bank is to make a profit, and if gambling with your money and mine increases their profit they will do it if they can get away with it. There were other regulations, such as stricter limits on insider trading, that also could be brought back.

But there is a simpler and more direct remedy for the gambling. It is to impose a small tax on every financial transaction, made just large enough to take most of the profit out of the gambling. Speculators commonly operate on very small margins, so a fraction of a percent might be enough to stop most of it. Legitimate trading would be hardly affected by such a small charge, because legitimate trades do not need to happen very often. Such a charge is known as a Tobin tax, after the economist who proposed it many decades ago.

There are current proposals for this form of tax, but their sponsors seem to miss the main point. They call them 'Robin Hood' taxes, because they want to transfer some of the wealth from rich financiers to the rest of us. But much the biggest benefit of such a tax, properly implemented, would be to eliminate the 98% of trades that are parasitic and destabilising, so the financial markets would be much more stable and investment would flow more reliably into productive enterprise. If it worked properly, such a tax might not maximise revenue, because the frequency of financial trading would be much lower than at present. However the economy would function much more efficiently and profitably, so the overall benefit would be much greater and one of the main causes of gross inequality of wealth would be removed.

The financial markets are alleged to have great power over us. If the Government proposes something the financiers don't like then, it is said, the country will be punished by the the markets. The prices of government bonds and other financial 'instruments' might fall and the government will have less borrowed money to spend. We've already been over that – the government does not need to borrow from the private sector, it can create and spend as much money as it needs. So the threat from the financial markets depends on everyone involved maintaining the myth that the government must borrow from the private sector.

If the government behaves really badly, according to the markets, there might be a 'capital flight'. Overseas investors might withdraw their money and take it elsewhere. In this age of globalised everything, financiers can move their money when ever and where ever they want. Then our economy would slump, allegedly. Well, first of all, we don't need most of their foreign money. Second, we can still control the flow of money through our borders, if we choose. Financiers keep track of every cent. Foreigners do business here at our pleasure and under our rules. If they want to continue, then they follow the rules.

You don't think it could ever happen? During the Asian currency meltdowns of the late 1990s Prime Minister Mahatir of Malaysia stopped the flow of money in and out of the country. Whereas neighbouring countries suffered dramatic flights of capital and their economies were thrown into recession, Malaysia rode out the panic and resumed business with little long-term effect on its economy. Such rules would require some credible enforcement, at a level such that financiers would think twice about the risk of being caught. Collecting taxes is not easy either, but we don't throw up our hands and give up.

Prominent economists C. P. Chandrasekhar and Jayati Ghosh recently wrote

> It is hard to think of a more masochistic economic strategy on the part of governments than complying with the rules of neoliberal finance.[115]

They were writing about the misadventures of 'emerging' and 'developing' countries in trying to benefit from 'liberalised' finance open to the global financial system. Somehow the net flow of wealth always seems to be to the wealthy creditor nations, even in schemes that are notionally about development or debt relief. Australia is not officially known as a 'developing economy', but our high dependence on raw commodity exports and the colonial mentality of our rulers ensure we suffer many of the same problems.

Would it really be feasible for us to be more independent in the world? Wouldn't we be at the mercy of bigger countries, especially China? The countries of Southeast Asia all have to contend with the power of China, they have been doing it for millennia. Even tiny Singapore. There is no credible threat of invasion, even from China. China's economic might is growing. We would need to use careful diplomacy, but we have things

China wants and we are not without bargaining power. We are in far more danger through our entanglement with the US, and its reckless confrontation with China. Malcolm Fraser thought so.

We would be in significant danger if we tried to extract ourselves from our entanglement with the US. It would respond with propaganda, with subversion, with trade penalties and with measured and disguised force. We might be wise to leave Pine Gap and a few other spy operations in place, because they are a vital part of US surveillance of the world, we are told, and the US might respond with overt force if we told them to leave. There would certainly be a hysterical propaganda campaign, with local right-wing media joining in. Nevertheless, with sufficient resolve, we can certainly stop the US using us as a military staging ground and we can stop being its deputy sheriff.

Some would label a move to greater independence as *nationalism,* and imply that is necessarily a bad thing. To dedicated neoliberal globalisers it would be a bad thing, but their view is invalid, as has already been discussed. Some imply that nationalism implies a more aggressive stance in the world, and there are examples of those, but nothing advocated here requires more aggression. Rather the reverse. We could extract ourselves from the serial aggression of the United States and be much less of a threat to our neighbours and the world. The independence advocated here is simply the freedom to run our affairs ourselves as we see fit.

10

Peace making

Everything is about balance. Everything is about harmony. Everything is about peace making. – **Aunty Anne Poelina**[116]

There is either love or violence. There is either love or a cry for love. – **Stan Dale**[117]

Human madness is the howl of a child with a shattered heart. – **Robin Grille**[19]

All through the unprecedented slaughter of World War I there were many efforts to get a negotiated end to the fighting, including by the Pope and US President Woodrow Wilson. Most of the soldiers wanted to stop fighting. Many anxious and grieving families wanted it to stop. However politicians and most British newspapers, many of them owned by Lord Northcliffe, spewed hatred and lies, girding and goading a majority of the population to support continued fighting until total victory was achieved.

Behind closed doors another logic was in play. The elite understood that if they were to agree to peace without a clear victory then the people would think the horrendous loss of life had been for nothing. The elite's hold on power would be threatened. The longer the fighting went on the more at risk was their power.[118] All efforts to broker a peace were rejected, many out of hand.

I was born late in World War II and so grew up in the nineteen fifties, just ahead of the postwar 'baby boomers'. My awareness emerged into a world with strong memories of 'the war', but at peace and with growing prosperity.

The war had been a 'good' war, it seemed: both Hitler's Germany and the Japanese to our north had behaved aggressively and atrociously and the rest of the world needed to beat them back decisively. Every year on Anzac Day there were ceremonies to celebrate the victory and to honour 'the fallen'.

In the big cities there were big Anzac Day marches of former servicemen, and a few women. At the head of the march would be a small contingent of old men, veterans of the Boer War, but it was not at all clear to me what that war was about. Behind them would be a long column of late-middle-aged men who had fought in the First World War. Then an even longer column of younger men who had fought in World War II. There may have been a contingent of veterans of the Korean War. It was all quite impressive. The family radio would be tuned into the ABC's commentary of the city march, calling out each unit of the armed forces and reciting something about where each had served, marching band music rising and receding in the background.

If I thought about it at all as a kid it was probably to know that the world was as it should be. My parents often talked about the Depression, through which they had lived as young adults, as well as the war. To them it must have seemed to be a golden era, and it was, compared with the preceding decades and, in retrospect, compared with the less benign world and gradually building crises that came after about 1970. Of course there were many who were doing it tough, even in a prosperous country like Australia, but I was oblivious to them. Australia was in a blessed peace and I hoped I would never have to take my turn being sent off to a war somewhere.

The big commemoration was on Anzac Day, 25th of April, because, we were told, that was the day in 1915 when Australian soldiers landed on the beaches of Gallipoli, Turkey, and fought with great valour for many months, suffering heavy casualties. This, we were assured, had forged the disparate colonies, that had come together to form the Federation of Australia in 1901, into a united and honourable nation. I never did quite understand that, there seemed to be some leap of logic I did not quite get.

As I grew up I realised I did not really know what WWI was about. WWII was about beating Hitler, and the Japanese, but nobody ever seemed to say why all the earlier fighting in Europe, except that the Germans were bad then, but they did not seem to have been as bad as Hitler.

By the time I was a young adult at university we were embroiled in yet another war, this time in Vietnam. The merits of being involved in this war were clearly debatable from early on, when the United States was sending 'advisers' to help the South Vietnamese fight the North Vietnamese. Our government propounded the 'domino theory', that if Vietnam fell to communism then the dominos would fall until the wicked commies were on our doorstep.

Then the US went in full bore and our government announced young men would be conscripted into the Australian Army so we could do our part 'fighting communism'. I was three months older than the first intake of twenty-year-olds. Quite a few of my friends were in later ballots and some were conscripted. The Menzies government broke a long commitment not to send conscripts overseas. We learnt that this had been a bitterly divisive issue during World War I, with two referenda to allow conscripts to be sent overseas being rejected.

Opposition to the war and its supposed justification got louder, and I was in no doubt what I thought - we were not threatened and we should not be involved.

What was Gallipoli really about? It was about a deal in which Britain and France sought to tempt Tsarist Russia to fight the Germans, their reward being Constantinople and the straights joining the Black Sea with the Mediterranean Sea. So our brave troops were really fighting for Russia, though they did not know it. Even the timing of the landing was adjusted to help persuade Italy to join the fight. The Turks were well forewarned of the invasion, and well prepared. The landing was a slaughter but the invaders gained a foothold. They never gained any more. After many months their depleted ranks were withdrawn, to be moved to the trenches in France, which were even worse. The operation was a massive failure. The mastermind of the failure was one Winston Churchill, but his career was not ended, as is the way of aristocratic elites.[118]

What was World War I about? It was a contest among European imperial powers for power and territory. Britain and France, once the German advance was halted, sought to defeat Germany and carve up Germany's colonies between them.

The fighting started in August 1914 with the widespread expectation, on both sides, that the soldiers would be home by Christmas. By Christmas a million young men were dead and the conflict was a stalemate. On Christmas Eve along many parts of the front, carols began to be sung, in German, English and French. Troops weary of the slaughter emerged from the trenches and joined in no-man's-land. Carols were sung, friendships were formed, soccer was played. Fully two-thirds of the English line engaged in an impromptu truce. However the authorities back home soon ordered the slaughter to resume.[18]

There were efforts by many to negotiate an end to the fighting, mentioned already. Among those who strove to stop the fighting were a diverse collection of women from many countries, including from both combatant sides and from Australia. They met in The Hague, Netherlands, in April 1915 and issued principles for peace. US President Wilson was receptive. After the war the women reconvened and formed the Women's International League for Peace and Freedom. Their list of principles were a significant input to the formation of the League of Nations, which in turn fed into the United Nations. They remain active in the cause of peace, if widely ignored, including in Australia.

Some in Germany understood that its failure to achieve a quick victory was a disaster. Discreet feelers were put out by back channels, as is the way, exploring the possibility of a negotiated peace. The British and French leaders rejected those approaches out of hand. Whenever there was any public suggestion of a truce the Germans were vilified anew and the cry was for a heroic total victory. The slaughter continued.

A particularly powerful push for peace came in December 1916, through the agency of US President Woodrow Wilson. The potential for peace became widely known, as notes from Germany and the US were published in newspapers around the world. The British elite perceived a dire threat, to their power, that had to be averted at all costs. Foreign Office advisers agreed: even a short-term truce would tip Europe into peace, because once talks had started they could never be broken off, so powerful would be the demand for peace rising from the suffering people of Europe.

> Europe was teetering on the edge, between peace and war. All who sat in the grand high-ceilinged rooms of power knew the unspoken secret: to begin negotiations meant that peace would break out – irresistibly – and the old order would be overwhelmed by the forces of change.[118]

World War I has been called the seminal catastrophe of the twentieth century.[18] Had the fighting stopped there might have been no Russian revolution, no Lenin and Stalin, no punishment of Germany, no Hitler, no World War II with even greater loss of life, no cold war with nuclear confrontation threatening to exterminate all humanity ... . Doubtless we would have found other ways to inflict disaster and misery, but it is plausible they would have been less extreme.

The Russian Bolsheviks negotiated a truce with Germany, on unfavourable terms, and the fighting on the eastern front stopped. The 'Entente' powers (Britain and France mainly) refused to deal with the Bolsheviks because of course socialists were a threat to the power of the elite. Wilson reluctantly brought the US into the War.

Germany slowly weakened, but that only encouraged the elites to continue the slaughter. The German elite lost prestige, and then lost power to socialists and others. The new government was desperate to negotiate a truce, but the Entente refused to deal with them, because that would have boosted the prestige of German socialists, which would in turn encourage socialists in other countries, who would then be a threat. They kept the fighting going until the German socialists lost prestige, for failing to deliver peace, and a new right-wing clique took power.[118] At that point the British and French elites were willing to contemplate a surrender, from people of their own kind.

In Australia the steady, competent and under-rated Andrew Fisher[119] regained government for Labor early in the war, but had to resign because of faltering health. He was replaced as leader and Prime Minister by the volatile and fanatical Billy Hughes, who screeched the 'knock-out blow' cause of the elite, both at home and on visits to England. Hughes' fiery speeches made him a useful tool of the elite. Hughes conducted not one but two bitterly divisive referenda seeking to allow conscripted Australian soldiers to be sent overseas, and lost both. After the second loss he deserted Labor and formed a government with conservatives.

After the German surrender Hughes called for the humiliation of Germany and for requiring Germany to pay heavy reparations to the Entente powers. The folly of this course was attested by economist John Maynard Keynes, among others. Hughes also called for Japan to be excluded from any peace settlement, though it had been involved on the side of the Entente powers. Japan was seeking to be recognised as a power on equal terms with the Western powers. Although his rhetoric tended to the extreme, Hughes spoke for many in Australia, who were in fear of invasion by 'Asian hordes', this having been the motivation for the White Australia policy, the first act of the new Federal parliament in 1901.

So Hughes spoke for the humiliation of Germany and for snubbing (and thereby insulting) Japan. Hughes was far from the only voice in these matters, but he was prominent. Both policies fed the resentments that festered into World War II. The intemperate and racist Hughes thus contributed to Australia being actually threatened, for the only time so far, and by the feared 'Asian hordes'.

Hughes also saved much of the old order in Australia. A major part of this, apart from being on the winning side, was the creation and propagation of the myth that Australia was forged as a nation on the beaches of Gallipoli, that in that slaughter we cast off the convict and colonial 'stains' and took our honourable place among nations. This was an expression of the inferiority complex of colonials craving the approval of the English elite.

Australia had in fact been a leader in social and political innovation over the preceding several decades, broadening the franchise, providing social welfare and ensuring a fairer sharing of the wealth of the new nation[120]. As in any society there were diverse streams, and the new attitudes co-existed with the old attachments to Empire and racism, but Australia until 1914 was an innovative, positive country growing in confidence and forging its own path. The war smashed all that. The wealthy elite re-asserted its power, through Hughes and his overtly conservative successor Stanley Bruce. The colonial and cultural cringes are with us still.

It is clear that war can be promoted. The behaviour of the European powers in the lead up to World War I is proof of that. It is also clear that war can be prolonged, as the English and French elites demonstrated during the same war. The converse is that the chances of war can be reduced. Perhaps war can even be averted, through different choices.

The United Nations has contributed to some reduction in war and conflict, though it is not allowed by the dominant powers to inhibit their own ambitions to violence. It is a positive influence in reducing poverty, suffering and ignorance, though again it is up against larger forces that promote them.

One way in which the UN has been explicitly useful, if only occasionally and marginally, is by providing 'peace-keeping' forces to keep warring parties separated. These forces are usually drawn from the armed forces of several countries who operate under a UN flag and who are commonly enjoined from anything other than immediate self-defence. Such interventions, often in civil conflicts or wars, have provided valuable time and space in which diplomacy may move the parties towards a resolution of some sort. So peace-*keeping* forces can have a positive influence, but they still comprise soldiers equipped for violence, and they address situations that are on the brink of violence.

Peace *making* goes well beyond this. It would seek to address and resolve disputes before they reach the level of violent conflict.

Traditional diplomacy can serve this role, and there are many who are steeped in its intricacies. Although it is usually presented to the world as promoting peace and understanding, diplomacy is very much involved in the power struggles among nations. Too often it is, to reverse the usual characterisation, war pursued by less violent means. It is routine that diplomatic and trade missions placed in other countries also harbour spies.

Diplomacy may keep rivalries and power struggles from boiling up into violence as they otherwise might, but in this sense it deals with symptoms. The underlying problem is the struggle for power over others. So long as that is there, the potential for war will remain. We cannot expect to cure that disease anytime soon, but understanding where it comes from will enhance our abilities to contain it and limit its destructiveness. We need to look deeper.

Perhaps the world is not really so complicated. I have found in life that some of the important things are simple, though not easy. Simple to understand, but not easy to act on.

Bullies gain power from other people. If there are not many people he won't get much power. If there are millions, he may get a great deal of power. His power depends on other people, and on those people allowing him to have their power. If people refuse to do what the bully wants he is powerless. That happened in East Germany in the 1980s. Most people hated the regime, but they did not know how many other people also hated the regime. There came a time when some brave people started to put their heads up, and the more who did the more others realised they were not alone, so they put their heads up too. Soon it was obvious that most people wanted the regime gone and refused to go along with it any more. The regime's power evaporated and it quietly yielded. People started to tear down the Berlin Wall.

A man with great power is, almost always, a fearful man. He is afraid he will lose his power, and then he fears he will no longer be safe. Therefore he devotes great energy to undermining those who might challenge him. He knows his power derives from his society, so he wants it to grow and become stronger, so it will not be threatened by the strong men of other societies. He tells his people they are threatened by another society so that they will rally behind him. A war might break out.

Or perhaps he realises a neighbouring society is wealthy but not very strong, and he can have his people invade it and steal a lot of their wealth. The Etruscans made the mistake of living next to early Rome. They were the first to succumb to Rome's realisation that it might become richer and stronger by invading neighbours. Rome was far from the first city-state to try this, rulers of cities had been trying it out for about 4,000 years already. But the Romans were supremely successful at it for many hundreds of years. We are exhorted to admire and emulate their behaviour.

A person who has been traumatised by the actions of others is an untrusting person. He or she will do whatever they can to keep themselves feeling safe. They might become a control freak, a manipulator or a bully. They might withdraw and refuse to engage in emotional connection, for fear of being emotionally hurt again. Empathy, the social glue, may be deficient or absent. Traumatised people cannot form into a healthy society, because a healthy society requires trust. Trust does not mean leaving yourself completely vulnerable, but it does mean reaching out for real emotional connection. A society with a trust deficiency will lack the confidence and discernment to select emotionally secure leaders. It will respond to demagogues who promise protection and safety, even though such demagogues continually undermine the security of people's lives.

Insecure people are more easily manipulated because they have fewer reserves and less time or ability to connect with their fellows. A recurring ploy, much in evidence in the recent past, is to promise protection and security while imposing policies that are claimed to enhance people's security but actually undermine it. The artificial scarcities of employment and money keep people running on the treadmill in the vain hope of getting off it.

The challenges we have with the behaviour of large groups come back to relationships. Traumatised and neglected people are not good at relationships, so they compensate by seeking to dominate. The most potent way to improve our relationships is to raise emotionally secure children.

There is quite a lot of attention given to what is called *early childhood education*. It is recognised that the quality of a child's experience in its first few years has a big effect on the rest of its life. However the discussion is not really matched with political action and resources, a symptom of our political culture's focus more on crises than on long-term strategies. On the political side of the discussion there is also a strong flavour of raising productive little economic units. This is evident in the term 'education', and by the fact that the subject is often discussed in conjunction with child care provided to get women out of the home and into the labour force, regardless of what each woman wants, what might be a good overall balance of home life and work life, and what might be best for young children.

We could do better by looking at how to raise healthy, whole human beings, and by extending more of our political attention back to infancy and before.

From birth, babies learn to socialise. They don't just eat and sleep, they have periods of alertness during which they look for eye contact and learn facial communication. Many parents naturally engage with their babies at this stage, but not everybody fully realises how interactive babies are. I didn't. Newborns are familiar with their parents' voices and ready for more contact. They engage with eye contact and mutual gazing (for up to a few minutes) and love skin to skin contact. When they have had enough they may turn away or otherwise signify they need a break. This early interaction actually helps their brains to develop.

By alerting parents to the subtle signs, babies can be helped to lay a firm social foundation for their lives. This early socialisation is profoundly important. It is the beginning and enabler of good relationships throughout life, and it is the foundation for other learning. Robin Grille, author of *Parenting for a Peaceful World*[19], goes so far as to argue that a baby who develops strong social attachment as an infant will be incapable of being violent later in life.

Grille brings a deep and well-informed perspective to the subject. His book details not only a great deal of careful study of the needs and behaviours of infants, but also recounts the history of child raising in Western societies over the centuries.

It is sobering to learn that not so many generations ago children were regarded simply as small adults, or as a nuisance, or a heavy burden, particularly in poor families. Child labour, beatings, abandonment, infanticide and sale into servitude were not at all uncommon within families, not just in workhouses. Even in rich families children were handed over to nannies and subjected to strict discipline and little affection.

Such cruel or uncaring experiences traumatise children. Not being well socialised they are unable to form good relationships. A tragic modern example occurred in Romania under the Ceauçescu regime, where orphan children were deliberately deprived of personal affection, apparently so they would have allegiance to the state instead of to parents. Both their social and their intellectual development were severely stunted, and many actually died of emotional neglect. Less extreme experiences still leave children socially and emotionally limited, so they in turn are less able to raise emotionally healthy children. In this way such traumas are passed down the generations. With this perspective, it is not a wonder that Europeans have been so cruel to each other, and then to the rest of the world.

Part of Grille's purpose in recounting such history is to emphasise how much better we do today. Generally, each recent generation has done better than the previous one, so that the inherited trauma is gradually being healed. He says in the first half of the 20th century children were still subjected to fairly strict discipline. Later in the century physical punishment was dropped but, he says, children were still being shamed or emotionally manipulated into 'being good'.

It is now becoming more common for parents to engage respectfully, empathetically and honestly their children rather than laying down rules by one means or another. He calls this the *helping mode*. The idea is to help children's innate abilities, to socialise and to relate well, to develop undistorted by a need to conform. Of course young children still need guidance, but this can be done with clear, strong and respectful boundaries. An important part of children's learning is to respect other people's needs and boundaries. Grille says helping mode interactions are two way and mutually respectful.

Although we do better these days, there are still important lessons for us. The traumas of the wars of the 20th century have not yet been erased. The huge attention in Australia on the centenary of Gallipoli focused heavily on the sacrifice of the young men, but less on how their trauma has come down the generations through disrupted family life. Still less was there a focus on avoiding needless involvement in current wars. Now we are being conditioned to expect another war, one that could be catastrophic.

Grille says[19]

> So much of the past needs to be re-evaluated in terms of collective adaptations to early trauma. Megalomania, sociopathy, and credulous adoration of charismatic leaders are but some of the results of childhood neglect and abuse. Humanity has been split into delinquent leaders and those who are mesmerised by or submissive to their power. ... When we contemplate the horrors of dysfunctional human relations, past and present, we should not say 'this is humanity' but instead 'this is traumatised humanity'. Human madness is the howl of a child with a shattered heart. (p. 95)

We are a strange species. We are much more flexible in how we raise our children than other species. This allows us to be very adaptable, and to undergo rapid social evolution. Unfortunately it also allows ill-informed and misguided practices to become established. The highest priority of every other species on the planet, after immediate survival, is to produce offspring and to give them the best possible start in life. Any species that neglects its offspring won't be around for long.

Giving babies a good start in life begins with parents-to-be, giving them good information on health, on birth choices and on what to expect after baby is born. Health is fairly well covered these days, but birth has become the subject of an unfortunate and rather polarised debate.

Although there is often also emotional support available for parents-to-be and for new parents, these are often different services. However a pilot program has shown the value of consistent support through pregnancy, birth and early parenting. Called *Relaxing into Parenting*[121], the same group of parents and facilitators meet regularly through the whole process. This allows the parents to make friends and share experiences, reassures them they won't be just thrown in the deep end after the birth, and gives them a familiar group with which to share the early stages of parenthood. Often the group continues to meet beyond the time of the formal program.

The health of a pregnant woman and baby is usually monitored by doctors and nurses, but often it is different people who take over after birth. Continuous and consistent support from the same person or people is important for reassuring mothers approaching, during and after birth. A familiar and trusted midwife who attends the whole process can provide such care.

Birthing mums need to choose a birthing situation they are comfortable with. The location might be a hospital, a quiet birthing centre or at home, with backup. The attendants might include a doctor, a midwife or a doula. For low-risk pregnancies the risks are comparable for each situation[122]. Hospitals have backup facilities close at hand, but for many mothers hospitals are less conducive to the birth process. Home is more familiar and reassuring, and backup is routinely available these days, though not quite as immediate. A birthing centre is in between.

In the Netherlands, home birth with a midwife is the default, with doctors and hospitals only involved when indicated. The government also provides help in the home for eight days after the birth: the helper is a qualified nurse who is experienced with newborns and who also does any household things that need doing, so the mother can focus on the newborn. One mother said she couldn't feel anxious because she had support with everything she might be anxious about.

People experienced in natural and gentle birthing know that birthing mothers need most to feel secure and 'unobserved', in the words of Dr.

Michel Odent[123], in other words private and unjudged. If the mother is anxious or afraid, or even if an anxious person is in the room, a shot of adrenalin may shut down the birthing hormones and inhibit the birthing process. If a mother feels observed or uncomfortable her attention may be drawn out of herself and to her surroundings, and again the process may be inhibited.

Unfortunately the medicalised hospital system is not so good at supporting the full range of choices[124]. Often the environment is bright, busy and not very personal. If this reassures the mother, then good, but for many mothers it is intrusive and unsettling. If anxiety slows the birthing process then medical staff, generally not as experienced in the natural birthing process, may begin medical intervention with artificial hormones, pain killers and so on, which further disrupt the delicate natural sequence. This can progress through a cascade of interventions leading to caesarian birth. In Australia the number of caesarian births has risen dramatically to 30-50%, and more in some hospitals. This is well above internationally recommended rates of 10-15%.

The subject of birth is intensely personal. Discussion of options is delicate, because mothers, quite understandably, are not receptive to any implication their choice may not have been the best choice. We all make the best choice we can in every moment of our lives, given what we know at that moment, so this is not to judge anyone's choice. Nevertheless there are real issues that we had best deal with. Unfortunately there are quite a lot of stories of mothers being traumatised by their experience, or of babies in difficulty. This is true of hospital births and of home births. Even more unfortunately, a rancorous debate has broken out in Australia with each side throwing horror stories at the other. This includes senior obstetricians who should know better. The whole thing is being driven by our old familiar devil, fear.

It seems, particularly from the caesarian statistics, that birth has become too medicalised in Australia. It would be healthy to tip the balance back to more natural childbirth. The New Zealand experience is instructive. New Zealand allows mothers a choice of a doctor or a midwife to attend their birthing. To the surprise of some doctors, it turned out a substantial proportion of women prefer midwives. In Australia it is difficult for midwives to operate outside of hospitals because of draconian insurance requirements, among other things, and they may practise in hospitals only within quite restrictive rules dictated by the medical staff.

The individual choices of each mother need to be honoured at the same time as it is made clear there are benefits and risks in any choice. The medical focus tends to be heavily on the physical welfare of the baby, with less attention to the mother's welfare, particularly her emotional well-being. A significant amount of emotional trauma shows up in the months following hospital births. It may be a significant source of postnatal depression, although paradoxically that may tend to disguise its source. Obviously a depressed or disabled mother is not good for the welfare of the baby either.

One of the most potent things we can do in Australia to promote a decent and loving society is to give more consistent support, emotional, professional and financial, to the birth and early years of our children, obviously with much of that support provided to and through their parents.

Most of us did not have the sort of start that Grille and others suggest is possible. As a society we are learning slowly, and sometimes we regress. Our parents did the best they knew how at the time. What to do? Are we condemned to live out our slightly or largely traumatised lives dysfunctionally? Not at all. It is best if we are not traumatised in the first place, and little children are the most adaptable, but we can all heal some of our trauma at any stage of our lives, if we are game to take on the challenge.

Nothing I write here will heal you, at least not directly. This is because the healing process works through our emotions, not our rational minds, in my experience. It is a very personal business, so I will refer to some of my own experience. I did not have a traumatic childhood but my father was emotionally distant and my mother a bit too coddling. There were also incidents that were humiliating, or painful in other ways, as there would be for most people. As a young and middle-aged adult I was emotionally and socially stuck in some ways, because I avoided, consciously or unconsciously, letting myself get into situations that reminded me of those old incidents, or that might trigger those old feelings of humiliation or fear. I was somewhat reserved, somewhat shut down emotionally, but prone to bursts of anger. As I got older I more often recognised times when I got flustered or angry, but usually only after the fact. Looking back on them some hours or days later I would wonder why I hadn't responded more calmly. In retrospect I could see how I might have responded more constructively or reasonably, but the next time I got triggered I would just react again. I could see I was in a pattern but I didn't know how to get out of it.

Through a friend I got myself to some experiential 'personal development' workshops. They sounded like a good thing but getting myself there the first time was hard, I was very fearful. Once there I and everyone were invited through a series of exercises, opportunities to talk openly or small, gentle situations that might recall or trigger old 'stuff'. We were encouraged to emotionally support each other, to be non-judgemental, just to really hear each other.

What I found was that if I could actually allow old, scary feelings to come up and wash through me again then they would peak and subside and my new-found friends would still be there, smiling and supporting, the sun would still be shining outside, the world would still be going along and I had survived. I would not be instantly cured of that particular old fear, but after that it would be less potent. I could think about facing it again, and each time I did its power over me would wane a bit more.

Emotional hangups occur because old fears cause us to shut parts of ourselves away. We don't allow ourselves to go into those old, dark places. We are less than the person we could be. We adopt avoidance behaviours and compensating behaviours. We might become reserved or we might talk a great deal about nothing much, anything to avoid stumbling into that place of fear or humiliation. Such ploys keep us functioning after a fashion, but we may not function well and we may hurt those around us, by withholding or by lashing out, even though we don't really mean to. I used to keep a lid on a lot of my emotions, but they were not to be denied and the pressure would build: every now and then I would be triggered, the lid would blow and I would lash out, verbally. My relationships suffered.

My experience is probably pretty ordinary in our society. Lots of people have such fears, many have had much worse experiences and have to deal with much greater emotional challenges. Some people heal themselves, perhaps with the support of close friends. It is not hard to recognise others who are struggling, stuck as I was in a pattern they don't know how to get out of. They may be rich and powerful or they may be poor and battling. Many seem not to know they are in such a pattern. We all like to think of ourselves as sensible, reasonable, rational, whatever.

The degree to which we are driven by our emotions is probably much greater than we like to admit. On the other hand if you look around our society, or watch the nightly news, you might suspect that our whole society is strongly driven by repressed and unrecognised emotional reactions. Robin Grille's claim that our society suffers from past traumas gains some credibility.

Over a decade or so I attended many of those workshops, first just to experience them and later to be a helper. The power of my old fears gradually lessened. I could tell, from the reactions of others, that I was more pleasant to be around, people more often sought me out. I learnt to be more open with my feelings and preferences, which makes for better relationships. I can still get triggered of course, but less often and less intensely, and I usually recover more quickly. Life is better and I have been in a rewarding relationship now for over a decade.

I would distill two key things out of my experience. One is that *love and fear cannot co-exist*. If I can find the place in me to act out of love, then I can push fear aside and be open with you. If I allow fear to take over and drive me, then I am reactive and cannot be properly loving. What do I mean by 'love' in this context? I mean being willing to trust there is a well-intentioned, vulnerable human being before me: by being open and clear about myself, I hope the other person will feel welcomed rather than threatened, and will respond positively. Often they will, but they may not; what they think of me or say to me does not define who I am. That is for me to do, though that's easy to say and not easy to do. And of course I need to keep myself physically safe, but I do not often encounter a physical threat.

The second key thing is that *we often misunderstand each other*. What you intend me to understand may not be what I think you meant, especially if your words trigger an emotional reaction in me. Then I may think you are belittling me or otherwise verbally attacking me. If I speak my reaction I will probably trigger a reaction in you, a hostile exchange may result and hurtful things may be said that we soon regret.

There are techniques we can use to slow important conversations down so we hear what each other really means. A basic one is called *reflective listening*. You speak, using 'I' statements, in other words just about your experience, not your judgements of anybody else. Then I paraphrase what I think you just said: I reflect back to you. If I don't have it quite right you can clarify. Then I reflect again until you are satisfied I have accurately understood you. Then it is my turn to speak and we reverse roles. It can seem stilted, and it is not easy to do if there is an emotional charge between us, but it saves us from going away angry because of what we *imagine* the other person said, rather than what they really meant.

I would go so far as to say that something like 90% of the misery we human beings suffer (and that is a lot of misery) is inflicted on each other because of misunderstandings. This applies from family and friends all the way up to struggles between nations.

Different approaches may work for different people. The workshops I attended were by the Human Awareness Institute in California, founded by Stan Dale[125], which were also run in Australia for quite a few years. We are not just stuck, we can still change at any age. The personal reward for healing old wounds is a more fulfilling life. The reward awaiting the world is to lessen the hold of fear over our societies, and to reduce the levels of conflict.

We *make* peace by choosing to act from a loving place, so we are not driven by fear.

11

Good growth

... there are many inputs on most farms and many of them are imported. They include vehicles, machinery; a tonne of chemicals ... ; all manner of widgets, including parts, pumps, pipes and other paraphernalia. And fuel. Australia imports 90 per cent of its fuel. You can't put a crop in without fuel. – **Gabrielle Chan**[126]

Nature will just drive it for you. Most of the time, all we've got to do is get out of the bloody way and stop interfering and it'll fix itself.
– **Colin Seis**, quoted by Massy[127]

Catching fish in the south Pacific, processing it in China and selling it frozen in Australian or European supermarkets is crazy. Catching North Sea fish, with heaven knows what pollutants in it, and selling it frozen in Australia while most of us live within 100 km of much bigger and hopefully less polluted oceans is crazy. Exporting and importing the same thing simultaneously is crazy. Such things happen all the time in our modern, globalised food system.

Australia produces vastly more food than we can eat, and a lot of it gets exported. Agriculture is a major export industry, and both the Government and the National Farmers Federation want agricultural exports to rise from $60 billion per year to $100 billion over this decade. It is far from clear this is possible, and even less clear it could be done and still leave us with a viable landscape.

If we think of food production in terms of dollars, price on the shelf, export earnings and ever-rising productivity then we will destroy our productive land. The reason is simple. Productive land is a living system, and it has a certain capacity for things to grow in it. The economy, as presently mismanaged, is supposed to keep growing every year, indefinitely. At some point the land will be over-exploited and its productive capacity will start to fall. If efforts to increase production continue the land will quickly spiral down to low productivity, basically because the soil will be degraded and then removed by wind and water.

All multicellular organisms grow, but they grow only so far and then slow or level off. As their life ends new organisms grow to replace them. The natural living world has been doing this for a billion years, and it resulted in a profusion of species across this abundant planet. That form of growth is healthy, it ensures the continuation of life indefinitely.

An economy that grows by 4% per year will double in about 20 years. In the next 20 years it will double again, and in the next double again, and so on until something gives. If an economy double its present size does not seem outlandish, how about an economy 8 times larger in 60 years, even as we struggle with severe global warming effects that are happening now, with worse already in the pipeline. Growth that repeatedly doubles the size of something over a certain period, also known as exponential growth, is unhealthy. Attempting to maintain exponential growth, beyond a certain point, is crazy.

If some of the cells in your body try to grow exponentially it is called cancer. If a bacterium or virus multiplies exponentially through the human population it is called an epidemic or a plague. If the mouse population keeps doubling in a region of monoculture grain cropping it is called a plague. Exponential growth does occur in living organisms, but beyond a certain point it is pathological, unhealthy.

The financialised economic system we have at this critical point in human history deals in abstractions. Money is an abstraction, and it can be multiplied indefinitely. Mainstream economic theory is an abstraction.

Abstractions have their uses: Newton's 'law' of gravity is an abstraction, but it happens to provide quite accurate guidance about how the world works in many situations, though not at cosmic scales. Abstractions are only helpful if you keep very clear that they are abstractions, and their application to the real world will have definite limits. Unfortunately our economic managers don't understand that. Hence we have economic 'growth' that is very unhealthy for children and other living things.

The productive capacity of land can be raised or lowered, depending on how it is treated. If we treat it badly its capacity will decline. If we treat it well, or use artificial enhancers, its capacity may increase, though not without limit. We have done both in Australia.

Early in European settlement the productivity of the land fell sharply in many areas because the pre-existing system of management by First Australians was disrupted and the systems used by early settlers were not appropriate for Australia. Better systems were gradually worked out, so that settler productivity stabilised and rose, but there was still a long term decline in productivity in many areas. Mechanised farming and, after World War II, chemical farming raised productivity in the better areas but still there was an underlying decline in soil and land quality. Australia's climate fluctuates more than that of Europe, and normal dry spells were called drought. Because the land was commonly managed more for exploiting the good seasons than for weathering the dry seasons, 'drought' often led to soil being exposed to wind and water. Much of our precious top soil has washed or drifted into surrounding oceans and sometimes coated New Zealand's glaciers in dirty brown.

Since WWII productivity has been raised by the application of manufactured chemicals - fertilisers and pesticides. For several decades farmers' incomes were boosted, and the nation's income benefitted from increasing exports of food and fibre. However in recent decades farmers have been going out of business at increasing rates. Several fundamental problems have emerged:

- the use of artificial inputs is addictive;
- pests evolve automatically whereas industrial controls are always playing catch-up, and they are falling further behind;

- farmers are squeezed by inappropriate market forces, and the land suffers;
- long supply lines make our agriculture highly vulnerable to disruption;
- the apparent efficiency of industrial agriculture is due to shifting and hiding costs.

Farmers are often quite conservative in some ways, yet over time Australian farmers have been very willing to adapt, as Gabrielle Chan has portrayed well[126]. What follows is not a critique of farmers, I am from a farming family myself. Farming is always a chancy business, and as well farmers have been struggling with human forces well beyond their control. It may be confronting to face up to difficult problems, but ignoring them is worse.

Central to these problems is that soil is a living system. In a shovelful of healthy soil there may be more living organisms than there are people on Earth. Tens of thousands of subterranean species of invertebrates, nematodes, bacteria and fungi are constantly filtering our water, recycling nutrients and helping to regulate the planet's temperature. Soils are some of the most complex ecosystems on Earth, containing nearly a quarter of the planet's biodiversity[128]. But under monoculture grain crops a toxic soup of insecticides, herbicides and fungicides is wreaking havoc[129].

• ***Pesticides kill soil micro-organisms and*** artificial fertilisers disrupt soil micro-ecologies. The natural soil fertility is thereby disrupted and it may take some time for it to recover. Pesticides may indiscriminately kill herbivorous bugs and their natural predators like spiders, but typically the herbivore populations recover more quickly than predators so they may soon be a worse problem than before.

Because of such dynamic responses to artificial inputs, the inputs may need to be repeated frequently: more fertilisers added and more pesticides applied. In this sense the use of artificial inputs is addictive. Inject the drug once and you're hooked, you have to keep repeating it and it's hard to break the cycle.

Consumer capitalism cultivates addictions. If only you buy the latest device, or beauty treatment, or fancy car you will feel better about yourself. But buying stuff does not fix our self esteem (which they undermine by insinuating that we are ugly and socially inept), so soon you are looking to buy another fix, and they have just the thing for you. The big ag input companies got onto a beauty: apply their fertilisers and pesticides and get a rush, but it soon wears off and you have to buy more. I read quite some time ago that pesticide potency had increased about 30 times since WWII, and the amount applied had increased by 10 times, or perhaps it was the other way around. Either way you need 300 times the potency do deal with the critters, and you are hooked ever more strongly. The cost of pesticides is increasing. Profits of pesticide suppliers are booming, but farmers struggle to make ends meet[126]. Some farmers are breaking the addiction and finding they can do well, but it's not easy.

• ***Biological evolution is driven by natural*** selection. A pesticide will kill many of the target pests, but usually not all. The survivors are less susceptible to the poison and they are the ones that propagate descendants, so the descendants will tend to have lower susceptibility, or, as it is commonly phrased, more resistance. By repeatedly applying the poison and eliminating the more susceptible, the more resistant specimens are left standing. Whether you want to call this *natural* selection is a bit of semantics we don't need to get into here.

This process has become well known in medicine and agriculture. Repeated use of antibiotics has bred *superbugs* that are increasingly resistant, even to the most recent antibiotics. Doctors are warning we may soon enter an era in which we are as helpless against bacterial diseases as our forebears were a century or two ago. The process has been accelerated by the – sorry – insane practice of routinely feeding antibiotics to healthy animals in feedlots, because animals crowded into feedlots are highly susceptible to any disease that might get in.

The same process has occurred with herbicides. Repeated and routine application of glyphosate (*Roundup*) is breeding *superweeds* that are increasingly hard to eliminate. Manufacturers may update their chemicals, but the options for viable poisons are narrowing. Perhaps poisons based on attacking quite different aspects of organisms might be developed, and the day of the superweeds will be deferred for a while longer, but the fundamental dynamic will be the same.

Chemical and pharmaceutical companies are always playing catch-up with nature. The spread of the Covid-19 virus has illustrated the process. As the virus spread, scientists raced to develop vaccines, which they did in remarkably short time. However before the world could be vaccinated the delta variant appeared and spread even faster. Then came the omicron variant, faster again. Anyway vaccine only confers partial resistance, and resistance declines with time.

Here is the essence: the virus is conducting trillions of experiments every hour, as it multiplies within infected people. It may be an extremely rare mutation that makes the virus more infectious, but once that mutation occurs it will tend to spread faster than earlier versions, and soon enough it will be the dominant strain. Pharmaceutical companies cannot anticipate what the next virus variant might be, they have to wait and see, and then see if they can counter it. It is a game of catch-up. In the meantime we hope the next variant does not produce higher mortality.

In nature, predators and prey *co-evolve*. If the wildebeest get a bit faster and a bit smarter about not walking into danger, some of the lions will go hungry. Only the fastest, smartest lions may survive, but then their descendants will do a little better and the wildebeest advantage will shrink. Conversely if the lions get a bit of an edge then they will multiply, fewer wildebeest will avoid being eaten, and only the smartest, fastest wildebeest will survive. If the lions have too much of an edge the wildebeest population may dwindle and then lions will go hungry. It's never a simple one-to-one cause and effect of course, it's all about fine statistical margins, but the effect is to keep the lions and the wildebeest close to a dynamic balance: each is slowly changing but neither gains too much advantage.

So it is with viruses and their hosts, crop munchers and their predators, and the complex, multi-level ecosystems in the soil. If you try to intervene in complex dynamic systems you may provoke an unexpected response. Your insecticide may kill a lot of the crop munchers, but also their predators. Herbivores tend to breed faster than predators, so before long you may have more crop munchers than before, fewer spiders to eat them and a worse problem than when you started. Perhaps you need to think about organic or regenerative systems that retain and take advantage of the natural evolutionary dynamics that are always at work. It is not an easy switch to make though. We'll get to that.

• ***In 2011, Coles and Woolworths conducted*** a milk war. They reduced the price of milk to $1 a litre. Of course they did not just sell the milk at a loss, they also squeezed the dairy farmers to accept less for the milk they supplied. Most small farmers most of the time in Australia operate on a slim margin. The result of the milk war, combined with the deregulation of the milk industry in 2001, was the elimination of 30,000 dairy farms, 75% family-owned, replaced with 7500 farms mostly owned by foreign companies.[130]

In 2017 a dairy farmer named Shane, from Kyogle in NSW, posted an angry video on Facebook[126]. He had just received his milk cheque for the previous month. He calculated he had worked for $2.46 an hour. TV reporters seemed to regard Shane's situation as simply an unfortunate act of nature, showing no curiosity as to why his income was so low. Financiers, most economists and many politicians simply shrug at such examples and imply Shane should find another occupation. But Shane was not receiving a fair price for his production. A fair price would give him and his family a decent living and leave enough so he could properly care for his land.

Coles and Woolworths so dominate their market they can dictate the price they pay to suppliers. To stay in business producers have to cut their own costs to the bone, which means they cannot properly care for their land to sustain its fertility. Effectively, they are forced to mine the nutrients from the soil. As prices are pushed ever lower, even this short-term strategy fails and producers go out of business. At this point the retailers look overseas for cheaper produce.

'*ColesWorth's*' scorched-earth tactics are repeated in every industry they touch[130], where they squeeze suppliers until only a few large and dependent ones are left standing, and if those suppliers fall over then they look for suppliers overseas.

This situation then begs the question of why Coles and Woolworths dominate our retail grocery market. The answer is that *competition eliminates competitors*. Once a firm becomes bigger than most of its rivals, it can undercut the prices of each smaller rival, eliminating them one by one.

A healthy economic system produces wealth, and produces it in a way that can continue indefinitely. Coles and Woolworths are not producing wealth, or rather are not paying for wealth *production*, they are forcing the unsustainable *extraction* of wealth. Wealth is being *extracted* from our soils and from our rural communities and families.

This is what you get if you let competitive markets operate without restraint. The only criterion for survival is to have the lowest price on the retail shelf. To achieve that the retailers off-load costs onto employees, suppliers, the land and the nation. The artificial scarcity of customers keeps the supermarket executives forever scavenging for tiny savings here and there, no matter what the costs to our society.

• ***Examples abound of things produced*** in one part of the world, processed in China and sold somewhere else entirely. Obviously this involves very long supply lines, which is wasteful. It also makes our system vulnerable to disruption, for example by a pandemic, storms, wars, terrorists, international political reprisals or stupid accidents like a giant freighter getting stuck in the Suez Canal for many days.

The quote from Gabrielle Chan that opens this chapter reveals how this vulnerability has been taken to another level. The greater part of our vaunted food production system is dependent on the importation of many inputs, large and small, from pumps to fuel. This means there are many more points at which the system might be disrupted. This is a pretty gob-smacking realisation. Perhaps it's a wonder the system has kept working at all through the pandemic.

As the world becomes more threatening, due to our own folly, we need systems that are more resilient to disruption. This means reducing the length and number of supply lines we depend on. It means having redundancy, so there is more than one source of supplies, more than one expert, more than one firm to do essential things.

Resilience is not compatible with ultra-efficiency of the narrow kind conceived by economists and politicians. William McDonough cites the example of a cherry tree[131]. It does not produce only one or only five flowers and seeds, conserving its energy to grow more 'efficiently'. Cherry trees have learnt through very long experience that reproduction is critical to survival of the species, so it puts a lot of its energy into reproduction. The result is that every tree produces thousands of flowers and seeds. It indulges in a great deal of redundancy in order to maximise the chances of some of its offspring surviving and continuing the species. Furthermore each seed will have a slightly different genetic make-up, ensuring that the tree's offspring will have a better chance of coping with whatever changes the world throws at them.

• ***Although economists claim their abstract theoretical*** markets ensure efficiency, the malfunctioning markets we have in the real world are extremely inefficient. The long supply lines are themselves extremely inefficient in time, fuel and greenhouse gas emissions. A substantial fraction of all food produced is wasted, because some of it is 'imperfect', because of losses in long supply lines and because it fails to sell. Unsold food could at least be composted and returned as nutrients to farms, but much of it is excessively packaged in plastic. The cheapest option (always the preferred option) is to dump the whole toxic mess in land fills.

At the same time many people in the world are still hungry. The clichéd claim that we must improve agricultural productivity so as to 'feed the world' is nonsense. There is plenty of food, but it is in the wrong places, and some people don't have the income to afford it. World hunger will be solved by helping, or allowing, people to produce their own food locally. Very often traditional food production is displaced by 'cheaper' industrial food that undercuts local markets and is unhealthy as well[132]. Industrial agriculture is driven by profit, not by ensuring everyone has enough to eat.

Industrial agriculture appears to be more 'efficient', in dollar terms, only because it shifts many costs onto people, society and the natural world. Many of our small- and medium-sized family farms do not get enough income to properly care for their land and to provide a reasonable income to their owners, so the land is being mined of nutrients and the people are being exploited. Having food processed in China can only work because the Chinese workers are paid a pittance, as are Indian textile workers: they are exploited. The productivity and biodiversity of the natural world is degraded by overly-extractive industrial agriculture and the planet is critically endangered by fossil fuel emissions.

A striking admission of exploitation is recounted by Richard Manning[33]. He interviewed the CEO of Archer Daniels Midland, Dwayne Andreas. ADM is the world's largest grain purchaser and processor, owning all the steps from farm gate to food manufacturer. Facing such an oligopoly, farmers have little choice but to grow what ADM wants, when it wants it, and to accept whatever price ADM offers for their crop. Manning asked why ADM did not just take over the corn farms as well. Andreas replied that it would be illegal for ADM to exploit the farmers to the degree they exploit themselves.

There is a more basic reason not to export large quantities of food, rarely noted. It is that we are exporting nutrients from our soil. Organic systems operate through local recycling. This means food grown here needs to be eaten here. Then the organic 'wastes' from sheep, cows and us can be returned to the soil and the nutrients recycled into the next generation of food. This simple truth cuts across most of Australia's history: we have always exported large quantities of food and fibre and we still do. This will not be changed quickly, but we need to recognise the long-term need. As we help the world to feed itself, and to recycle its own nutrients, so we also can move towards more localised food production and consumption. This will become more challenging as the climate warms and there may be much less surplus to export anyway. It will however be better for employment and local communities. At the same time we could be moving to using native pastures and grains, and grazing native animals, so recovering well-honed local systems of nutrient recycling.

Markets can only work properly if the price of goods covers the *full* cost of production. Our present system shifts and hides many costs, and people and the world are suffering. The market is distorted, some people are making large profits while others struggle, and the system is destroying its own base.

If this seems to imply that food should cost more, that is correct. Does this also mean poor people must go hungry? No, it means poor people should have higher incomes. There is plenty of wealth around, it is just being captured by the very rich through market manipulations of this kind.

Remember how we looked in Chapter 2 at the effect of pushing wages down so the economy slows? If wages are increased, the economy can pick up. The effect of the supermarket chains pushing down the prices they pay suppliers is the same: as suppliers are paid less so the economy slows. We, as a society, can increase the minimum wage so people can afford properly-costed food. Then small farmers will get a better income and they and the land will be healthier. The economy will pick up. The artificial advantage of big agri-business, due to cost shifting, will decline. Absurdly long supply lines can be eliminated and food production can become more localised and the food healthier.

We can adjust the economic system so it functions more as it is supposed to, and it will then better support the localisation many people are struggling to develop[52]. American farmer, writer and philosopher Wendell Berry has written

> I think good farming is a high and difficult art, that it is indispensable, and that it cannot be accomplished except under

> certain conditions. Manifestly, good farming cannot be fostered or maintained under the rule of the presently dominant economic and cultural assumptions ...
>
> ... I am a member, by choice, of a local community. I believe that healthy communities are indispensable, and I know that our communities are disintegrating under the influence of economic assumptions that are accepted without question by both our [political] parties – despite their lip service to various noneconomic 'values.'[133]

The 'high and difficult art' of farming used to be practised more widely, when farming was done mostly as small family operations. Not by all, by any means, but most farmers had some emotional attachment to their land, especially if it had been in their family for several generations, and most did their best to manage it so it retained its fertility. This was not easy in Australia's more erratic climate with soils that lacked key minerals present in European soils. Mixed farming, with grain, pasture and an assortment of animals was common. The results were mixed, but the better farmers did a good job.

As the mechanical and chemical farming fashions took over and then the economy was 'reformed' to privilege finance and short-term profit over everything, the pressure was on to 'get big or get out' and it became harder to care for the land. Despite this, some dogged spirits pursued alternative approaches more supportive of living systems. Permaculture[134], developed by Bill Mollison in Tasmania, was an explicit break from the trend to growing monocultures, and was intrinsically small-scale. People here and abroad explored doing without the poisons that had become pervasive, and developed organic agriculture. As an appreciation of soil structure and complex soil ecosystems of microbiota developed people developed 'no-till' farming. This left the soil structure intact and, most importantly in our dry and erratic climate, avoided exposing bare soil to wind and running water. As damage to the land became more widely appreciated the Landcare movement was developed in the 1980s[135], by farmers, conservationists and governments more enlightened than those of today.

More fundamental shifts also have been underway. The shift away from monocultures has been applied also to pastures and, potentially, to grain and other crops. In Australia this has led to renewed attention to native grasses and other plants, that are adapted to our unique soils and climate and that thrive when the native soil ecologies are allowed to regenerate. A consistent goal among a fairly diverse array of approaches is not only to slow and halt the degradation of land, but to regenerate its natural health. This is now commonly called agro-ecology or *regenerative farming*[127].

One profound re-conception of farming has been underway for some time. The dominant form of Eurasian farming, for millennia, has used monocultures of annual plants and tilling of ground. Richard Manning, the deer hunter we met earlier, calls it *catastrophe agriculture*[33]. If a local catastrophe wipes out the local flora the exposed ground is first colonised by quick-growing annuals. Later, as the area becomes more habitable, perennials will establish and they will eventually dominate.

An advantage of annuals for agriculture is that they all mature at the same time. People would have been harvesting the ancestors of wheat and other grains long before settled agriculture got going, but those grains really came into their own as settlement developed, because they were predictable, storable and divisible. A local strongman boss would know when to send his tax collectors and enforcers out to claim his share of the harvest[46]. Perennials tend to produce for a longer period so they don't suit tax collectors as well.

On the other hand perennials have their own advantages. Australian perennial grains are deep-rooted, which allows them to survive dry periods better. Their deep roots generate deeper soils and store more carbon. The better and deeper soil structure can then store more water[127]. Perennials do not require tilling, which allows soil ecosystems to survive better, especially if artificial pesticides and chemicals are avoided. Australian perennial grasses stay green in summer, providing feed when exotic annuals have withered in the heat and dry.

Efforts to cultivate perennial grains and pastures have been underway for some time. Overseas, Wes Jackson in Kansas has been working since 1976 to recreate diverse prairie-style polycultures of perennial grains, pulses, and oilseed-bearing plants grown in ecologically intensified, diverse crop mixtures[136]. In Australia Charles Massy has surveyed a range of innovative farms, many of which cultivate perennial polycultures as pasture[127]. Author and landholder Bruce Pascoe is actively developing and promoting the cultivation of perennial native food plants that are well adapted to Australia's unique conditions[35,137].

Polycultures are more resilient to pests than monocultures, because pest species cannot become as densely established and predators can survive better and control pests naturally.

Regenerative farming may be the most fundamental approach. The term regenerative agriculture can mean many things, but at its core it aims to increase the number of micro-organisms in the soil, which in turn increases the amount of carbon, water and nutrition in the soil, according to Jamieson Murphy[138]. It features in many of the farms surveyed by Charles Massy[127] and other approaches use at least some of its principles. Massy uses five concepts to explain how it works.

- the solar energy function, focussed on maximising the capture of solar energy by fixing as many plant sugars, via photosynthesis, as possible;
- the water cycle, focussed on the maximisation of water infiltration, storage and recycling in the soil;
- the soil-mineral cycle, focussed on cultivating biologically alive and healthy soils that contain and recycle a rich lode of diverse minerals and chemicals;
- dynamic ecosystems, focussed on maximum biodiversity and health of integrated ecosystems at all levels;
- the human-social aspect, focussed on human agency triggering landscape regeneration by working in harmony with natural systems.

Jamieson Murphy, writing in Farm Online[138], distills five practical principles:

- do not disturb the soil by ploughing or tilling
- maintain cover on the soil, preferably green and growing
- maintain living roots in the soil
- create as much diversity as possible
- integrate animals into the system

Living cover is fundamental because plants are the foundation of the living world and they feed the soil ecology. Deeply penetrating living roots store carbon, maintain soil structure and pass nutrients to the myriad organisms in the soil. For every gram of carbon in the soil there can be eight grams of extra water stored. Diversity promotes resilience both directly and by helping to maintain diverse creatures above the surface that limit pests and provide other services.

Herbivorous animals are important because they close the recycling loop of nutrients. A grazing pattern mimicking African ungulates has been found to work well even with Australian native pastures: the animals are kept in concentrated mobs that are moved frequently, so the pasture is not eaten too far down and it then has extended time to recover and regrow.

Many farmers use a multi- species cover crop that may only be in the ground for eight or nine weeks, before being rolled or crimped to make way for a cash crop. Multi-species cover crops have been found to be three times more water efficient than a monoculture crop, and they draw in three times the amount of carbon[138].

Massy recounts Australian farmers trying many variations of alternative approaches that better mimic natural ecosystems[127]. Switching from chemical-industrial methods may not be easy. You have to go cold turkey on artificial inputs, and it can take some time for the native ecosystem to re-establish. One farmer, Colin Seis in the central west of NSW, made the switch because his place was completely burnt out and all he had was whatever would grow by itself. Even so, farmers are often surprised by how quickly native pastures can re-establish. A commonly repeated refrain is 'You just have to learn to get out of the bloody way'. Yields are not necessarily high at first, but operations can be as profitable or more so because the high cost of inputs is greatly reduced or eliminated.

John Weatherly transformed his property on the NSW southern tablelands over a period of decades, planting trees, allowing native systems to re-establish and attracting many birds and other creatures large and small into a highly bio-diverse and resilient landscape. The result was that the carrying capacity (of cattle) nearly doubled, even though twenty percent of the land was tree-covered. Among the many benefits were increased soil protection, reduced salinity, enhanced habitat, natural weed control, increased livestock forage and more nutrient recycling[127].

Such a brief sampling of Massy's book *Call of the Reed Warbler*[127] cannot do it justice. It is a large book rich with information, both general information and the specifics of many particular locations. If you want information of any depth and breadth you need to read it.

Substantial yields from regenerative farming are not to be discounted, as soil fertility can continue to build over a long period. One of the longest trials comparing organic farming with conventional agriculture has run at the Rodale Institute in Pennsylvania for more than 30 years[139]. They found over the first few years organic yields were lower than conventional yields, but then the build-up of soil organic matter and quality raised the organic yields to equal or exceed the conventional yields. On all significant criteria, organic did better over the longer term. Not only can organic yields match conventional yields, but they are better in years of drought. They build rather than deplete soil organic matter, and so are sustainable. Their organic farming uses 45% less energy, is more efficient and produces 30% less greenhouse gas. Crucially, because their inputs are fewer and less expensive, organic farming systems are more profitable than conventional.

A study in Iowa comparing yields of corn and soybeans, two of the USA's principal crops, found results comparable to the Rodale study. K. Delate reported in 2007 that yields from organic methods equalled or exceeded yields from conventional methods[140]. They found organic soils cycle nutrients more efficiently, making them available when and where the plants need them. Profitability was also greater, and soil quality improved steadily through the nine-year organic trials.

Another survey in 2007 showed that organic farming methods in developed countries consistently produce yields similar to conventional methods[141]. A key input is to use *green manures,* meaning nitrogen-fixing cover plants that are ploughed under. The study found ample nitrogen was being supplied this way. A different study in 2007 showed that artificial nitrogen fertilisers are commonly applied excessively, and this actually depletes soil carbon and degrades soil fertility, as well as creating marine dead zones where rivers run out to sea[142].

Such results set a benchmark for industrial and non-industrial systems of farming, of which there are many variations. Rodale's 30-year report, in 2015, gives clear messages:

> The key to sustainable agriculture is healthy soil, since this is the foundation for present and future growth. Organic farming is far

superior to conventional systems when it comes to building, maintaining and replenishing the health of the soil. For *soil health* alone, organic agriculture is more sustainable than conventional. When one also considers *yields, economic viability, energy usage, and human health,* it's clear that organic farming is sustainable, while current conventional practices are not.[139]

European settlers have never come fully to grips with the role of fire in Australia. Disastrous fires have been regular events through our history as settlers, with the occasional catastrophe. There have been many enquiries and many reports, some with clear and strong recommendations. Most of the advice has been ignored.

The Black Summer fires, from August 2019 to February 2020, were of a different order. More people have woken up to the message of those fires, but that includes few politicians it seems. The message is that our forests and woodlands will be degraded and destroyed as global warming inevitably causes more fires on that scale - or even worse. Our farmlands will be increasingly hazardous places to be through bad summers, and that land also will be degraded, not to mention the destruction of stock, homes, infrastructure and small towns.

You can go through the numbers, but they don't mean much on their own: 10 million or 20 million hectares burnt, depending on who's counting. Look at a map and you see a substantial fraction of the eastern forested highlands and escarpment was burnt, perhaps 20% of temperate and sub-tropical forests. It takes hours to drive through the larger burn zones. Do it, and grieve.

Nearly two years later there is green and there are birds, but much of the green is epicormic growth on tree trunks and fast-growing ground cover that is very different from the old forest understory. Those forests would take a century or more to recover to mature forests. The areas burnt are so huge there must be local extinctions, because they can't be reseeded and repopulated from a few kilometres away, the nearest unburnt similar forest may be tens of kilometres away. If it burns again within the next couple of decades, as is likely, there will be permanent losses.

Large areas of former mountain ash forest in Victoria never recovered from the 1939 fires[143]. Mountain ash actually depend on fire every few centuries to open their tough seeds and begin a new generation, but the 1939 fires were so intense they destroyed the seeds along with everything else.

There is growing recognition, among those with some direct interest in the landscape, that we need to learn from First Australians, who practised regular, small-scale mosaic burning as part of their management of Country. The burning, rather more sophisticated than might be implied by the term 'fire-stick farming', had multiple purposes, including arranging the mix of pastures and woodlands and the mix of plant and animal species. Limiting the density and extent of 'fuel' that would carry a big fire was but one intended result.

There is growing interest in such *cultural burning* – having it done in small areas of woodland or forest, and learning how to do it. Learning how to do it well is no small order. First Australians had, and many still have, intimate knowledge of their patch of Country: every species, their seasonality, their susceptibility to fire and so on[144]. Burns must be done in the right season and the right weather conditions[66]. The knowledge involved is highly localised, different for every place.

The European approach to land is very different. For a start we insist on dividing farmland up into small rectangles, separated by fences commonly with wooden, combustible posts. The rectangles often have little relationship with the biota that were there before, or even with watersheds, a fundamental natural division of landscape. Forests are divided more coarsely, but still with only crude reference to biota and landscape. The practices of 'fuel reduction burning' and forest management more generally, and the cultures of agencies and firefighting organisations are obviously far from the First Australians' approaches. This is not a condemnation, simply a recognition that, for all their good work and with whatever good intention, learning and practising some of the art of cultural burning will not be easy.

Some state governments have made some moves to encourage better management and burning practices, but on the scale of what is required they are small. Governments, of course, are based in cities and their attention is dominated by city interests, not to mention internal power struggles, petty partisan point scoring, abstract ideologies and belief systems, covert corruption and the systemic corruption of serving the interests of big donors to the old parties. There are serious moves to replace the old parties with Independent representatives who will actually focus on the interests of electorates and the country. May it come to pass, and may we have governments that recognise the parlous situation of the land and the planet and act as if that matters.

On the other hand decades of ignorant management have taken a heavy toll. New South Wales substantially cut the number of rangers managing its National Parks a few years ago. A friend who had been working a nearby Park for many years was induced to retire, and the work was covered by more distant rangers lacking his intimate local knowledge. When the Black Summer fires came he saved his own small place but his valuable knowledge was not called upon because he was no longer an employee. The managerialist, city-based, cost-cutting mentality is entirely incompatible with caring for our landscape.

Overall there is a lack of interest and imagination. To really make a difference we would have to change some basic things, but our present politicians are only interested in tinkering.

For example, when fire roared out of the hills and into Canberra in 2003 it destroyed 500 homes. It was obvious, if not much remarked, that golf courses and other playing fields stopped the fire. What if we put a greenbelt all along the western side of the city? It could include golf courses, playing fields, parkland and whatever other uses people think of. When next a big fire roars in, which could be in a few decades or in the next dry summer (the previous big fire was in the 1960s), it would be stopped or greatly diminished. Maintenance of the green belt would be a cost to the city, and sports people might have to travel a bit further than previously. Is that a very big price to pay for avoiding the terror and destruction of another big fire?

It is disappointing to read that new suburbs are being built next to woodland with no buffer zone. The local government is contemplating adding many more suburbs on the western side where they would be even more vulnerable, though this possibility is only in the exploration stage.

As the stricken forests of Eastern Australia slowly recover, we could create broad bands through them in which trees and undergrowth are kept much thinner and fire would travel much less catastrophically. A network of bands a kilometre or two wide would break up the flammable forest and improve the chances of actually containing a big fire. It would be a step towards cultural burning, which could be taught in parallel. This seems like a rather obvious strategy at least to consider and trial, but I have seen no such suggestion.

Greg Mullins, former fire chief and member of the Climate Council, asked in an online discussion, in December 2021, 'Are we any safer'? Early in 2019 Mullins organised a group of retired fire chiefs and requested a meeting with the Prime Minister to discuss what they perceived as an extremely dangerous approaching fire season. They reiterated the request several times but the PM never responded. The fire season was even worse than they feared, and firefighters did not have the air tankers and other equipment and organisation they were advocating. Even as the catastrophe progressed the PM refused to respond, except with the notorious line delivered from his holiday in Hawaii 'I don't hold a hose, mate.' Granted Scott Morrison may be our most ineffectual, disconnected Prime Minister ever, this is still an astounding level of apathy. We are no safer.

This chapter is about possibility, as is the whole book. It is not a detailed instruction manual, and the difficulty of the challenges involved is recognised. Yet if we are to continue to live in this wide, brown land we simply must stop degrading its soils and start regenerating them. We must stop destroying the bush, whether it is to graze yet more exotic beasts for export earnings, to grow cotton with stolen water and multiple poisons, or to build yet more sprawling, unsustainable suburbs. We must learn to manage the forests, the woodlands, the farmlands and the rangelands so they can regenerate.

Regeneration means healthy soils with rich microbiota, soils that naturally hold much more carbon and water than most do now. Regeneration means biodiversity in crops and pastures, and biodiversity in nearby bushland that is preserved, healthy and regarded as an integral part of a farm. Regeneration means restored biodiversity in semi-arid and arid lands, in the great, wet forests of the east and south and in everything in between.

There is no time left, we must start rapidly learning and doing what it takes. That may seem like a huge task, yet there are steps that can be taken quickly that will get us well on the way. Just ceasing to senselessly 'clear' bushland, ceasing to subsidise unhealthy and destructive practices like feedlots, ceasing to let big financial firms, many foreign, run our land for quick (and brief) profit rather than for health would already make a difference.

Promoting the learning and adoption of practices that are already regenerating land might quickly accelerate as its benefits become obvious. Instead of methane-emitting cattle and sheep we could be learning to harvest kangaroos and emus, whose meat is lean and healthy and to which the land is well adapted. We could pick up on fledgeling efforts to grow and harvest native grains that are highly nutritious and well adapted, so they do not require fertilisers and pesticides[137]. Any such development will be best done by First Australians, but in any case their intellectual property would need to be recognised and properly compensated.

We can live well without destroying our life support system.

How else can it be?

12

Cycling

At Interface, we are on a quest to become the first sustainable corporation in the world, and then we want to keep going and become the first restorative company. . . . ultimately, I believe we have to learn to operate off current income the way a forest does.

– Ray C. Anderson[145]

Increasing energy end-use efficiency ... is generally the largest, least expensive, most benign, most quickly deployable, least visible, least understood, and most neglected way to provide energy services.

– Amory Lovins[146]

We saw in Chapter 3 that the living world produces no persistent toxins and recycles all materials. It also lives off energy income, from sun, wind and water, and not from ancient energy capital, in the form of fossil fuels. As we are part of the living world, we must return to living as the rest of the living world does, if we are to have an indefinite future. The prospect of 'renewable' energy is well along, though still obstructed by those captive to old ways, and though we can still learn to use it less wastefully. The other requirements, recycling and no toxins, are less well appreciated.

From the perspective of the ways of the past couple of centuries these will seem to be immense challenges, if not impossibilities. Even if such things could be done, how could we get the modern industrial system to do them? What kind of draconian regulation and enforcement would be required?

As with other changes surveyed already, there are people already doing what is needed, or at least making serious progress in the right direction. Our system is actually very wasteful in important ways, and that is both challenge and opportunity. Eliminating waste and hidden costs, and properly pricing products, might get us a long way towards what we want. Then a few key changes of perspective and requirement can do much to move us further along. Rather than brute, retroactive regulation by centralised bureaucracies, both socialist and capitalist, we look for the points in the system where a judicious intervention can trigger a major shift in priorities and practice.

Interface Inc. is a large carpet manufacturer. In 1994 the CEO of Interface, the late Ray Anderson, had an epiphany while reading Paul Hawken's book *The Ecology of Commerce*[147]. Anderson in 2010 recounted how he decided he wanted to transform his company from an Earth degrader to an Earth restorer[148]. His most far-reaching change was to switch from *selling a product* (carpet tiles) to *providing a service* (floor covering). In other words, rather than simply selling and installing office carpet, Interface undertakes to maintain attractive floor coverings as a continuing service.

In adopting this role, Interface *reversed its own incentives*. Before the change, its profit was proportional to the amount of carpet it sold. Not only that, there was an incentive to make the carpet as cheaply as possible so it would need replacing as often as possible. After the change, its incentive was to make the carpet as durable as possible because Interface, not the customer, was paying for the replacement of worn carpet.

Having placed on itself the requirement for its carpet to be durable, Interface developed new synthetic materials that were not only more durable but more readily recyclable, and redesigned its carpets' fabrication so its materials were more easily separable. It found it could then recycle its materials more cheaply than buying more petroleum products extracted from the Earth. It developed non-toxic dyes that also turned out to be cheaper, so a source of serious chemical pollution was eliminated.

How much did these planet-saving, warm-fuzzy-inducing good works cost? Less than nothing. Manufacturing costs were significantly reduced and margins increased. In fact Interface prospered. Four years after it began this quest in 1994, Interface's revenues had doubled, its employment had nearly doubled and its profits had tripled. In 1999 it was a billion-dollar company with manufacturing facilities in seven countries. By the early 2000s it was selling more than 40 percent of all the carpet tile used in commercial buildings.

Interface intends to go much further. It aspires to eliminate all waste, to use only the power of the sun, and even to mine old waste landfills for the millions of tons of carpet fibre previously dumped there.

By offering an end-use *service*, attractively covered floors, rather than a product, carpet, Interface took upon itself the imperative to improve durability and reduce the quantity of materials it extracted from the Earth. Our whole system at present is geared to maximise material throughput, in other words to maximise material wastes. Through creative shifts in incentives, of the kind Interface has demonstrated, our system can incorporate the imperative to minimise wastes and toxins.

We can, if we are smart, harness markets to help us to live healthy lives in a healthy society and a healthy biosphere. Why would we want to do anything else?

To quote Ray Anderson again:

> We look forward to the day when our factories have no smokestacks and no effluents. If successful, we'll spend the rest of our days harvesting yesteryear's carpets, recycling old petrochemicals into new materials, and converting sunlight into energy. There will be zero scrap going into landfills and zero emissions into the ecosystem. Literally, it is a company that will grow by cleaning up the world, not by polluting or degrading it.

The notion of an industrial ecosystem is very poorly appreciated in Australian policy circles. Firms are not isolated, they are part of a dense network of suppliers, customers, banks and so on. Innovations depend on the conjunction of key products and ideas that may be very specific to a particular place and time. Policy should be to cultivate the ecosystem, instead of the present crude conception of isolated firms responding only to price signals. Such ideas were elaborated by Hawken and others in 1999[149].

Closely related is the potential for a recycling industrial system. Firms may recycle their own products, as does Interface Carpet, but the greater potential is to recycle each other's outputs, as occurs in natural ecosystems that recycle 100% of their materials. In *Cradle to Cradle,* McDonough and Braungart advocate moving to a near-100% industrial recycling system[131]. A key facilitator is to design products so they can be readily reborn after their useful life.

There is the prospect of an industrial system in which most materials are recycled and reused indefinitely (not just once), either through the industrial system or through the organic world. Architect and designer William McDonough calls this movement the *Second Industrial Revolution.*

If all materials are to be recycled then there must be no waste, no pollution and limited use of non-renewable materials. Since the industrial revolution, our industrial system has been mainly a once-through system: dig up, manufacture, use, dump. Traditional economies and the biosphere do not function in this way, and we need to transform our industrial systems so they emulate the biosphere.

In order to achieve total recycling, design must take account, from the beginning, of the need to recycle components and materials. The engineering must be more than *cradle to grave,* it must be *cradle to cradle,* as McDonough and Braungart put it[131]. In other words, products must be designed with a view to how they will be reborn after they have worn out. Every component must be recyclable or reusable. Design should permit disassembly to be easy and inexpensive. Toxic materials should be totally recoverable, or ultimately designed out of a product. Return of old products to manufacturers will have to become as routine as distribution of new products is now.

Most of these things have been done commercially to some degree for some time. Even in the 1990s BMW in Germany was redesigning its vehicles for easier disassembly. By 2002, over 90% of components in German-manufactured cars were required to be reclaimed by manufacturers. Parts are bar-coded to identify type of materials and instructions on reuse. The numbers of component materials and plastics is being reduced for easier separation and remanufacture. The aim is 100% reusability. In Japan, legislation required all parts of durable goods eventually to be labelled to indicate their recyclability and manufacturers were required to establish resource recovery centres. In response, Japanese companies were redesigning products, using recycled and recyclable materials and designing for ease of disassembly. Matsushita's washing machines could be disassembled with a single screwdriver. An additional incentive to German and Japanese citizens is that tipping fees at landfills average ten times higher than in the U.S., where they are only about $30 per ton.[149]

Australian cities are very inefficient in every respect - greenhouse emissions, people's time, amenity, cost. The general principles for building a smart, pleasant, efficient city have been known for a good while, and are being improved all the time[150], but we make very little use of them. This seems to be due to a combination of ideology, lack of ambition, the resulting ignorance, lack of coordination among levels of government, and our combative political system, in which each side tries to dismantle what the other has been doing.

A key principle is to mix the main uses within neighbourhoods. As William McDonough puts it, *transportation is a symptom of being in the wrong place.*[131] We can, with better design, arrange our lives so usually we don't have far to go.

If there are transport nodes, housing, shops, entertainment, offices and other businesses all close together, then people need to travel less and they can even walk to many of their activities. Housing might be medium density, but if it is interspersed with parks, shops and entertainment then residents can have much of the best of our current city and suburban duality. If there is a good public transport system, then longer journeys through the city can still be accomplished easily, comfortably and efficiently.

The inner parts of Melbourne still provide much of this amenity, with tramlines and suburban train stations within walking distance, plenty of park space and medium density housing, although much of the housing stock is old and not very efficient.

Melbourne was one of the few cities in Australia and North America to retain its tram system in the face of a deliberate campaign by the automotive industry to buy public transport systems, run them down and then close them down. This set in motion the leapfrogging process James Kunstler has called *suburban buildout,* in which people move progressively further away from a city centre in search of a pleasant hideaway.[151] One would think that after a century we might have noticed it doesn't work. Instead we have the insanity of people driving for two hours or more every day through congested, inefficient and unhealthy traffic. As complaints rise, the reflexive response of authority is to bulldoze or tunnel more roads through the mess, but that only perpetuates the process.

Many cities in Europe have been showing us a better way for a long time, but our politicians are oblivious to most things beyond our shores. The pandemic might finally be jolting us out of the folly of moving tides of people every day from a wide radius into a small, congested city centre and then dispersing them back at night for an abbreviated time with their family.

There are plenty of examples from around the world, but one of the more striking comes from the regional Brazilian city of Curitiba. It is not a rich city by our standards. A carefully integrated city plan was implemented in the 1970s involving development along main axes with a bus system running on central dedicated roadways. Disruption of existing buildings along narrow streets in the city centre was minimised by using three parallel pre-existing streets, the inner one as an express bus route and the outer ones for one-way private traffic. Both commercial and residential development was encouraged along the city axes.

The benefits of foresight were dramatic in Curitiba's case because the city's population tripled to 1.6 million (over 2 million counting surrounds) and ridership on the bus system grew from 50,000 in 1974 to 800,000 passengers per day by 1996. About 75% of the population uses the system each day. Innovations in the bus system itself have been important contributors to its success. These include the dedicated roadways, enclosed 'tube stations' that function like train stations, simplifying ticketing and speeding loading and unloading, and the use of articulated and bi-articulated buses. The system has about four times the throughput of conventional bus systems. Express bus lanes carry peak loads of 20,000 passengers each per hour, similar to a subway.

The capital cost of Curitiba's bus system was more than 100-fold lower than an underground rail system would have been, and about 10 times lower than conventional surface rail. Fares are very low: a flat 20 pence-equivalent (about $US0.45) over the whole city in 1996, but the system still paid for itself. The city provides the infrastructure and the buses are run by private companies. The private operators are paid per kilometre served, rather than per passenger carried, which maximises coverage of the city and convenience for passengers.

Other benefits of Curitiba's bus system are the cleanest ambient air in any Brazilian city, 30% lower petrol consumption per capita and the lowest car drivership despite the highest car ownership in Brazil, and a large amount of open space (52 sq m per capita). The latter is also due to the broader integrated city plan, which involves zoning, flood control, welfare, education and an innovative combination of trash collection, recycling and nutritional assistance in poorer neighbourhoods.[152]

A feature of Curitiba's planning, and a principal ingredient in its success, has been the major effort to involve the populace and gain their trust and support. There were major efforts to explain the benefits of integrated planning and of environmental compatibility, starting with school programs. The progress of programs is regularly monitored. Mistakes are identified and corrected. Information and government services are readily available through conveniently located 'shopfronts', hotlines and other services.

Curitiba shows how imaginative planning, that actively involves the populace, and an imaginative approach to integrating city functions spreads benefits beyond those immediately affected and through the broader community[153]. It all came about through the imagination and initiative of one man, Jaime Lerner, who got himself elected mayor back in 1971.[154] If they can do it, we certainly can.

Our sprawling cities are rather different from Curitiba, and we won't shift them into a better mode any time soon, it will be a work of generations, but Curitiba illustrates what good design can accomplish. If we take advantage of available expertise, for example at Curtin University[150], we can make the new parts of our cities more sensible, compact and liveable. If we did that, more of us could *cycle* to work.

Energy efficiency - the most neglected, quickest, and possibly cheapest option still. Even though renewable electricity with low greenhouse gas emissions has become cheaper than other forms of energy, it still makes sense not to waste it, so we don't need to build as much generation capacity.

Household appliances are more energy efficient than they used to be. Today we have an energy star rating system on fridges and washing machines, thanks to people who campaigned to improve the designs.[152]

Australian houses have been described as 'glorified tents'. There are more deaths from cold in Australia than in Sweden, because many older houses do such a poor job of keeping occupants warm in our relatively mild winters[155]. It is cheaper for builders to leave out insulation, to not take the trouble to tightly seal the structure and to not worry about passive solar design features. Builders don't have to pay the heating bills, so they have a perverse incentive to build wasteful buildings. Regulations were required to overcome this market failure. We have a star system to rate the energy efficiency of houses, and some requirements that new houses have to meet prescribed standards. As a result our heating and cooling bills are smaller, for only a modest extra investment. Still, our houses fall well short of the possible, partly because the star system is a box-ticking exercise rather than requiring the building's features to integrate well and achieve actual performance benchmarks.

Back in the 1990s, Amory Lovins estimated that poor building design in the US had resulted in the installation of about *$1 trillion-worth* of unnecessary air-conditioning equipment[152]. This figure was based on the estimate that buildings could readily save 80-90% of their cooling costs for little or no extra capital cost, just by using design features that had been shown in practice to be effective. Lovins found that perverse incentives commonly apply to those who conceive, approve, finance, design, build, commission, operate, maintain, sell, lease and renovate buildings. Wasteful buildings are more profitable for them all. Regulation is a crude counter. A better solution is to write energy efficiency into the contract in the first place, with the professionals' fees dependent on the building's actual performance meeting agreed criteria.

Even greater benefits from thoughtfully integrated design can be achieved by considering the people who use a building. A lighting retrofit in a mail-sorting office not only saved energy, but improved employees' view of what they were doing and reduced distracting and fatiguing noise. Typically about 6 times as much is spent on the people occupying a building as is spent on the building itself, expressed as rental cost. Energy costs are even less, only about 1% of people costs. Energy savings are usually worthwhile investments by themselves. However improvements in the work environment have been found to improve employee productivity by 6-16%, which means that the financial benefit is at least ten times the direct savings in energy costs. A 1% improvement in employee productivity would cover the entire energy cost, and a 16% improvement would cover the rent.[149]

Retrofitting old buildings has more benefits than may at first appear. When the life-cycle of a building is considered, a great deal of energy and greenhouse gas emissions can be saved by re-using old buildings that already 'embody' a lot of energy. Even though a new building may be more efficient than a retrofitted old building, the large initial energy cost of knocking the old one down and building a new one may not be made up for decades, anything from 10 to 80 years according to one estimate.[156]

There has been considerable progress over the past couple of decades in finding affordable ways to reduce household energy use, and there is a large literature out there. Just one example is the use of mud brick or rammed earth construction, which is usually cheap, uses local materials, is easy to build and can be made very energy-efficient.[157]

Zero-energy houses are being built, for a cost comparable to a conventional Western house. The concept is being extended so they require no water supply, process their own wastes and even grow food indoors through severe winters.[158] Such houses may have a different aesthetic, but they can also be more attractive than your average tract house. A consistent theme of people who live in high-efficiency houses is that they are more pleasant to be in, because they have more even temperatures without hotspots and coldspots, and the well-directed natural lighting is more pleasant. The concepts are being adapted further to dramatically reduce the cost so they will be within reach of third-world people.

If we require manufacturers to take back their products at the end of the products' life then their incentive is to make the products durable, easy to repair, and easy to recycle. Interface carpet has shown the way. Private firms *can* be very adaptable, if they have no alternative. They would soon have the systems in place to accomplish the change.

Good design, of appliances, houses or cities, makes life more comfortable and saves money as well. We can be more comfortable, save money and save the planet all at the same time. The flip side of that is that we are being forced to pay extra so we can trash the planet.

13

Our place

We ought to be angry, with a deep and determined anger, that a country as rich and skilled as ours should be producing so much inequality, so much poverty, so much that is shoddy and substandard.
– **Gough Whitlam**, 1972 election speech, quoted by Elizabeth Reid[159]

Whitlam's words, from 1972, apply even more strongly to Australia today. We ought not only to be angry, but ashamed of our present condition. Not only have we failed to progress, we have gone backwards. It is a major failure of governance. It reflects badly on all governments since, without exception, though more on some than others. It is a measure of the folly of the ideas by which we have been misgoverned.

The difference between then and now is that Whitlam had a vision large enough to actually change our society, and change it for the better according to the ideas developed here. Now there is no vision worth mentioning, certainly no vision that is anywhere near big enough to address our dire situation.

It's true the Whitlam Government was accused of incompetence, even of personal immorality. This is not to say there were not mistakes and questionable actions, but its record is decidedly less disastrous in the cooler hindsight of the present, as discussed in previous chapters. And its alleged offences are quite overshadowed by the irresponsibility, incompetence, corruption, irregularity and disregard for the law of the Morrison Government in particular.

What kind of society are we that imprisons ten-year-olds? That indefinitely imprisons innocent families, people who have sought shelter with us? What kind of government seeks a legal ruling that it owes no duty of care to our children? Why do we allow some people to distort our social conversations, to create division for their own profit and power? What kind of system creates widespread homelessness in a wealthy society?

The exclusive promotion of selfish competition has been an economic failure and a social disaster. Competition and cooperation need to be kept in a healthy balance. If people are not paid decent wages they have less to spend, and the economy falters. On the other hand the wealthy channel much of their excess wealth into speculation, rather than into productive enterprise. The result is soaring inequality and a faltering economy.

The world's business model is broken. Unfettered financial markets supercharge anarchy and greed. If we don't soon resume a proper place in the natural world, that world will brutally force us into a much more difficult state. The natural living world is our life support system. If it sickens, we sicken. If it dies, we die.

Some indigenous Australians I know say, paraphrasing, 'You were born here, so you're part of this land too, that's just how it works.' Others say 'We're not going away. You're not going away. Let's walk together into the future'.

Walking together implies mutual respect. We non-indigenous people can choose to respect people of an ancient and rich culture, people who carry, still, a great deal of wisdom, and whose accumulated cultural experience has valuable lessons for all of us. It does require of us that we acknowledge the violent dispossession our forebears inflicted. The reconciliation required is between we non-indigenous settlers and our own history. It is not about guilt, it is about acknowledging that the land and advantages we enjoy today were bought at the cost of a holocaust inflicted on the people who were already here. That applies to every non-indigenous person in the country, whether they arrived yesterday or their forebears arrived on the First Fleet. We are living on stolen land, and sovereignty was never ceded by the First Australians. If we acknowledge that, then they will be able to respect us, if they choose, and we can stand with them with a full heart.

First Australians have said, in the Uluru Statement from the Heart, 'We invite you to walk with us in a movement of the Australian people for a better future'. This is an act of the greatest generosity, after all the horrors they have endured. Are we ready to meet their generosity with our respect?

Are we ready also to respect the land we are part of, more than two hundred and fifty years after 'Jimmy Cook' was observed sailing off the east coast and more than two hundred and thirty years after the first European boat people arrived to settle? Most Australians still cluster on the edge of the continent. Our cities have been allowed to grow so large and so sprawling it is not so easy for most of us to directly and regularly experience the land we live in. Yet we all know it is different from other lands. We all know it has unique and remarkable flora and fauna. Even in the big cities we learnt first hand in the Black Summer of 2019-20 and the freak floods of 2022, if we did not know already, that it is a wilful land of flood and fire.

Our settler forebears feared this land, so different from what they were used to. They tried to transform it to be like 'home'. They made big changes, but only some of the changes worked, and the character of the land is still stubbornly there, pushing up through the pavements we lay and the foreign landscapes we impose.

If we choose to respect First Australians then we will ask them what they need, and work with them as they figure out how they want to be. If we choose to respect the land then we will listen to it and closely observe it so we learn what it needs. We will then be able to work with it so we can live as part of it. Some people are well down that path, and they have important news for us.

If we choose to respect First Australians and the land can we, the non-indigenous, choose to respect each other? Can we ask each other what we need and what we want? Can we *listen* to each other so we actually hear? Shut up and just listen?

There is a process that has been called Kitchen Table Conversations, though I would rather call it Listening Circles. A dozen or so people, no more, gather around a kitchen table or other quiet, undistracted place. Each person in turn simply speaks what they want – from the local community, from their society, whatever requires a collective will and agreement to bring about. The point is not to debate. The point is simply to hear what we each *really* want. It is common for people to discover they want many of the same things.

We are so much in the habit of arguing, in our culture, that it can take a conscious effort to stop mentally lining up counter-arguments to what another person is saying, so our minds are free to just hear them. If, when we do that, we discover that underneath it we all want a lot of the same things, does that mean most of the arguing we do is pointless? Perhaps we don't have to be so acrimonious. Perhaps the tribes we divide ourselves into are not really necessary, and are obstructive and harmful.

The particular version of listening called Kitchen Table Conversations originated in Victoria in the 1990s in response to draconian actions by the State Government[160]. It was used by *Voices for Indi* in the rural seat of Indi[75] in the lead up to the 2013 Federal election and resulted in the unexpected win of Independent Cathy McGowan. She was re-elected in 2016 and her successor Independent, Helen Haines, was elected in 2019 and again in 2022. Independent Zali Steggal famously unseated a former Prime Minister in the 2019 election, using the KTC process to build support.

Similar organisations sprang up in many electorates and at least six more were successful in the 2022 election. There was a distinct possibility that Labor would not achieve a majority, in which case the Independents could wield a lot of influence. As it turned out Labor has a slim majority of two, but it will still need to be considerate of the Independents.

Politics need not be conducted in the old adversarial way. The old way has become more and more superficial, divisive and toxic, and the old parties more corrupted by special interests. The *Voices* movement is showing that much of the political conflict is unnecessary, and that we can deal with each other through respectful listening and then calmly working towards a mutually acceptable path forward. That is how candidates are chosen in the KTC process, and many political issues can be addressed in the same way.

The group *Australia ReMade*[161] has used an approach comparable to KTCs in a survey of attitudes extending right across the country, not just in a single electorate[162]. They used interviews and focus groups to pose two questions to a selected diversity of people. First, what do you want available to you and your communities? Second, forgetting who pays for it, who do you think should provide this? People consistently named housing, healthcare, education, jobs, access to nature and access to the internet as basic priorities. Many other things were also named, from good footpaths through emergency housing and getting the money out of politics to a sense of community identity.

But then people would pause, reflect, and go deeper. Out of those deeper reflections came three core wishes:

The opportunity to **connect** with each other and with place;

The ability to **care** and be cared for;

Pathways to **contribute**, locally and nationally, to who we are as communities and as a nation.

Connecting, caring and *contributing* are foundations of building *public good*. These values are widely held in our society, but our current political culture mostly functions at a much more superficial level. The superficiality often undermines the public good.

It is notable that the *Voices* movement is concentrated so far in Coalition electorates. The more 'conservative' people are the ones rebelling. Many of them are what is sometimes called 'small-l' liberal, inclined to favour private enterprise but also to be socially tolerant, more like what Menzies proclaimed the Liberal Party to be when he founded it. Many of the current *Voices* campaigns especially want strong action to counter global warming, along with action on abuse of women and on corruption. Liberal Party voters see that their party has been hijacked by extremists and they are doing something about it.

Not only are the old tribal groupings being challenged, but the old political labels are becoming less relevant. In some ways Labor is more 'conservative'. Many of the Greens' policies are closer to Menzies' Keynesian policies than either modern Liberal or modern Labor. We can just talk about what we want, never mind the labels.

Nor do the old labels apply to the economic approach that emerges in this book. There are markets but they should not be left to run untended: the private sector can be guided by adjusting the financial incentives under which it operates, so the markets actually behave more in the way markets are claimed to behave, but commonly don't, and so their results align more with society's goals. There can be a significant government sector, as in the *mixed economies* of the postwar decades, and the Government can be active but should not micro-manage. We have learnt during the fire, pandemic and flood emergencies that there are roles we want governments to take. There can be social supports, but devolved as much as possible down to communities. Perhaps, taking a lead from agriculture, it might be called *regenerative economics*: economics that cultivates the regeneration of the world.

This is not socialism: there are markets where markets are appropriate. It is not old capitalism and certainly not neoliberal market fundamentalism: there are markets but they are not left to run free or, the common reality, to be manipulated by special interests for their own benefit. Markets can be guided by managing the incentives that operate within them. Government's job will be to keep the incentives aligned as much as possible with the democratic will of the people.

A carbon emissions market is an example, though they have been severely criticised by both sides. Most such markets have been very poorly designed, the European mechanism being quite ineffectual, and much criticised by 'the left'. Australia had a fairly well designed carbon price mechanism and it worked for a brief time, but it interfered with the wealth extraction of the mining lobby and was repealed by 'the right'. If it had been made clear from the start that the poor would be compensated, and helped to reduce their energy use, it would have had a chance of being established and doing its job. It would be a 'great big tax on everything' only for those who refused to adapt to it and reduce their emissions, which would be a good investment anyway.

Some market incentives can be adjusted without taxes or subsidies. If manufacturers are required to take back their product at the end of its useful lifetime then they have an incentive to make it durable and easy to repair or recycle, as Interface Carpet demonstrated.

We can thus move beyond the old ideologies that have led to so much destructive conflict. There will still be a contest between those who have or want great wealth and the rest of us, but we can join that contest with much greater clarity of purpose. Great concentrations of wealth and power are *not* good for everyone, they stunt the economy as well as depriving others of their reasonable share of wealth.

If it is true that the driving force of the relentless material growth of the present economic regime is *artificial scarcity,* originating in the old European enclosure movement but implemented in many other ways in modern economies, then we have identified the off switch. We can turn off the machine that is consuming the planet.

The artificial scarcity that keeps us on the treadmill can be overcome by ensuring that everyone has at least a sufficiency for a modest but dignified life. It is not true that people do not want to be usefully occupied. With some assurance of security people would be able to avoid the deadening work of *bullshit jobs*[59], unless they chose to do them and were appropriately compensated. The frenetic overproduction that is consuming the world could then decline back to what we reasonably need, and to what the planet can sustain.

We can also bring clearer understanding to other aspects of economies: to the financial and monetary systems, how to properly measure or document the effectiveness of policies and the state of our society, and to treat land appropriately in its own special category.

The financial markets are dominated by speculation, which makes them parasitic and destabilising. They should not exist to allow the rich to play wild gambling games with our wealth, they should exist to enable investment into useful activities. They can be restrained by imposing small transaction taxes that remove most of the profit from the speculation. Legitimate trades need only occur much less often so the impost of a small transaction fee will have little effect, but a more stable and productive economy will be of great benefit to everyone. The objective of the transaction fees is primarily to slow and stabilise the financial markets, not to raise revenue.

Governments with sovereign money power can create and spend as much money as is needed for beneficial operations. Inflation can be controlled using taxes to remove money from circulation, as needed.

A primary objective should be to maintain full employment, which means only around 1% unemployment, as was true in the postwar decades. Budget surpluses imply private sector deficits and slow the economy. Budget 'deficits' are normal and desirable and need not impose any debt on our grandchildren.

Private banks are granted the great privilege of creating and issuing money, at essentially zero cost. They should be regulated at least as much as they were in the postwar decades, when they comprised a smaller segment of the economy. The amount of money (credit) they issue should be carefully limited so as not to fuel inflation, as has occurred in the property sector. They should not be able to gamble with other people's money; separate investment funds may exist for that purpose. Beyond that, they ought not to charge interest on money created out of nothing. Fees should be modest and reflect what is, at its core, a fairly basic service. Banks occupy a critical role in our society, and they should not be able to hold us hostage: they need to be carefully and firmly managed so they perform their legitimate role, and no more.

The *national accounts* should feature a triple bottom line system, with a balance sheet for each of the economy, society and the environment, with both qualitative and quantitative assessments included in the latter two. These should be annually reported and taken as measures of the quality of our lives, society and environment. The GDP should have no part in such assessments; it may be of limited use to technocrats monitoring activity, but might well be dropped entirely, to remove the temptation to strive for quantity for its own sake.

We don't manufacture space on the Earth's surface, it is just there, so there is no innate production price attached to it. This has led it to be treated as an item of speculation. Such speculation is a major source of wealth inequality, and it has nearly reversed the housing gains for ordinary people from the postwar burst of prosperity. Unimproved land, or the unimproved space occupied if it is improved, could be held in trust and leased to users. Land trusts might belong to local communities or to higher level collectives. Land taxes accomplish some of the same purpose but less efficiently.

The legitimate role of government needs to be re-asserted. Government arises from a society and can take whatever form we agree on. Government is the means by which we organise ourselves. If government is not working well then we should set about improving it rather than just shrinking it. It is obviously not true that private enterprise is always better or more efficient than government, and some roles cannot sensibly be privatised. Diminishing government below a minimum merely creates space for bullies and warlords, also known as billionaires and corporations, to exert power over us, as is evident all around us at present, to anyone who can remove the scales from their eyes and look.

Parliaments are the locus of our notionally democratic governance, but at present they are very compromised, by entrenched interests and a toxic culture. The interests enter through long-established networks of influence and through money. Networks of influence have been vividly described by Cameron Murray and Paul Frijters in *Game of Mates*[163]. Both channels severely restrict the range of views brought to bear in policy, and the monetary influence amounts to a flagrant systemic corruption, in which 'donors' give to parties and Ministers claim their decisions are not influenced by the one-step-removed source of the money they desperately want for campaigning. Much of the money is hidden, but even so examples of overt immediate corruption, in which the link from donor to policy is plain, have become common. This reached the level of openly plundering the public purse for the benefit of sponsors, on the claimed basis that because the Morrison Government was elected it could do what ever it liked.

The networks of influence strongly affect who gets into parliament and how many favours they owe. The continuing domination by older white men is an obvious symptom, as is the toxic culture, which is acrimonious, highly untrusting, sexist and often overtly sexual. The old parties are the main channels for the toxic culture and the improper influence.

The election of community-based Independent candidates who challenge the old parties is a promising and refreshing development. These candidates seem to be little involved with old networks of influence and with corrupt money. They are explicitly challenging the entrenched interests by drawing on grass roots campaigns. They will have a positive influence on the culture of government and parliament. In the longer term if greater numbers of such grass-roots Independents are elected then both the corrupt influence and the toxic culture might be substantially disrupted, and that would be very healthy for the whole country.

There is another kind of Independent, mostly in the Senate, who have achieved their positions through minority 'populist' campaigns and the complicated workings of the preferential voting system, so they do not have the healthy legitimacy of the grass-roots Independents.

On the other hand the Greens are also a significant force, generally based in the grass roots, healthy and uncorrupt in their functioning. Their success in 2022 in increasing their number from one to four in the House and from nine to twelve in the Senate means they can also be a powerful force for healthy change.

The other big players in our politics are the media. It is arguable that the commercial mass media are more powerful than the political parties (though they are strongly aligned with the Liberal Party) and more regressive, being dedicated to the wealth and power of their proprietors ahead of any interest of our society. We need to understand that media of all kinds occupy a critical place in our human societies, being the means to extend our communal conversations to large societies. These conversations are fundamental to our humanity, as they serve our highly social nature. It is a profound folly to allow a few privileged people to control or strongly influence the nature of those conversations. We owe nothing to present proprietors and need to break their stranglehold. One of the best ways to do that would be to vest ownership in large numbers of the consumers of media, with democratic management processes prescribed, so the media are more likely to serve their audience and less likely to fall under the control of a few individuals.

If we are to properly take charge of our affairs we need to move beyond the dependent colonial mindset. We do not need foreign investment; if we can assemble the resources for a project it is easy to issue the money that will facilitate it, and we can do so without incurring any foreign debt. Neither should we be selling off our land and property to foreigners. We can *trade* with the world as needed to earn foreign credit, rather than as an ideological article of faith. We can work towards locally-based enterprises being locally autonomous instead of controlled by foreign headquarters, although there is a big deficit to overcome and it won't happen quickly.

Our relationships with other countries need to be within our control and not outsourced to a foreign power. This is not anti-anybody, it reflects the simple fact that our own interests are not the same as any other country's. This should be obvious, as we have a historically European culture adjacent to Asia, and have a diverse and unique mixture of people and cultures. We are far too closely entangled with the United States and we are endangered by the US approach to the world and by its internal instability. Extracting ourselves will not be simple or quick, but it needs to be a priority.

With a firm and respectful approach we can deal with powerful countries without fearing or provoking aggressive responses; we have considerable leverage over our international relationships. Other medium-sized countries do it. We do not need to be fearful and reactive, and those responses are reliably counter-productive anyway.

Stepping up to our full independence will require leaving behind colonial-era symbols like the flag and national anthem. I have written new words for a national anthem (see Appendix II), words that celebrate our uniqueness while avoiding chauvinism and immature boasting. These particular words may not be everyone's choice but they illustrate how far we can move away from the old imperial-era words we are currently saddled with.

We also need to cut the constitutional apron string. We need our own head of state. We need a constitution reflecting our modern situation. We badly need a bill of rights to limit the abusive government behaviour that has become more extreme and routine in recent decades. We could tinker with the present constitution, or we could step up to a bigger opportunity and take up the invitation in the *Uluru Statement* to walk together.

Mark McKenna proposed a reconciled republic[164] and I agree, possibly for somewhat different reasons. We are actually in a constitutional limbo. First Australians never ceded their sovereignties, but they do not have the power to enforce them. The invaders' sovereignty has no basis in English law. In English law at the time of invasion a land could be claimed if it was unoccupied, or if a non-coercive treaty was signed with the prior inhabitants, or if the land was seized in a declared war. The pretence of *terra nullius,* that the land was unoccupied, has been demolished. The invasion was not a declared war. No treaty was made.

In this situation it makes good sense for First Australians and invaders to reach a *negotiated* agreement for *joint* sovereignty. We can recognise their prior and continuing occupation and they can recognise our obvious presence, but in a way that respects both sides. That would be a serious reconciliation of our interests, going well beyond the tokenism of present proposals.

Such an undertaking, to reach a settlement between indigenous and settler populations, might well provoke panic and hysteria among reactionaries and ideologues. They would claim (again) that our back yards would be taken from us and we might all be sent back to where our ancestors came from. The key word is 'negotiated'. The settlement would be negotiated. Outrageous claims would not be accepted by the other side. First Australians do not exactly have a strong hand. Good will on both sides would be required, to ensure no serious inequities remained.

Here we are in this unique and remarkable land, with these unique and remarkable histories and with people from all over the world living peacefully together. There is plenty to mark and to celebrate.

Even more substantive, and needed, would be to change our society so it treads lightly on the land, and on the planet. A transition to clean electricity is well along. The use of clean energy in industry, transport and housing can be rapidly progressed, if we just decide we want to do that, remove the obstructors and bring in the many people who can facilitate it. If we adjust the incentives operating in our economy to support that goal we might be surprise how soon we approach zero greenhouse gas emissions. Some time in the 2030s is quite plausible, and that might be enough, replicated around the world, to hold global warming close to 1.5°C, which in turn might be enough to avoid an apocalyptic runaway.

Reforming market incentives to support comprehensive recycling of materials would address many other ways in which we assault the land, our life support system: over-extraction, dumping of valuable or nuisance materials, emitting toxins, destroying habitat, polluting land, water and air. Done well, such reform would not be draconian, it would present our business people with many opportunities. The example of Interface carpets is but one of many, mostly below the radar of the mainstream media.

Those who would claim the changes required are beyond us ought to take stock of the changes that have been forced on us over the past four decades. Whole industries have been rapidly dismantled or made inoperable and other industries have been dramatically changed. Daily life has become considerably less secure for many people.

We will begin to properly *settle* into this land when we learn to use its immense native potential for sustainable production. Quite a few farmers of various kinds across the continent are learning to use native pastures that need no artificial additives[127]. Another big step, not yet seriously pursued it seems, would be to replace destructive exotic grazers like cattle, sheep and mainly feral species like goats and pigs, with benign native grazers like kangaroo and emu. Efforts to recover, restore and use the many food plants that First Australians used have barely begun[137]. If we had started twenty or fifty years ago we would be well along; if we start now we can be well along within twenty years as the need for resilience in a hostile climate rises.

A major part of settling into this land has to be a constructive use of fire. It is becoming apparent the forest and woodland landscapes are very degenerated from what they were in 1788, and much more dangerous[137]. The need for change is incontestable but we trap ourselves in our dependence on European-style land use. There have been big changes before and there can be big changes again. It will be challenging, but we do not have a choice, if our countryside is to remain habitable through this century.

We need to restrain and eventually eliminate overt plundering of the land. This may well need legislated and enforced restrictions, or requirements for sustainable use. However a fair amount might be eliminated simply by disrupting the corrupt nexus of politicians and exploiters that operates at present, stealing water, extracting coal and gas, polluting aquifers, degrading farmland, trashing bushland and so on.

One thing that these land-use changes will require, and facilitate, is a much greater localisation of food production, work and living. This would make us more resilient, more secure and healthier. Much of what we need to do is labour intensive, to use the old industrial framing, but that does imply more jobs. Framing it another way, it is an opportunity to live more fulfilling and healthy lives in stronger local communities. This does not mean drudgery, nor isolation, we can still use appropriate technology, and we can still remain connected with each other and with the great fund of knowledge in our global culture.

We will fully settle into this wide brown and green land when we begin to feel immersed in it. Whether we are conscious of it or not, we are intimately connected with it. If we develop more awareness of the myriad connections we have with forests, woodlands, grasslands, arid lands and their creatures and physical features then we will necessarily treat them with more respect. We will conceive ourselves as *part* of the land. We will be in *our place*: not a place that we own, but our proper place, the place we belong.

Developing that awareness is harder for those in our huge, sprawling cities, but if we cultivate it, it will grow. If we make our cities more hospitable to living things, including ourselves, it will grow. As the awareness grows and spreads, so we will be walking with First Australians into our joint future. With their deep and subtle awareness, developed over an immense span of time, to remind us and teach us, we can learn to thrive with the rest of our land thriving around us. It is the best and priceless gift we can give our grandchildren, and theirs, on into the distant future.

If we dispense with stories that no longer serve us, or that have never served us, and replace them with stories that play to our innate abilities, to our better nature and to the requirements of the living world around us, then a rather better society can eventuate. We create so many avoidable miseries with our misguided blundering that even a modest reduction of them could quickly lead to a striking improvement.

This is not about utopia: we could improve our lot a great deal and still be well short of any such fantasy. There will always be differences and disputes, they are part of the richness of our uncertain lives, but we could manage them better so they don't run out of control.

We can stop or reduce the deliberate cultivation of dispute, sensation and fear, so we might have a more understanding and level-headed view of our fellows. We can ensure that enough of our jointly generated wealth flows to everyone so no-one needs to live in misery, stress and shame. We can begin to take control of all our own affairs. We can cease provocative behaviour towards other nations, and respect their legitimate needs, regardless of how they are trying to meet them, and we can do so without condoning abusive behaviour towards their citizens. We can cease to degrade the land and ensure it is improving. We can quickly reduce our assaults on the ailing planetary system that is our only home in the universe.

We can let go of silly fantasies about (a tiny number of us) escaping to and surviving on other planets, which is quite impossible at this stage of history and which may remain forever so. Anyway we would only ruin them in turn unless we change our ways. Why does this even need to be said? Because some of our boy-child billionaires have never grown up.

So let us examine our presumptions, many of which may serve us badly. If any of the claims made here are correct, then let us act on them; if any are plausible, let us debate them, but let us not continue to hide from our dire situation.

This book is about possibility. It is not just about what we can do tomorrow and accomplish next year, though a fair amount would fit that category if we got on with it. The book is about breaking through the myths that constrain us, getting below the superficial slagging and slogans that absorb much of our attention, seeing how things really work and realising we can do things in rather different ways that are far more positive and rewarding.

There are many things that might have been included in this book. Hopefully it has covered most of the important issues, but its purpose is not to be a complete compendium. Its purpose is to give a flavour of what is possible, to highlight and signpost alternatives that are obscured in the dark confusion of the present.

There *is* a path out of the dark confusion. We may only be able to see the beginning of it from here, but if we step onto that path our lives should immediately begin to improve, and we will soon see the next stage of it unfolding before us.

If we all just say it can't be done, we'll be right.

If enough of us just get on with it then the benefits will soon be apparent and others will join in.

But this book is also about necessity. We can debate the details, but there is no doubt that we must rapidly wind back the destructive system we are part of, starting now. We must reform it so it stops destroying life and begins to support life, all life, human and other.

It is that simple.

Appendix I: A field bereft of intellectual integrity

Through this book I have been highly critical of what I call mainstream economics. Much of this mainstream can be technically identified as neoclassical economics, but it also includes things not related to the core neoclassical theory of free markets, such as treating the GDP as accounting and having an incorrect understanding of banking practice. Some of the foundational claims of the neoclassical theory are based on plainly false premises and many of its conclusions are blatantly contradicted by the behaviour of real economies. Even so this litany of problems still does not convey the full depth of the field's profound deficiencies, nor the strength of the field's grip on political power.

Neoclassical economics and its related topics comprise a hermit discipline. It is deeply ignorant of other fields of knowledge, despite cherry picking some parts, like behavioural psychology, that it uses out of context for its own purposes, usually failing to appreciate the full import of the fragments. It purports to be a scientific discipline, and proffers its pervasive use of mathematical modelling as evidence. There are several problems with this claim.

Its model of science is the dualist and reductionist approach of Descartes and Newton. Thus in the dualist view human beings are regarded as separate from the rest of the natural world. In the reductionist view, human economies can be understood as mechanisms, and each aspect of an economy can supposedly be understood by isolating it from other factors and seeing how it behaves. Models of all the different aspects can then be put back together, like a clockwork, to see how the whole economy behaves.

Even fundamental physics has moved on from reductionism to a radically different conception of dynamic networks of events and interactions. Parts cannot be isolated from other parts or from human observers. But neoclassical economists, in attempting to emulate Newton so as to produce 'laws' and rigorous mathematical models, have got it wrong, at both the fundamental and trivial levels. They have failed to appreciate that the essence of science is the back-and-forth between modelling and observation. You create a mathematical model and then you compare its implications with what you can observe, to see if it gives you useful guidance on the world's behaviour.

The life sciences, apart from economics, have (mostly) come to realise that they must treat living systems in their wholeness: systems reduced to their parts are dead systems. The whole is greater than the sum of its parts. Technically, a living system exhibits emergent behaviour that is not innate in its parts, only in the interactions of its parts to comprise the whole. The notion that an economy is a living entity comprising people, plants and animals and that it is intimately interconnected with human society and with the rest of the biosphere is quite alien to mainstream economics.

Economists concentrate almost wholly on modelling using untested and often plainly inappropriate hypotheses. They keep doing rigorous versions of deducing the implications of their assumptions, and are under the delusion that because they are doing mathematics they are doing science. But they are only doing the deductive stage of science. Missing is the comparison with observations, to either correct or abandon a model. Their ability to formulate hypotheses based on observations is stunted, because mostly they keep using the same old assumptions going back over a century. In real science there is a creative, non-rational phase of perceiving a pattern of some kind in observations. This perceived pattern might then be described using mathematical equations. Only then does mathematical deduction come into play, after which comparison with more observations is pursued.

Worse still, even the mathematics has mistakes in key places, according to Steve Keen[30]. For example, in using calculus to construct aggregate demand curves they conclude that the sum of infinitesimal positive contributions is zero. With this logic, as Keen says, you can conclude that the Earth is flat because the curvature of the bit you're standing on is infinitesimal.

For rank ignorance it is hard to surpass William Nordhaus, the guru of the economics of global warming and a pseudo-Nobel prize winner. To analyse the effects of global warming he first excluded about ninety percent of the economy on the grounds that it was conducted indoors and so would not be affected by the climate. He thus confused climate with weather. Agriculture and some parts of mining he allowed would be affected. He set the template for a long series of studies that routinely conclude that even 3-4°C of warming would reduce the (growing) GDP by only a few percent relative to what it would have been without warming. So we would get rich a little more slowly. He failed to appreciate that even the 1.3°C of warming we are currently experiencing is causing unprecedented fires, floods, droughts and storms and imposing heavy costs in lives and disruption. Evidently he doesn't think rebuilding low-lying ports and cities because of rising sea levels is important, or will cost very much. Or he just doesn't think. He failed to take into account tipping points, in which there is a serious danger that natural processes will begin to reinforce human-induced warming and an uncontrolled runaway warming will take to planet to 4-6°C warming, which would radically transform the human and natural environments. He made other assumptions and mistakes just as egregious, as challenged by Steve Keen[165].

Behind all this deficiency of scholarship are the more human deficiencies of infatuation and self interest. The central result of the neoclassical theory of markets is that they might bring about a *general equilibrium* in which all supplies balance all demands. This can be shown to be an optimum state that maximises outputs for given inputs of 'land, labour and capital'. This is the reason for the claim that free markets are the best way to organise our societies. It is the supposed justification for the neoliberal political ideology of rugged individualism and free markets.

The field became infatuated with this result, not only because of its apparent justification for laissez-faire policies but also because of its mathematical elegance. For about 150 years the field has been desperately striving to exclude anything that disturbs the equilibrium. This is why it uses such absurd assumptions as that we are all fully informed and rational, in a certain sense, that there are no economies of scale, that there are no social interactions and that time does not flow, or if it does then all future possibilities can still be assigned probabilities. If the future is unknown, if there are economies of scale, if we are not fully informed or if we interact socially and 'non-rationally' then instabilities arise and the general equilibrium is lost. If instabilities pervade the system, as they appear to pervade real economies, then you are dealing with a complex self-organising system that is far from equilibrium, unpredictable in detail and with radically different behaviours from the general equilibrium. It is the difference between a rocking horse and wild horses.

In desperately preserving the general equilibrium in its abstract theoretical world, neoclassical economics has completely divorced itself from relevance to real human affairs. Its models are irrelevant to real economies, and its claims are highly misleading.

It will be evident to anyone who understands science even a little bit that this is not a scientific approach. The field claims to be scientific on the basis that it uses rigorous mathematics to deduce consequences from its models, but mathematics is not science, it is a tool used in the course of doing science. Neoclassical economics seems to be modelled on the widespread misconception that Euclid's geometry, which is a branch of mathematics, is an obviously true description of the world. However it was eventually realised that Euclid's geometry is only one of many possible geometries and one has to compare with observations to see if its descriptions are useful. Most of the time they are, but Einstein discovered that one must use Riemann's geometry (of space-time) to describe cosmic-scale phenomena and very strong gravitational fields.

Neoclassical economics claims to be scientific, and cites its use of mathematics as evidence. However it is not science, it just dresses itself up with mathematics to look like science. In other words it is pseudo-science.

Prominent New York Times commentator and pseudo-Nobel winner Paul Krugman likes to say that neoclassical models help to systematise one's thinking. That may be true but if the models are wildly unlike real economies then one's thinking will be wildly misled. The field likes to appeal to a 1953 paper by Milton Friedman[166] in which he attempted to justify the idealisations used in neoclassical economics by claiming, among other things, that all models are wrong and that a theory should be judged on the resemblance of its conclusions to real economies rather than on the absurdity or otherwise of its assumptions. The paper is a hopelessly confused attempt to discuss the art of making judicious approximations that lead to useful insights, which is a very legitimate part of science. However, wildly inappropriate assumptions will lead to wildly misleading conclusions.[167] It is not hard to find examples in which its conclusions are wildly at variance with observed economies: its exclusion of the possibility of a financial market crash is an obvious one.

Neoclassical economics is not even as useful as Ptolemaic astronomy. Ptolemy developed an elaborate system to calculate the positions of the planets in the sky. It is a big and clumsy system that still does not get all the detail of planetary motions. It has been superseded by the conceptions of Copernicus, Kepler and Newton that yield much more accurate descriptions using a much more concise theory. Nevertheless Ptolemy's system still gives a passable description of planetary motions. It is science, just not as concise and accurate as Newton's version.

Neoclassical economics is not science. It is as though it predicted that some of the planets would go around the sun the other way (and I don't just mean the brief episodes of apparent retrograde motion as viewed from Earth). You might think you are on a rocking horse that will come back to balance by itself if you stop rocking it, but you might find you are really on a wild horse that throws you violently to the ground.

Neoclassical economics has no place in universities. It is a fraudulent field. Its claims are plainly and blatantly untrue. It has no intellectual integrity. Many of its practitioners may just be sorely misled by the teaching they have received, but its leading thinkers should still have the integrity to address the fundamental deficiencies that have been pointed out by many critics over a long period[12,30,31,168]. When its deficiencies become obvious, as they did during the Global Financial Crisis of 2008, they don't change their theories, they change the subject and carry on, as James Galbraith puts it[12]. Neoclassicists have come to dominate most economics departments and the most prominent academic journals. Anyone who dissents is banished to the fringes of the field. Galbraith says there is 'a politburo for correct economic thinking'.

Neoclassical economics has come to dominate public policy as well. This can only be attributed to its usefulness to the very rich, because its message to them is that they should keep making money as fast as they can. They pay the economists well to keep putting that message out.

Obviously the false neoclassical doctrines need to be eliminated from public policy as well.

Appendix II: Anthem words

If we are to finish growing up, as a nation, then we need to move on from the old words of the national anthem, *Advance Australia Fair,* which were borne of the attitudes of the British Empire in the 1870s. Some people have modified those words to remove some of the more dated and inappropriate expressions, but the chauvinist sentiment of the original still comes through.

I think it is better just to start again, taking a more contemporary, more inclusive view of ourselves. We can also move beyond the need to trumpet our worth, or superiority, because that just perpetuates the old inferiority complex.

So I have written some words to celebrate who we are, what we are and what we might aspire to. At least they can demonstrate a different perspective and approach. If they help to stimulate others to have a go, then good. I think the old tune serves well as an anthem. It is not so hard for the average punter to sing and it tarts up well for grand occasions. You may use the words but please acknowledge my authorship.

Australia We Share

An ancient land from Rock to sand
A Dreaming old and wise
White, brown and black from other lands
New ways from old arise.
From whips and chains through gold and fleece
Invention, sweat and care
A new refrain to grace the world:
A fair go and fair share.
To Dream together, old and new,
Australia we share.

A wilful land of flood and fire
Of forests lush and tall
Of rivers slow and jewel reef
And creatures fit for all
This land abounds in nature's gifts
Of beauty rich and rare
From aeons past a heritage
For us to take due care.
We all are now custodians
Australia, we care.

(Geoff Davies, 30 April 2013; http://betternaturebooks.net/oz-identity/new-anthem-words/)

Bibliography

1 Uluru. *Uluru Statement from the Heart,* 2017. https://ulurustatement.org.

2 Dowse, S., *Then, now, and what might come,* in Women and Whitlam: Revisiting the Revolution, M. Arrow, Editor. 2023, NewSouth. p. 352.

3 Diamond, J., *Collapse: How Societies Choose to Fail or Succeed*. 2005, New York: Viking.

4 Horne, D., *The Lucky Country*. 5th ed. 1964/2005: Penguin Group.

5 Ray, P.H. and S.R. Anderson, *The Cultural Creatives*. 2000, New York: Harmony Books.

6 Watts, J., Humans 'pushing Earth close to tipping point', say most in G20. *The Guardian,* 2021, 17 August https://www.theguardian.com/environment/2021/aug/16/three-quarters-g20-earth-close-to-tipping-point-global-survey-climate-crisis.

7 Hamilton, C. and E. Mail, *Downshifting in Australia: a sea-change in the pursuit of happiness*. Discussion Paper 50, 2003, Australia Institute: Canberra.

8 Huntley, R., Culture capture. *The Monthly,* 2021. Schwarz Media: Issue **184**(December), https://www.themonthly.com.au/issue/2021/

december/1638277200/rebecca-huntley/fossil-fuel-industry-s-grip-australian-hearts-and.

9 Campbell, R., E. Littleton, and A. Armistead, Fossil fuel subsidies in Australia. 2021. *Australia Institute,* https://australiainstitute.org.au/post/australian-fossil-fuel-subsidies-hit-10-3-billion-in-2020-21/.

10 Biddulph, S., *Fully Human; a new way of using our mind*. 2021: Pan Macmillan. 280 pp.

11 Krasnostein, S., The most hated man. *The Monthly,* 2021. Schwartz Media: Issue (June).

12 Galbraith, J.K., Who Are These Economists, Anyway? *Thought & Action,* 2009(Fall): p. 85-97, http://qa16.nea.org/assets/docs/HE/TA09EconomistGalbraith.pdf.

13 Burt, R., Margaret Thatcher interview. *Sunday Times,* 1981, 3 May.

14 Keay, D., Thatcher interview. *Woman's Own,* 1987: Issue (31 October).

15 Beinhocker, E.D., *The Origin of Wealth*. 2006, Boston: Harvard Business School Press.

16 Greene, J., *Moral Tribes: Emotion, Reason, and the Gap Between Us and Them*. 2013: The Penguin Press HC. 432 pp.

17 Kahneman, D., *Thinking, Fast and Slow*. 2011: Farrar, Straus and Giroux. 512 pp.

18 Bregman, R., *Humankind, a hopeful history*. 2020, London: Bloomsbury Publishing. 463 pp.

19 Grille, R., *Parenting for a Peaceful World*. 2008, Richmond, UK: The Children's Project.

20 Galbraith, J.K., Who Are These Economists, Anyway? *Thought & Action,* 2009(Fall): p. 85-97, http://www.nea.org/home/37170.htm.

21 Falzon, J., Solidarity in the face of a neoliberal inferno *Eureka Street,* 2020, 3 March https://www.eurekastreet.com.au/article/solidarity-in-the-face-of-a-neoliberal-inferno.

22 Conifer, D., Josh Frydenberg was alerted less than three months into JobKeeper that unqualified companies were receiving support. *ABC,* 2021, 3 Nov https://www.abc.net.au/news/2021-11-03/josh-frydenberg-jobkeeper/100589318.

23 Reich, R.B., The Limping Middle Class. *New York Times*, 2011: Issue (3 Sept 2011), http://www.nytimes.com/2011/09/04/opinion/sunday/jobs-will-follow-a-strengthening-of-the-middle-class.html?src=rechp.

24 Tracker, R. *Human Rights Measurement Initiative,* 2021. https://rightstracker.org/en/country/AUS?as=hi.

25 McKnight, D., *Beyond Right and Left*. 2005, Sydney: Allen & Unwin. 298 pp.

26 Hocking, J., Letters of an insecure and indiscreet John Kerr make a mockery of the claim that the Queen played 'no part'. *Pearls and Irritations*, 2020, 19 July https://johnmenadue.com/jenny-hocking-letters-of-an-insecure-and-indiscreet-john-kerr-make-a-mockery-of-the-claim-that-the-queen-played-no-part/.

27 Coventry, C.J., The "eloquence" of Robert J. Hawke: United States informer. *Australian Journal of Politics and History*, 2021. **67**(1): p. 1-21.

28 Hutchens, G., Lift the minimum wage and employment still rises? How to anger the establishment and win a Nobel Prize. 2021. *ABC,* 13 October https://www.abc.net.au/news/2021-10-13/nobel-prize-in-economics-2021-david-card-minimum-wage/100531994.

29 Kelton, S., *The Deficit Myth: Modern Monetary Theory and How to Build a Better Economy*. 2020, UK: John Murray. 325 pp.

30 Keen, S., *Debunking Economics: The Naked Emperor Dethroned?* Second, revised and expanded ed. 2011: Zed Books.

31 Galbraith, J.K., Dismal economics. 2021. *Project Syndicate,* https://www.project-syndicate.org/onpoint/economics-captured-by-neoclassical-magical-thinking-by-james-k-galbraith-2021-07.

32 Ubuntu, P., Ubuntu philosophy. *Wikipedia,* 2022, https://en.wikipedia.org/wiki/Ubuntu_philosophy.

33 Manning, R., *Against the Grain: How Agriculture Has Hijacked Civilization*. 2004, New York: North Point Press.

34 Gammage, B., *The Biggest Estate on Earth: How Aborigines made Australia.* 2011: Allen & Unwin. 434 pp.

35 Pascoe, B., *Dark Emu. Black seeds: agriculture or accident?* 2014, Broome, WA: Magabala Books Aboriginal Corporation. 176 pp.

[36] Kelly, L., *The Memory Code: The Traditional Aboriginal Memory Technique That Unlocks the Secrets of Stonehenge, Easter Island and Ancient Monuments the World Over*. 2016, Australia: Allen & Unwin. 336 pp.

[37] Wilson, E.O., *The Diversity of Life*. 1992, Cambridge, MA: The Belknap Press of Harvard University Press.

[38] Koestler, A., *The Ghost in the Machine*. 1967: Hutchinson. 384 pp.

[39] Wolff, R., *Original Wisdom: Stories of an Ancient Way of Knowling*. 2001, Rochester, Vermont: Inner Traditions International. 197 pp.

[40] Abram, D., *The Spell of the Sensuous*. 1996, New York: Vintage.

[41] Hickel, J., *Degrowth: a theory of radical abundance,* in Economics and the Ecosystem, E. Fullbrook and J. Morgan, Editors. 2019, World Economics Association.

[42] Lee, K., How John Howard contributed to the aged care crisis. *The Australian Independent Media Network,* 2019, 7 May https://theaimn.com/how-john-howard-contributed-to-the-aged-care-crisis/.

[43] Pagone, T. and L. Briggs, The Final Report of the Royal Commission into Aged Care Quality and Safety 2021, 1 March https://agedcare.royalcommission.gov.au/news-and-media/final-report-calls-fundamental-and-systemic-aged-care-reform.

[44] Quiggin, J., Face the facts: competition and profit don't work in health, education or prisons. *The Guardian,* 2016, 12 Sept https://www.theguardian.com/commentisfree/2016/sep/12/face-the-facts-competition-and-profit-dont-work-in-health-education-or-prisons.

[45] Rothschild, M., *Bionomics: Economy as Ecosystem*. 1990, New York: Henry Holt. 423 pp.

[46] Scott, J.C., *Against the Grain: a deep history of the earliest states*. 2017: Yale University Press. 312 pp.

[47] Alt, J.D., *The Millenials' Money*. 2016, Indianapolis IN: Dog Ear Publishing, www.dogearpublishing.net. 111 pp.

[48] Tharoor, S., *Inglorious Empire: What the British Did to India*. 2016, New Delhi: Aleph Book Company. 294 pp.

[49] Zinn, H., *A People's History of the United States*. 1980: Harper Perennial Modern Classics. 729 pp.

50 Picchi, A., 50 years of tax cuts for the rich failed to trickle down, economics study says. *CBS News,* 2020, 17 Dec https://www.cbsnews.com/news/tax-cuts-rich-50-years-no-trickle-down/?fbclid=IwAR33jymA4DTNZbPbU2o41WNn4EXfE1pZIZcNpK5hhZ0VwzMX8rCwDAA3BJo.

51 Barlow, T., *The Australian Miracle, an innovative nation revisited.* 2006, Sydney: Pan Macmillan Australia. 278 pp; McLean, I.W., *Why Australia Prospered: the shifting sources of economic growth.* 2013, Princeton, NJ: Princeton University Press. 296 pp.

52 Norberg-Hodge, H., *Local is Our Future: Steps to an Economics of Happiness.* 2019: Local Futures. 160 pp.

53 Colborn, T., D. Dumanowski, and J.P. Myers, *Our Stolen Future.* 1997, London: Abacus.

54 Cribb, J., Idiocracy: how the decline in human intelligence is undermining democracy. *Pearls and Irritations,* 2021, 19 October https://johnmenadue.com/idiocracy-is-the-decline-in-human-intelligence-undermining-democracy/.

55 Daly, H.E. and J.B. Cobb Jr., *For the Common Good.* 2nd ed. 1994, Boston: Beacon.

56 Hamilton, C. and H. Saddler, *The Genuine Progress Indicator.* Discussion Paper 14, 1997, The Australia Institute: Canberra.

57 Hamilton, C. and R. Denniss, *Tracking well-being in Australia - the Genuine Progress Indicator 2000.* Discussion Paper 35, 2000, The Australia Institute, www.tai.org.au: Canberra.

58 Waring, M., *If Women Counted.* 1988, San Francisco: Harper & Row.

59 Graeber, D., *Bullshit Jobs: a Theory.* 2019: Simon & Schuster. 368 pp.

60 Cobb, C., M. Glickman, and C. Cheslog, *The Genuine Progress Indicator, 2000 Update.* 2001, Redefining Progress, www.redefiningprogress.org: Oakland, CA.

61 Hamilton, C., *Downshifting in Britain: a sea-change in the pursuit of happiness.* Discussion Paper 58, 2003, Australia Institute: Canberra.

62 Berg, A.G. and J.D. Ostry, Equality and efficiency. *Finance and Development,* 2011. **48**(3): p. 12-15.

63 O'Sullivan, J., *Submission to the Productivity Commission Inquiry into Infrastructure provision and funding in Australia*. 2019, Productivity Commission, https://www.pc.gov.au.

64 O'Sullivan, J.N., The burden of durable asset acquisition in growing populations. *Economic Affairs*, 2012. **32**(1): p. 31-37.

65 Graeber, D. and D. Wengrow, *The Dawn of Everything*. 2021: Farrar, Straus and Giroux. 692 pp.

66 Yunkaporta, T., *Sand Talk: How indigenous thinking can save the world*. 2019, Melbourne: The Text Publishing Company. 280 pp.

67 Wrangham, R., *The Goodness Paradox: How evolution made us more and less violent*. 2019, London: Profile Books. 380 pp.

68 Sutton, P. and K. Walshe, *Farmers or Hunter-gatherers? The Dark Emu Debate*. 2021: Melbourne University Press. 288 pp.

69 Davies, G., Dark Ostrich: the attack on Bruce Pascoe's Dark Emu. *Pearls & Irritations*, 2021, 14 July https://johnmenadue.com/__trashed-11/.

70 Diamond, J., *Guns, Germs and Steel*. 1999, New York: W. W. Norton.

71 Buck, J. and S. Villines, *We The People: Consenting to a Deeper Democracy*. 2007, Washington D.C.: Sociocracy.info. 277 pp.

72 Boswell, R., Valedictory. *Senate Debates*, 2014. *Commonwealth of Australia*, 17 June https://www.openaustralia.org.au/senate/?gid=2014-06-17.122.3.

73 Betts, K. and B. Birrell, Politics and the population question during the pandemic. 2021. *The Australian Population Research Institute*, October https://tapri.org.au/wp-content/uploads/2021/10/TAPRI-survey-Oct-2021-final-V3.pdf.

74 Paine, T., *Common Sense, The Rights of Man, and other essential writings*. 2003, New York: Signet Classics.

75 Indi, V.f. *Voices for Indi*. http://www.voicesforindi.com.

76 Climate. *Climate 200*, 2021. https://www.climate200.com.au.

77 West, M. *Revolving Doors*, 2020. https://www.michaelwest.com.au/revolving-doors/.

78 Ludlam, S., *Full Circle*. 2021, Carlton, Vic: Black Inc. 378 pp.

79 Wallace, C., 'Palace letters' reveal the palace's fingerprints on the dismissal of the Whitlam government. *The Conversation,* 2020, 14 July https://theconversation.com/palace-letters-reveal-the-palaces-fingerprints-on-the-dismissal-of-the-whitlam-government-142476.

80 Blaine, L., *Top Blokes: The Larrikin Myth, Class and Power. Quarterly Essay,* ed. C. Feik. Vol. **83**. 2021: Black Inc. 156 pp.

81 Manne, R., Bad News: Murdoch's Australian and the Shaping of the Nation. *Quarterly Essay,* 2011(43): p. http://www.quarterlyessay.com/issue/bad-news-murdochs-australian-and-shaping-nation.

82 Schultz, J., *The Idea of Australia.* 2022, Crows Nest NSW: Allen & Unwin. 460 pp.

83 Young, S., *Paper Emperors.* 2019: NSW Press.

84 Davies, G.F., *Economia: New Economic Systems to Empower People and Support the Living World.* 2004, Sydney: ABC Books. Electronic copy available at http://betternature.wordpress.com/.

85 Bradley, M., Legally speaking, our political parties are mere tuckshop committees. *Crikey,* 2022, 6 April https://www.crikey.com.au/2022/04/06/legally-political-parties-mere-tuckshop-committees/?utm_campaign=Daily&utm_medium=email&utm_source=newsletter.

86 Dalton, T., *Love Stories.* 2021: Fourth Estate. 340 pp.

87 Hudson, M., Rent-seeking and asset-price inflation: a total-returns profile of economic polarization in America. *Review of Keynesian Economics,* 2021. **9**(4): p. 435-460.

88 Fox, R. and R. Finlay, Dwelling Prices and Household Income. *Reserve Bank of Australia Bulletin,* 2012(December Quarter): p. 13-22.

89 McLeay, M., A. Radia, and R. Thomas, *Money in the modern economy: an introduction.* 2014, Bank of England.

90 King, M., *The End of Alchemy: Money, Banking and the Future of the Global Economy.* 2016, New York: W. W. Norton and Co. 430 pp.

91 George, H. and B. Drake, *Progress and Poverty.* 1879/2006: Robert Schalkenbach Foundation.

92 Brennan, F., *Canberra in Crisis.* 1971, Canberra: Dalton Publishing Company.

93 Turnbull, S., *A framework for designing sustainable urban communities.* 2007, International Institute for Self Governance.

94 Davies, G., *Economy, Society, Nature: An introduction to the new systems-based, life-friendly economics.* 2019, Bristol, UK: World Economics Association. 379 pp.

95 Riegel, E.C., *Flight From Inflation.* 1978, Los Angeles: The Heather Foundation, Box 48, San Pedro, CA 90773.

96 Greco, T.H., Jr., *New Money for Healthy Communities.* 1994, Tucson, AZ: Thomas H. Greco, Jr., P.O. Box 42663, Tucson AZ 85733.

97 Frazee, G., Did Trump's tax cuts boost hiring? Most companies say no. *Public Broadcasting Service (US),* 2019, 28 Jan https://www.pbs.org/newshour/economy/making-sense/did-trumps-tax-cuts-boost-hiring-most-companies-say-no.

98 Mitchell, W. and T. Fazi, *Reclaiming the State.* 2017, London: Pluto Press. 302 pp.

99 Keen, S., The New Liberals Housing Affordability Policy. *Patreon.com,* 2022, 13 Jan https://www.patreon.com/posts/new-liberals-61077693.

100 Blum, W., *Killing Hope: U.S. Military and CIA Interventions Since World War II.* 2004: Common Courage Press. 471 pp.

101 McCoy, A.W. and B. Reilly, Washington on the Rocks. *Tomgram,* 2011, April 24, 2011 http://www.tomdispatch.com/blog/175383/.

102 Menadue, J., The United States empire is almost always at war. *Pearls & Irritations,* 2021, 30 Dec https://johnmenadue.com/the-united-states-empire-is-almost-always-at-war/.

103 Pilger, J., The Great Game of smashing countries. *Pearls and Irritations,* 2021, 26 August https://johnmenadue.com/the-great-game-of-smashing-countries/.

104 Pilger, J., *A Secret Country.* 1992, London: Vintage. 409 pp.

105 Phillips, A.A., The Cultural Cringe. *Meanjin,* 1950. **9**(4): p. 299-302.

106 Lang, J.T., *The Great Bust.* 1962, Sydney: Angus & Robertson.

107 Haigh, B., The all-American coercive diplomacy: bullying by any other name. *Pearls and Irritations,* 2021, 30 Sept https://johnmenadue.com/the-all-american-coercive-diplomacy-bullying-by-any-other-name/.

108 Daley, P., Declassified documents show Australia assisted CIA in coup against Chile's Salvador Allende. *Guardian Australia,* 2021, 11 Sept https://www.theguardian.com/politics/2021/sep/11/declassified-documents-show-australia-assisted-cia-in-coup-against-chiles-salvador-allende.

109 Patience, A., History is repeating itself: Billy Hughes on Japan and now Scott Morrison on China. *Pearls and Irritations,* 2021, 20 Sept https://johnmenadue.com/history-is-repeating-itself-billy-hughes-on-japan-and-now-scott-morrison-on-china/.

110 Fraser, M. and C. Roberts, *Dangerous Allies.* 2014: Melbourne University Press.

111 Soos, P., Do the crime, do the time? Not if you're a banker in Australia. *The Conversation,* 2014, 30 Oct https://theconversation.com/do-the-crime-do-the-time-not-if-youre-a-banker-in-australia-33548.

112 Verrender, I., A royal commission into banks could end two scandals. *The Drum (ABC),* 2015, 17 Aug http://www.abc.net.au/news/2015-08-17/verrender-a-royal-commission-into-banks/6701420.

113 Lewis, M., *The Big Short.* 2011, New York: W. W. Norton.

114 Foroohar, R., *Makers and Takers: the rise of finance and the fall of American business.* 2016, New York: Crown Business. 388 pp.

115 Chandrasekhar, C.P. and J. Ghosh, How emerging markets hurt poor countries. *Real-world Economics Review Blog,* 2021, 16 October https://rwer.wordpress.com/2021/10/16/how-emerging-markets-hurt-poor-countries/#comment-184662.

116 Poelina, A., Between Stories: TransCultural Conversations for Troubling Times • Session #3 of 3: DEEP TIME. 2021. *Anthropocene Transition Network Inc,* 1:55:46 https://click.mlsend.com/link/c/YT0xODQ0MTk4MTUxNTMyMDU4MjU4JmM9cTJrNCZlPTg4MDk0NTQ5JmI9ODQwMzk5NjU2JmQ9dDd6OGY5aQ==.BPByt_a9x6XD3-NAoWWqRqm3OB5X-xx2_oidXd2EL2M.

117 Dale, S., *My Child, My Self.* 1992, San Mateo, CA: Human Awareness Publications. 160 pp.

118 Newton, D., *Private Ryan and the Lost Peace.* 2021, Haberfield NSW: Longueville Media. 380 pp.

119 Bastian, P., *Andrew Fisher, an underestimated man*. 2009, Sydney: University of New South Wales Press. 419 pp.

120 Ham, P., A half-formed nation. *Griffith Review*, 2016. **51**: p. 174-188.

121 Health, A., Relaxing into Parenting Program. 2012. *Women's Centre for Health Matters*, http://www.wchm.org.au/announcements/relaxing-into-parenting-program.

122 Jonge, A.d. et al., Perinatal mortality and morbidity in a nationwide cohort of 529 688 low-risk planned home and hospital births. *BJOG: An International Journal of Obstetrics and Gynaecology*, 2009. **116**: p. 1177–1184. DOI: 10.1111/j.1471-0528.2009.02175.x.

123 Odent, M., Michel Odent - 2 of 3 on gentle birth. 2007, Nov 3 https://www.youtube.com/watch?v=8x8ip4VVGAI&feature=relmfu.

124 Young, K. and Y. Miller, Women's magazines could play a role in promoting natural births. *The Conversation*, 2015, 1 May https://theconversation.com/womens-magazines-could-play-a-role-in-promoting-natural-births-41021

125 HAI. *Human Awareness Institute*. http://www.hai.org.

126 Chan, G., *Why You Should Give a F*ck About Farming*. 2021: Vintage Books Australia. 314 pp.

127 Massy, C., *Call of the Reed Warbler: A new agriculture, a new Earth*. 2017, St. Lucia, Qld, Australia: University of Queensland Press. 569 pp.

128 Odoul, A., Soils and Biodiversity. 2015. *Food and Agriculture Organisation*, https://www.fao.org/documents/card/en/c/43b565e7-57c2-43c6-b4f0-812091486ed3/.

129 Donley, N. and T. Gunstone, **Pesticides are killing our soils**. *Scientific American*, 2021: Issue **August**, https://www.scientificamerican.com/article/pesticides-are-killing-the-worlds-soils/.

130 Knox, M., *Supermarket Monsters*. 2015, Collingwood, Vic: Redback.

131 McDonough, W. and M. Braungart, *Cradle to Cradle*. 2002, New York: North Point Press. 193 pp.

132 Uprety, A., Misleading commercials in Nepal make families replace nutritious local diets with processed food. *Nepali Times*, 2021, 19 Oct https://www.nepalitimes.com/opinion/we-are-what-we-eat/?

fbclid=IwAR3rrpdoLiMwoL_NmlHfdswcrFCHJFxOSxcwtPTYvBF_gOi8AVkFnjwCmG0.

133 Berry, W., *Another Turn of the Crank*. 1995, Washington, D.C.: Counterpoint.

134 Mollison, B., *Permaculture Two: Practical Design for Town and Country in Permanent Agriculture*. Reprint edition ed. 1999, Tyalgum, NSW 2484, Australia: Tagari Publications.

135 Landcare, A. *Landcare Australia,* 2015. https://landcareaustralia.org.au.

136 Jackson, W., *Becoming Native to This Place*. 1994: University Press of Kentucky.

137 Gammage, B. and B. Pascoe, *Country: Future Fire, Future Farming. First Knowledges,* ed. M. Neale. 2021, Port Melbourne: Thames & Hudson Australia Pty Ltd. 211 pp.

138 Murphy, J., The five principles of regenerative farming and how to apply them. *Farm Online,* 2021, 3 Jan https://www.farmonline.com.au/story/7048003/the-five-principle...=IwAR1tUolBiKm3rK50gOaKl_mH4BKNVyVb2RAGltJINs0lkuutY5vTbtVBGrU.

139 Rodale, I., The Farming Systems Trial: Celebrating 30 years. 2015. *Rodale Institute,* www.rodaleinstitute.org.

140 Delate, K., *Organic practices outpace conventional in long-term research.* 2007, Leopold Center for Sustainable Agriculture: Ames, IA, USA.

141 Badgley, C. et al., Organic agriculture and the global food supply. *Renewable Agriculture and Food Systems,* 2007. **22**: p. 86-108.

142 Khan, S. et al., The myth of nitrogen fertilization for soil carbon sequestration. *J. Environmental Quality,* 2007. **36**: p. 1821-1832.

143 Griffiths, T., *Forests of Ash: An Environmental History*. 2001: Cambridge University Press. 227 pp.

144 Steffensen, V., *Fire Country: How Indigenous Fire Management Could Help Save Australia*. 2020: Hardie Grant Explore. 240 pp.

145 Anderson, R.C., *Mid-Course Correction*. 1998, White River Junction, VT: Chelsea Green Publishing.

146 Lovins, A.B., *Energy End-Use Efficiency. www.interacademycouncil.net.* 2005: InterAcademy Council, Amsterdam.

[147] Hawken, P., *The Ecology of Commerce.* 1993, New York: HarperBusiness.

[148] Anderson, R.C., *Business Lessons from a Radical Industrialist.* 2010, New York: St. Martins Press.

[149] Hawken, P., A. Lovins, and L.H. Lovins, *Natural Capitalism.* 1999, Boston: Little, Brown and Company.

[150] Curtin, U. *School of Design and the Built Environment,* 2021. https://about.curtin.edu.au/learning-teaching/humanities/design-built-environment/.

[151] Kunstler, J.H., *The Geography of Nowhere.* 1993, New York: Touchstone.

[152] von Weizsäcker, E., A.B. Lovins, and L.H. Lovins, *Factor Four: Doubling Wealth, Halving Resource Use.* 1997, St. Leonards: Allen & Unwin.

[153] Rabinovich, J. and J. Leitman, Urban planning in Curitiba. *Scientific American,* 1996(March): p. 46-53.

[154] Green, J., Green cities on the cheap: Low-cost solutions for a sustainable world. 2011, 28 Dec http://www.grist.org/smart-cities/2011-12-28-green-cities-on-the-cheap-low-cost-solutions-sustainable-world.

[155] Roberts, N., Australian houses are just glorified tents in winter. *The Canberra Times,* 2015, June 11 www.canberratimes.com.au/action/printArticle?id=996902241.

[156] GREG HANSCOM, This old house: Why fixing up old homes is greener than building new ones. 2012. *Grist,* 25 Jan http://grist.org/cities/this-old-house-why-fixing-up-old-homes-is-greener-than-building-new-ones/.

[157] Ciancio, D., Cheap, tough and green: why aren't more buildings made of rammed earth? *The Conversation,* 2015, 30 April https://theconversation.com/cheap-tough-and-green-why-arent-more-buildings-made-of-rammed-earth-38040.

[158] Earthship, Radically Sustainable Buildings. 2014. *Earthship Biotecture,* http://earthship.com.

[159] Reid, E., *Whitlam and the women's liberation movement,* in Women and Whitlam, M. Arrow, Editor. 2023, NewSouth Publishing: Sydney. p. 28.

[160] Trust, V.W., *The Purple Sage Project.* 1999, Victorian Women's Trust, http://vwt.org.au/1998/11/purple-sage/.

[161] ReMade, A. *Australia ReMade,* 2022. https://www.australiaremade.org.

[162] Rooney, M. and L. Spencer, Reclaiming our Purpose: It's time to talk about the public good. 2022, March https://www.australiaremade.org/public-good.

[163] Murray, C.K. and P. Frijters, *Game of Mates: How Favours Bleed the Nation*. 2017: Publicious Pty Ltd. 204 pp.

[164] McKenna, M., *This Country: A Reconciled Republic*. 2004, Sydney: UNSW Press. 160 pp.

[165] Keen, S., Nobel prize-winning economics of climate change is misleading and dangerous – here's why. *The Conversation*, 2020, 9 September https://theconversation.com/nobel-prize-winning-economics-of-climate-change-is-misleading-and-dangerous-heres-why-145567.

[166] Friedman, M., *The methodology of positive economics*, in Appraisal and Criticism in Economics: A Book of Readings, B. Caldwell, Editor. 1953/1984, Allen and Unwin: London.

[167] Davies, G.F., Is the Neoclassical Theory Scientific? 2004, http://betternaturebooks.net.au/economies-general/scientific/.

[168] Davies, G.F., *Sack the Economists, http://betternaturebooks.net.au/my-books/sack-the-economists/*. 2013, Canberra, ACT, Australia: BWM Books. 238 pp.

About the author

Geoff Davies was born on some of the flattest country in this or any other wide brown land, coming from a line of battling farmers and drovers going back to first-fleet convicts. He grew up by the ocean and went to a rough small-town public school, then got a PhD and spent four decades as an academic scientist figuring out how the inside of the Earth drives tectonic plates. He appreciates his origins and still thinks ordinary Australians are mostly good-hearted and generous. He wondered why the world is so poorly governed and found that mainstream economics is misleading pseudo-science, and that mass societies can bring out the worst in us. He thinks we can organise ourselves to support our better angels, and live well and more peaceably within the world's abundant biosphere. There isn't really much alternative.

Professionally, after BSc and MSc degrees from Monash University, Geoff Davies gained a PhD from the California Institute of Technology and was a postdoctoral fellow at Harvard University. He held academic positions at the University of Rochester, NY, Washington University in St. Louis and the Australian National University, and retired in 2010. He was awarded the inaugural Augustus Love Medal for geodynamics by the European Geosciences Union and is a Fellow of the American Geophysical Union. He has published three books on Earth science, over one hundred scientific papers and has a Hirsch index of 42 (42 papers with 42 or more citations).